KT-157-820

RED SEA SPIES

'The true and most accurate story of the Mossad's Ethiopian Jewish rescue operation in Sudan.'

EFRAIM HALEVY,
Head of the Mossad 1998–2002

RED SEA SPIES

THE TRUE STORY OF MOSSAD'S FAKE DIVING RESORT

RAFFI BERG

ICON

Published in the UK and USA in 2020
by Icon Books Ltd, Omnibus Business Centre,
39–41 North Road, London N7 9DP
email: info@iconbooks.com
www.iconbooks.com

Sold in the UK, Europe and Asia
by Faber & Faber Ltd, Bloomsbury House,
74–77 Great Russell Street,
London WC1B 3DA or their agents

Distributed in the UK, Europe and Asia
by Grantham Book Services, Trent Road,
Grantham NG31 7XQ

Distributed in the USA
by Publishers Group West,
1700 Fourth Street, Berkeley, CA 94710

Distributed in Canada by Publishers Group Canada,
76 Stafford Street, Unit 300
Toronto, Ontario M6J 2S1

Distributed in Australia and New Zealand
by Allen & Unwin Pty Ltd, PO Box 8500,
83 Alexander Street, Crows Nest, NSW 2065

Distributed in South Africa
by Jonathan Ball, Office B4, The District,
41 Sir Lowry Road, Woodstock 7925

Distributed in India by Penguin Books India,
7th Floor, Infinity Tower – C, DLF Cyber City,
Gurgaon 122002, Haryana

ISBN: 978-178578-600-6 (hardback)
ISBN: 978-178578-641-9 (paperback)

Text copyright © 2020 Raffi Berg
Map illustrations © 2020 Kate Simunek

The author has asserted his moral rights.

No part of this book may be reproduced in any form, or by any
means, without prior permission in writing from the publisher.

Typeset in Adobe Garamond by Marie Doherty

Printed and bound in Great Britain
by Clays Ltd, Elcograf S.p.A.

CONTENTS

ABOUT THE AUTHOR

Raffi Berg is the Middle East editor of the BBC News website, a position he has held since 2013. He has a particular interest in events in Israel, from where he has reported extensively, in times of both peace and war. His first real introduction to the country came when he spent his gap year at the Hebrew University of Jerusalem, an experience which shaped the path of his future career. Raffi began as a journalist on radio in Liverpool in 1993, later moving to TV and international agency news before joining the BBC in 2001. Born in the north-west seaside town of Southport, he graduated in Modern and Medieval History at the London School of Economics (LSE) and in journalism at the University of Central Lancashire. When not working or travelling, he enjoys reading historical books and spending time with his wife Suzi and their two children at their home in north-west London.

In memory of my beloved friend Oliver.

LIST OF ILLUSTRATIONS

SELECTED INDIVIDUALS, ORGANISATIONS AND TERMS

PEOPLE
Individuals' military ranks correspond to the positions they held at the time of their last activity during the operations to evacuate Ethiopian Jews.

Nahum Admoni   Director of the Mossad, 1982–89.

Colonel Asaf Agmon   Israeli Air Force Hercules squadron commander. Flew on secret airlifts of Jews from Sudan and Ethiopia between 1977 and 1991.

Liwa Youssef Hussein Ahmed   Commander of the Sudanese Navy in the early 1980s.

Ferede Aklum   Ethiopian Jew who, together with Mossad agent Dani, orchestrated the secret migration to Sudan of thousands of Ethiopian Jews who were then smuggled out to Israel, from 1979 onwards.

Yazezow Aklum   Ferede Aklum's father.

Avrehet Aklum   Ferede Aklum's mother.

Rear Admiral Zeev Almog   Commander in Chief of the Israeli Navy, 1979–85.

Apke   Mossad employee and first manager of the Arous diving resort, December 1981 to March 1982.

Lieutenant Colonel Ami Ayalon   Commander of the Shayetet 13, 1979–81.

Colonel Dov Bar   Senior officer on board the INS *Bat Galim* during operation to evacuate Ethiopian Jews from Sudan in March 1982.

Milton Bearden   CIA station chief in Khartoum, 1983–85.

Menachem Begin   Israeli prime minister, 1977–83. Ordered the Mossad to bring the Jews of Ethiopia to Israel.

Lieutenant Colonel Yisrael Ben-Chaim   Israeli Air Force Hercules squadron commander. Flew on secret airlifts of Jews from Sudan and piloted flight which evacuated Mossad agents from Arous in April 1985.

Zimna Berhane   Israeli of Ethiopian Jewish origin who succeeded Ferede Aklum as go-between for the Mossad and a clandestine Ethiopian Jewish cell in Gedaref, Sudan, from 1980–81. Served in secret seaborne evacuations of Ethiopian Jews from 1981–83.

Yona Bogale   Ethiopian Jewish leader, activist and educator, from the 1950s to 1970s in Ethiopia, then in Israel, until his death in 1987.

Major Ika Brant   Israeli Air Force Hercules squadron commander. Served in Israeli Air Force Operations Department, 1982–85. Flew on airlifts of Ethiopian Jews from the desert in Sudan.

Major Ilan Buchris   Commander of the INS *Bat Galim*, 1970s–80s.

Angelo and Alfredo Castiglioni   Italian anthropologists and archaeologists. Founded and operated the Arous diving resort from 1974–77.

'Chana'   Member of the Mossad team and a manageress of the Arous diving resort from late 1983.

Dani   Mossad commander and instigator of Operation Brothers. Recruited and led the team of agents who operated the Arous diving resort and carried out secret evacuations of Ethiopian Jews from Sudan by land, sea and air, 1979–83.

Colonel Natan Dvir   Israeli Air Force Hercules squadron commander. Flew on secret airlifts of Jews from Sudan (1980s) and Ethiopia (1991).

Dr Jacques Faitlovich Foremost campaigner for Ethiopian Jews in the first half of the 20th century.

Muammar Gaddafi Libyan leader, 1969–2011.

Jacques Haggai Member of the Mossad team based at the Arous diving resort involved in operations in March and May 1982.

Chaim Halachmy Representative of organisations responsible for Jewish immigration to Israel. Helped bring out first groups of Jews from Ethiopia in 1977 and 1978, and connected the Mossad to Ferede Aklum.

Efraim Halevy Overall commander of Operation Brothers at Mossad HQ from 1980 onwards. Instigated Operation Moses in 1984 and facilitated Operation Joshua (Sheba) in 1985. Director of the Mossad from 1998–2002.

Joseph Halévy Professor of Ethiopic at Sorbonne University and first Jewish outsider to make contact with the Jews of Ethiopia (1867).

Major General Yitzhak 'Haka' Hofi Director of the Mossad, 1974–82.

Dr Baha al-Din Muhammad Idris Sudanese Minister of Presidential Affairs (sacked by Nimeiri in May 1984).

'Itai' Former Israeli Navy commando who served as a diving instructor at the Arous holiday resort from 1983.

Major General David Ivry Commander in Chief of the Israeli Air Force, 1977–82. Instigated the use of airlifts as a way to secretly evacuate Ethiopian Jews from Sudan.

David 'Dave' Kimche Head of Mossad division for handling relations with foreign intelligence services. Orchestrated the mission to smuggle Ethiopian Jews to Israel from 1977–81.

Lieutenant Colonel Gadi Kroll Commander of the Israeli Navy commando unit involved in the seaborne evacuation of Ethiopian Jews from Sudan.

Major General Amos Lapidot Commander in Chief of the Israeli Air Force, 1982–87.

Louis   Longest-serving member of the Mossad team based at the Arous diving resort mid-1981, participating in evacuations of Ethiopian Jews.

'ZL'   Swiss-based travel agent who marketed the Arous holiday resort for the Mossad.

Salah Madaneh   Head of Sudanese Tourism Corporation in Port Sudan.

Abba Mahari   Ethiopian Jewish priest, who is said to have led thousands of followers on an attempted journey from Gondar to Jerusalem in 1862.

Colonel Mohammed Mahgoub   Director General of the Sudanese Ministry of Tourism and of the Sudanese Tourism and Hotels Corporation. Leased the Arous holiday village to the European tourism company set up as a front by the Mossad.

Marcel   Mossad agent and Dani's deputy in Sudan. Joined Operation Brothers in late 1980, participating in evacuations of Ethiopian Jews. Served in the operation until late 1984.

Mengistu Haile Mariam   Ethiopian ruler, 1977–91.

Abu Medina   Caretaker at the Arous diving resort.

Mohammed   Head of the secret police in Gedaref.

Colonel Avinoam Maimon   Israeli Air Force Base 27 commander in the mid-1980s.

'Jean-Michel'   UNHCR representative in Gedaref, 1979–81.

Jean-Claude Nedjar   ORT project manager in Gondar, Ethiopia, 1978–82.

Jaafar Nimeiri   Sudanese president, 1969–85.

'Noam'   Manager of Neviot (Nuweiba) diving resort in the Sinai. Carried out initial survey of Arous diving resort in May 1981.

Dr Micki   Member of the Mossad team based at the Arous diving resort from mid-1982 until late 1984, participating in operations evacuating Ethiopian Jews.

Gil Pas   Member of the Mossad team based at the Arous diving resort from May 1982, participating in operations evacuating Ethiopian Jews.

Dr Shlomo Pomeranz Deputy head of neurology at Hadassah Hospital, Jerusalem, and Mossad agent. Joined Operation Brothers in Sudan in late 1980, served until 1983, participating in operations evacuating Ethiopian Jews.

'Ramian' Businessman in Khartoum who supplied vehicles used by the Mossad team to smuggle Ethiopian Jews.

Rubi Member of the Mossad team based at the Arous diving resort from mid-1981.

Ruth Recruited by the Mossad as head of the ICM office in Khartoum from February 1982.

Uri Sela Mossad agent who joined Operation Brothers in late 1980. Served undercover in Khartoum until April 1985, secretly evacuating Ethiopian Jews through the airport.

Haile Selassie Ethiopian emperor, 1930–74. Overthrown and murdered by the Derg.

Ariel Sharon Israeli defence minister, August 1981 to February 1983.

Gad Shimron Member of the Mossad team based at the Arous diving resort from December 1981, participating in operations evacuating Ethiopian Jews.

Shmulik Head diving instructor at Neviot (Nuweiba) resort and a member of the Mossad team based at the Arous diving resort from mid-1981, participating in operations evacuating Ethiopia Jews.

Shuffa Ethiopian Muslim merchant who delivered messages from Ferede Aklum in Sudan to his family in Ethiopia in 1979.

Omar el-Tayeb Sudanese vice president and head of the State Security Organisation (domestic intelligence agency).

David Ben Uziel (Tarzan) Mossad agent. Participated in operations evacuating Ethiopian Jews out of Sudan. Succeeded Dani as the head of the department in charge of Operation Brothers in October 1983.

'William'   Member of the Mossad team based at the Arous diving resort who participated in the first naval evacuation of Ethiopian Jews, in November 1981.

Yola   Member of the Mossad team and a manageress of the Arous diving resort from September 1982.

'Yoni'   Agent from the Mossad's Special Operations Division who made the first survey of the Sudanese coast with Dani and participated in the naval evacuation of Ethiopian Jews in November 1981.

'Yuval'   Member of the Mossad team based at Arous from April 1983, participating in operations evacuating Ethiopian Jews. Succeeded Dani as field commander.

ACRONYMS, ORGANISATIONS AND TERMS

Alliance Israelite Universelle (AIU)   Paris-based international Jewish rights organisation.

American Association for Ethiopian Jews (AAEJ)   Pro-Ethiopian Jewish activist group formed in 1974 (dissolved in 1993).

Berare   Amharic for 'Escapees'. Secret cells of Ethiopian Jewish youths in refugee camps in Sudan responsible for smuggling out evacuees at night-time to a waiting Mossad team.

Beta Israel   Hebrew for 'House of Israel'. Name by which the Ethiopian Jewish community has identified itself for generations and now widely used as the proper term of reference.

Canadian Association for Ethiopian Jews (CAEJ)   Pro-Ethiopian Jewish activist group formed in 1980 (dissolved in 1992).

Central Intelligence Agency (CIA)   US secret service.

Committee Men   Secret cell of Ethiopian Jewish refugee elders set up by the Mossad team in Sudan to organise evacuation lists and the welfare of Jews in the camps.

Derg   Military council which ruled Ethiopia from 1974–87.

Direction de la Surveillance du Territoire (DST)   Directorate of Territorial Surveillance. French domestic intelligence agency.

Ethiopian Democratic Union (EDU)   Counter-revolutionary movement responsible for attacks against the regime and others, including Ethiopian Jews, from mid- to late 1970s.

Ethiopian People's Revolutionary Party (EPRP)   Anti-Derg movement which waged an armed campaign against the regime and other perceived enemies, including 'Zionist' Ethiopian Jews in mid-1970s.

Etzel   Acronym for Irgun Zvai Leumi (Hebrew for National Military Organisation). Jewish underground group led by future Israeli Prime Minister Menachem Begin which operated against British forces in Mandate Palestine, 1931–48.

Falashas   Amharic for 'strangers' or 'landless people'. Name historically used by outsiders to refer to Ethiopian Jews. Considered derogatory by the Ethiopian Jewish community.

Hebrew Immigrant Aid Society (HIAS)   US-based Jewish organisation providing assistance in the resettlement, and in some cases clandestine evacuations, of refugees and Jewish communities in danger.

INS *Bat Galim*   Israeli Navy transport ship used in secret evacuations of Ethiopian Jews from Sudan from 1981–83.

Intergovernmental Committee for Migration (ICM)   Organisation responsible for the resettlement of refugees and displaced persons, whose office in Khartoum was set up and operated by the Mossad to move Ethiopian Jews out of the country from 1982.

Israel Defense Forces (IDF)   Collective name for the Israeli Army, Navy and Air Force.

Jewish Agency   Israeli non-governmental body responsible for helping Jews migrate to Israel.

Mossad   Israel's foreign intelligence agency.

Navco   'Fake' tourism company set up by the Mossad for the purposes of operating the diving resort at Arous.

Operation Brothers   Umbrella name for a series of clandestine evacuations by land, sea and air of Ethiopian Jews from Sudan to Israel from 1979–85, orchestrated by the Mossad.

Operation Joshua (or Sheba)   Secret airlift of the remaining Ethiopian Jews stranded by the abrupt halt of Operation Moses, from Sudan to Israel, on 22 March 1985.

Operation Moses   Secret mass airlift of Ethiopian Jews from Khartoum airport to Israel from 21 November 1984 to 5 January 1985.

Operation Solomon   Secret airlift by Israel of Ethiopian Jews from Addis Ababa, 24–25 May 1991.

Organisation for Rehabilitation through Training (ORT)   Geneva-based Jewish humanitarian organisation, providing assistance to developing communities around the world. Active in Ethiopia's Gondar region from 1976–81.

Shaldag   Elite unit of the Israeli Air Force, deployed in special operations inside enemy territory. Provided protection during airlifts of Ethiopian Jews from Sudan from 1982–84.

Shayetet 13   Hebrew for Flotilla 13. An elite navy commando unit which carried out seaborne evacuations of Ethiopian Jews from Sudan from 1981–83.

Tigray People's Liberation Front (TPLF)   Ethiopian rebel movement which fought against the regime from 1975 (eventually helping to overthrow the government in 1991).

Tribe of Dan   One of the twelve Biblical tribes of Israel from which, according to one theory, the Ethiopian Jews descend.

UNHCR   United Nations High Commissioner for Refugees (UN refugee agency).

MAPS

The region during the period of Operation Brothers

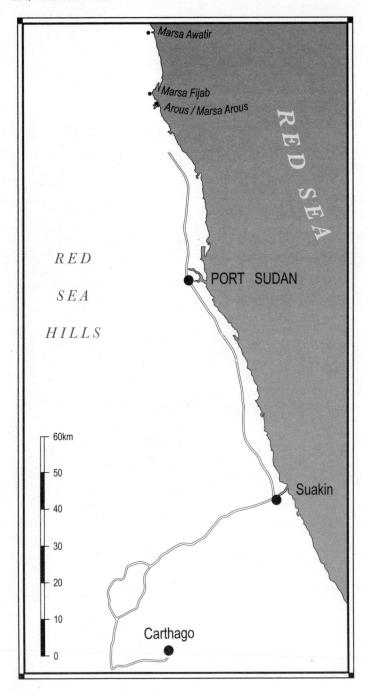

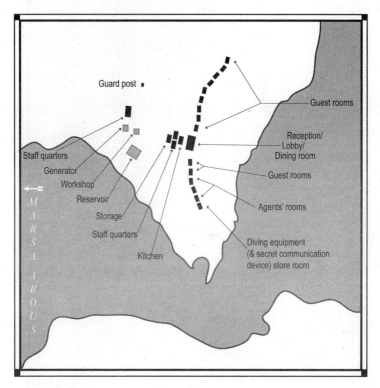

Arous resort

Left: Sudan's Red Sea coast

INTRODUCTION

The story of the spiriting of the Jews of Ethiopia to Israel is one without parallel.

As recently as 1975, the State of Israel, the declared nation state of the Jewish people, denied them the right to settle there.[1] Just two years later, Israel began a secret process involving its Air Force, Navy and foreign intelligence service to bring every Ethiopian Jewish man, woman and child it could to the Jewish state. So important was the cause that the people sent to carry it out constantly risked their lives to accomplish it.

In Israel, something profound had changed. For the echelons of the state it was a moment of awakening – but the Ethiopian Jews themselves had never been in slumber. For centuries, arguably millennia, the black Jews of the Highlands had steadfastly clung to the Jewish faith in the face of wars, oppression, invasion, poverty and famine. At the core of their beliefs lay a single driving force – an ancient dream to return to Jerusalem. The Ethiopian Jews maintained throughout the generations that they were Israelites, driven out of the land in biblical times. Their origins are an enigma, and until as recently as the mid-19th century they had survived so cut off from the rest of world Jewry that they thought there was no such thing as white Jews. They might not have survived at all were it not for the efforts of remarkable individuals, from benevolent French Jews in the late-1800s down to activists in North America a century later, and ultimately courageous decision-makers in Israel who instigated the operation to return them to their ancestral land. Nothing on such a scale had been done before, and it fell to the Mossad – Israel's much vaunted spy agency – to achieve it.

That is half of it. No such monumental event could have happened without the extraordinary actions, first and foremost, of the Ethiopian Jews themselves. They made it out not from within Ethiopia itself, but from Sudan, a Muslim-majority country tied to the Arab world, blighted by poverty and officially at war with Israel, the very country they were trying to reach. Whether lone souls, or entire villages, Jews walked hundreds of kilometres across inhospitable terrain to get to Sudan – not, according to countless accounts, to escape undeniable hardship and conflict in Ethiopia, but out of a conviction that they were walking to Jerusalem. Many died along the way and the conditions they found themselves in in refugee camps on the other side of the border were immeasurably worse than those which they had left behind. On top of this, it was all done by stealth. They left their homes in the middle of the night, risking arrest, torture and worse if they were caught, as many were, since leaving Ethiopia without permission was treated as a crime. Leaving to get to Israel was treated as treasonous. Even in the refugee camps they hid who they were, lest they be attacked or taken away.

The question arises as to why, then, they headed to Sudan at all. The answer lies in the fact that it was, from 1979, a secret gateway, a pathway to the Holy Land, unlocked by two men – one, an enterprising Ethiopian Jewish fugitive called Ferede Aklum; the other, an exceptional Israeli secret agent called Dani.

One cryptic letter, and an unlikely partnership, changed the course of history for the Jews of Ethiopia, and in many ways that of the State of Israel and the Mossad itself. It is the only operation of its kind, where civilians have been evacuated from another country, that has been completely led by an intelligence agency.

It was through danger and daring that Ferede and Dani laid the foundations for a secret network of Ethiopian Jews and an entire division of the Mossad, backed by naval and air support, to deliver thousands of Jewish refugees to a land they had yearned for for so long. As Dani put it to me in one of our many interviews: 'It was like two big wheels, two strong wheels, actually met – one was the old Ethiopian Jews' dream to go back to Zion and Jerusalem, and the other one was the Israeli Jews that came to help them fulfil this – it was the fusion of wheels that was the strength of this operation – that is why nobody ever gave up.'*[2]

It was also the result of a combination of bravery, ingenuity, subterfuge and guile – perhaps none more so than the ruse used as a years-long cover story by the Mossad to carry out the mission behind enemy lines. With astonishing inventiveness, the team of secret agents led by Dani set up and operated a diving resort on the Sudanese coast, masquerading as hotel staff by day, while smuggling Jews out of the country by night. Even more remarkable was the fact that it was done hand-in-hand with unwitting Sudanese authorities and under the very noses of the guests. How it happened is told in this book, pieced together from accounts of the agents and the people who stayed there themselves.

* Zion: a biblical term for Jerusalem and/or the 'Land of Israel'.

In the course of over 100 hours of interviews I conducted with past and present Mossad agents and Navy and Air Force personnel involved in the secret operation, both on the ground and behind the scenes, many made a similar, personal point: that they knew there and then that they were involved in something historic. All would say with modesty that they were 'just doing their job' but it was clear they were motivated by something much more visceral than that. More than once, these individuals would use the analogy of the biblical Exodus of the Jewish people who went from bondage in Egypt to redemption in the Promised Land. They felt they were carrying out something similar in the modern age.

The latter day event is often referred to as the 'rescue' of the Ethiopian Jews. This, however, is a characterisation which is rejected by the Ethiopian Jews themselves, a perspective which deserves to be acknowledged and respected. They were masters of their own fate. They elected to make the perilous journey, leaving behind their homes and their way of life, in pursuit of the Holy City, losing loved ones in terrible circumstances along the way. For this reason, and in deference to them, I do not describe what took place as a 'rescue' in this book.

By its very nature, the Mossad operates in an opaque and clandestine way, which was very much the case when it came to smuggling the Jews out of Sudan. For decades, the details of this operation, which paved the way for the historic mass airlift of Jewish refugees from Sudan, known as Operation Moses, were officially secret.[3] The fact that it *happened* is known; *how* it happened has not been written about before with the full cooperation of those who commanded and carried it out. Now is a moment in time when the story is surfacing, quite rightly capturing people's imaginations. It is an exciting tale, but as with all intriguing stories about covert activities, it may in time become muddied by half-truths and fictional portrayals. The real story does not need any such embellishment: it is dramatic and astounding in its own right. I chose to write this book for the same reason as those individuals who decided to take me into their trust did so – to document it in a truthful way so it stands as an authentic record of what took place. Some of the contributors have not spoken out about their roles before and none seek public recognition.[4] In this book, where there is dialogue it is faithfully reproduced as close to verbatim as possible, based on the recollections of those who were part of these conversations.

This book has taken me on an extraordinary journey of discovery and it has been nothing short of a privilege. I write it in tribute to both the Beta Israel (Ethiopian Jews) and the actions of the Mossad and Israeli armed forces which helped to bring them home.

1

CAT AND MOUSE

APRIL, 1985

It was after dark when the knock came on Milton Bearden's door. He was not expecting visitors and the rapping had an urgency to it, suggesting this was no social call.

Bearden cautiously opened up.

'We've got trouble!' said one of the three men standing there. Bearden did not recognise them, but he knew who they were.

'Come in,' he said instinctively, glancing around as he ushered them inside.

'Go upstairs. There's a loft. Get up there and stay out of the way.'

The three men followed his direction and disappeared out of sight.

Bearden knew he suddenly had an emergency on his hands. As he stood considering what to do, one of the men reappeared.

'Here,' said the figure, tossing Bearden a set of keys, 'you'd better get the stuff out of the van.'

Milton Bearden, the CIA's station chief in Khartoum, had been prepared for such a moment for the past two years. He understood his 'guests' were Mossad agents, and that they were on the run.

In hot pursuit were units of the Sudanese Army, aided by a Libyan hit-squad sent by the country's mercurial ruler Muammar Gaddafi to hunt down dissidents operating in the city.

The old order had been swept away days earlier when Sudan's longtime leader and US ally Jaafar Nimeiri was deposed in a popular uprising backed by the Army. A military council was now in charge, President Nimeiri and his acolytes accused of everything from corruption to high treason. Among the allegations was collusion with Israel, with which Sudan was in a formal state of war.[1] Now it was time for the new rulers to burnish their credentials among the Arab world and flush out Zionist spies, real or imaginary.

Bearden checked the coast was clear, then went out to the men's vehicle. It was packed with communications equipment, much to his chagrin. He lugged it all inside the house, hiding it in a back room.

The station chief went upstairs to talk to the men and discuss what to do. The contingency plan had been agreed at a meeting with Mossad officials in August 1983, shortly after he had taken up his post. In the event of a problem, Israeli agents in Khartoum knew to meet Bearden in the arcade of the Meridien Hotel, identifying him by his walking stick with a warthog tusk handle and a .44 Magnum casing tip, or to head to his house in the capital's New Extension district – in Bearden's words, 'at the snap of a finger, if everything starts to fall apart'.

Mossad had been operating secretly in Sudan for years, but owing to the political upheaval, its presence had finally been exposed.

As soon as it took power, the Sudanese military began making sweeping arrests in an anti-Nimeiri drive, purging the state security service and detaining hundreds of key figures associated with the ousted government. Among them was Nimeiri's former Minister of Presidential Affairs, Dr Baha al-Din Muhammad Idris, known as Mr Ten Per Cent on account of the cost of greasing his palm. Purportedly arrested while trying to flee the country with a Samsonite suitcase full of money, Idris is said to have offered his captors information in exchange for clemency.

'Leave me alone, and I'll give you something really big,' he said, according to Bearden, recounting conversations with trusted sources. 'There's an Israeli intelligence nest here in town. Arrest them, and you'll be heroes.'

It did not help Idris. He was later convicted of corruption and sentenced to ten years in jail, but it was enough to put the hit squad on the Israelis' trail.

Mossad chiefs in Tel Aviv knew they had to get their men out before their pursuers closed in. The question was how. The borders and airport had been closed – dump trucks had been parked on the runways to prevent any aircraft arriving or leaving – and outside telephone lines cut since thousands of protesters had taken to the streets demanding Nimeiri's removal.

Whichever way, it was not going to happen very quickly, and Bearden's immediate problem was to keep the men hidden. He employed household staff and could not be sure that they were not passing information to the authorities. The staff had gone for the night but would be back in the morning and inevitably wonder about the unannounced guests.

Bearden decided to pass the Israelis off as US contractors on temporary duty at the embassy, staying with him for the time being. He gave them Dallas Cowboys baseball hats 'and made sure they looked like Americans'. He also gave them weapons

– a Browning Hi-Power 9mm semi-automatic pistol and a 9mm Beretta submachine gun.

'There was a very active search for these guys going on,' Bearden recalls, 'and with my own intelligence assets I was able to monitor pretty closely the planning for this search – where these [Sudanese/Libyan] guys were going to be looking, which quadrant of town. I was able to understand what they were up to as well as they were.'

In the meantime, Bearden, CIA HQ in Virginia and Mossad chiefs were in contact, and they got to work on a plan. With conventional options closed, the men, it was decided, would have to be smuggled out of the country, albeit at great risk.

'Crates,' proposed Bearden. 'What about putting them in crates?' The idea was perilous and subjected to a 'very difficult decision-making process', as one high-ranking Mossad official with intimate knowledge of the discussions remembers. Time was short and after tense debate at Mossad HQ the plan was approved.

The CIA's technical services set to work on a design.

A few days after the men had turned up at Bearden's house, another knock came at the door. This time his wife, Marie-Catherine, answered. 'My name is Pierre. I'm French,' announced the visitor.

'Come in quickly,' replied Mrs Bearden, 'but I can tell you're not French – because I *am*,' she said. 'Go into that room and wait.'

'Pierre' was in fact another Mossad agent, sent to find out about the other three. 'There wasn't much he could do other than come to me,' recalls Bearden, 'so now instead of three, we had four.'

Bearden decided it was time to wrong-foot their pursuers.

'I knew which areas had just been canvassed for these guys, so it was a safe bet to take them right there,' he recalls.

He put the four men, dressed in their American garb, in a van and drove them to parts of town which search teams had already scoured. Monitoring the pursuers' movements, Bearden shuttled the agents between safe houses and his own home, for one or two days at a time, in a tense game of cat and mouse.

Ten days after it was shut down, the airport reopened, and the US embassy put in a request with the Sudanese authorities to allow a resupply plane in. The flight got the go-ahead and a C-141 flew in with stocks of equipment. There was something else on board: the aircraft was carrying the escape kit, and a CIA technician to put it together. Unloaded, the apparatus was taken to the embassy building on Ali Abdul Lattif Street in west Khartoum, where it was assembled.

The boxes were rigged with air tubes and small oxygen generators that could be activated from within as back-up. The plan was to hide the men inside the crates, place the boxes in oversized diplomatic pouches, seal them up and get the 'cargo' past Sudanese security to a waiting plane at the airport some 25 minutes' drive away.

'There was a 49–51 per cent chance of this working,' says Bearden. 'But these men [on their trail] were just not giving up, and they meant harm.'

The following day Bearden and the men, accompanied by two CIA officers and a driver, slipped out of his home before dawn and set off for the embassy. There Bearden and the technician helped the four agents climb into the boxes.

'They understood and showed no fear,' he recalls, 'I patted them on their heads and told them: "God be with you. Be bold, be brave, be strong."'[2]

The lids came down. The pouches were tied. It was time to go.

SEPTEMBER, 1973

The tall, slim man walked into the building on Dejazmach Belay Zeleke Road. The flag outside – white with two blue stripes and a star in the middle – signalled he had found the right place.

Ferede Aklum had travelled more than 900 kilometres from his home in Adi Woreva, a Jewish village in the highlands of Tigray, in Ethiopia's far north, to the Israeli embassy in the capital, Addis Ababa, to get a pass to a new life.[3] He had arrived full of hope, but his optimism quickly faded.

Visas to Israel, embassy officials told Ferede, were not issued on the spot. Applicants were required to show proof of their intended travel, such as an air or sea ticket, and that they had sufficient funds to support themselves once they got there. It amounted to several hundred US dollars, beyond the reach of impoverished villagers.

Despite the obstacles, Ferede was single-minded. He travelled back home and set about forging a ticket for a journey by boat to Israel and raising money, supported in his endeavour by his parents.

Ferede's father, Yazezow, was a well-respected district judge in Indabaguna, a mixed Muslim-Christian town with a small Jewish presence, near Adi Woreva.

An erudite and religious man, he studied both Ethiopian law and the Bible. The Ethiopian Jews were a devout community who considered themselves the descendants of the Jewish people who, according to tradition, stood at the foot of Mount Sinai and received the Ten Commandments, conquered

Canaan under Joshua and formed the Kingdom of Solomon with its Holy Temple in Jerusalem. Until the latter part of the 19th century, they self-identified not as Jews (*ayhud* in Amharic – Ethiopia's official language – historically a derogatory term in Ethiopia) but as 'Beta Israel' – House of Israel – or, put simply, Israelites.[4]

Although Judaism had been part of the fabric of Ethiopia for centuries, non-Jewish Ethiopians (and foreigners) referred to them as *falasha*, meaning 'strangers' or 'landless people'. The Beta Israel considered this degrading, even though in a religious sense they regarded themselves as living in exile and looked upon Jerusalem as their spiritual home. They spoke not of the Land of Israel (as it is known in the Hebrew Bible) but the Land of Jerusalem. They prayed towards Jerusalem, slaughtered their animals for food while facing in its direction and spoke about the holy city as flowing with milk and honey. Stories about the glory of Jerusalem were passed down from generation to generation, and poetry and songs were written in its praise. '*Shimela! Shimela!*' Ethiopian Jewish children would sing on catching sight of a stork, as migrating musters headed to the Holy Land, '*Agerachin Yerusalem dehena?*' – 'Stork! Stork! How is our country Jerusalem doing?'[5]

Like his own parents and grandparents before him, Yazezow believed the time would come when, in the words of the prophet Isaiah from the 8th century BC, 'the Lord will set His hand again the second time to recover the remnant of His people, that shall remain from Assyria, and from Egypt … and from Cush …'[6] At the time of Isaiah, Cush corresponded to present-day northern Sudan and possibly beyond, and it was where, according to one theory, Jews resided in ancient times before crossing into what is now Ethiopia.[7]

Yazezow would tell his own twelve children over and over again of Jerusalem's splendour, delicately depicting imagined scenes of the city in embroideries with threads of red, yellow and gold.[8]

With his parents' blessing, Ferede went back to the embassy. He produced his 'ticket' and cash, and got his visa. His hope renewed, Ferede then took a bus 1,200 kilometres north to Eritrea, where he bought a one-way ticket for a sea voyage to the Israeli port city of Eilat. For the 25 year old, it was the culmination of a lifelong dream. He checked into a guesthouse and waited for his boat.

The Beta Israel had heard about Israel's declaration of independence in 1948 and had danced jubilantly in the streets. There were around that time nascent contacts between Ethiopian Jews and other Jewish communities in the world – but in Israel itself, even by the 1970s, the Ethiopians were not recognised as 'real' Jews – neither by the state nor its Orthodox rabbinical establishment. As a result, they did not qualify to settle there under the 1950 Law of Return, which granted Jews anywhere in the world the right to Israeli citizenship.[9] In spite of this, a small number of Ethiopian Jews had made it to Israel by boat – some had got through, while others were caught and were turned back.[10] Ferede was prepared to take his chance. He had his pass – albeit a tourist visa – and was set to go.

Then two days before he was due to sail, calamitous news broke. Israel had been attacked by Syria and Egypt on the holiest day in the Jewish calendar – Yom Kippur – and was at war. All flights and sailings between Ethiopia and Israel were cancelled. Worse was to come when, some two weeks later, relenting to Arab pressure, Ethiopian emperor Haile Selassie severed diplomatic relations with Israel.

For Ferede it was a catastrophe. He went back home in a state of despair.

The Yom Kippur War, as it would become commonly known, was one of Israel's most difficult.[11] Taken by surprise, the Jewish state sustained heavy losses and struggled to beat back the attacking forces. By the time the fighting ended in a ceasefire twenty days after it started, Israeli troops had advanced to within 101 kilometres of Cairo and 40 kilometres of Damascus. Exhausted, Israel's sense of invincibility, shored up by its overwhelming victory in the Six Day War just six years earlier, had been punctured.[12] The nation had suffered a trauma and although the governing Labor Party was returned to office in elections just two months later, support was slipping. For the first time in Israel's political history, public opinion began to shift from the left to the right. The left was ideologically split over what to do with territory won from the Arabs in 1967, anti-government demonstrations against the failure of the ruling elite to anticipate the attack in 1973 were growing, and Israel's 'Iron Lady' Golda Meir resigned in April 1974 over the fallout from the war. Her replacement, Yitzhak Rabin, was beset by a series of corruption scandals in the party, and himself resigned weeks before elections in 1977 after it emerged that his wife illegally held a US bank account.[13] The conditions were ripe for change, and the polls in May delivered it. Israel witnessed a political earthquake. The country woke up to a new prime minister, and the dawn of a new era.

2

'BRING ME THE ETHIOPIAN JEWS'

A short, balding man with prominent features who wore distinctive large, heavy-rimmed glasses, Menachem Begin had been leader of the opposition in parliament for 29 years, having contested – and lost – eight previous elections. Now, as head of the right-wing Likud party, he had been swept to power.

Begin was widely perceived as being one of Israel's founding fathers. A staunch nationalist, he had led one of the most fearsome Jewish underground groups operating against British forces in Palestine, the Irgun Zvai Leumi (National Military Organisation), known by its Hebrew acronym Etzel.[1] In the 1940s, the group carried out attacks and reprisals to try to force the British out. Its most notorious attack was on the luxurious King David Hotel in Jerusalem, which housed the British military command, where in 1946 a bombing brought down the southern wing, killing 91 people.[2] Begin spent years as a wanted man, and came out of hiding only after the establishment of the State of Israel. He had arrived in Palestine in 1943, escaping the Nazi invasions of Poland and the Soviet Union, but his parents, elder brother and a nephew had not got out and were murdered by the Germans.

Begin's mentality was shaped by the Nazi Holocaust and the persecution – and defencelessness – of Jews. (He would reportedly tell US President Jimmy Carter later: 'There is only one thing to which I'm sensitive: Jewish blood.')[3] For him, Israel was not just the Jewish homeland, but a sanctuary for Jews under threat anywhere. The bringing of the Jewish diaspora to Israel was a Zionist goal and for Begin a creed. In a transitional meeting with outgoing Prime Minister Rabin and the head of the Mossad, Yitzhak 'Haka' Hofi, Begin was briefed on the intelligence agency's operations. Prime ministers could hire and fire Mossad chiefs, but Begin asked Hofi – who was reportedly prepared to resign – to stay on.[4] Begin told him to carry on all planned and active Mossad missions, and to add a new one to the list. 'Bring me the Jews of Ethiopia,' he said.[5]

The fate of Ethiopian Jews had become an issue while Begin was in opposition. In the 1970s, activist groups in the US and Canada, led by the American Association for Ethiopian Jews (AAEJ), spearheaded campaigns to prick public consciousness about the Ethiopian Jewish community and pressure the Israeli government to act. The AAEJ said it forced the issue up the prime minister's agenda, but this claim is emphatically rejected by Israeli officials in positions of seniority under Begin's administration.[6] According to a high-ranking Mossad figure who dealt with the prime minister personally in connection with the issue at the time, both Begin and Hofi acted out of a deep sense of moral obligation, dismissing the suggestion that they were pressured into it as specious.[7]

It is true that for decades the Israeli state and (to a lesser extent) the Jewish Agency – a non-governmental body which helped Jewish communities abroad and facilitated immigration to Israel – were at best ambivalent and at worst resistant to doing anything about Ethiopian Jewry. There was among political circles a sense that Ethiopian Jews' 'primitive' way of life was incompatible with that led by modern, integrated Israelis, rendering them too problematic and costly to absorb. Golda Meir herself reportedly said of the issue in 1969: 'They will just be objects of prejudice here. Don't we have enough problems already? What do we need these blacks for?'[8] Even as late on as 1975, the head of the Jewish Agency's Department of Immigration and Absorption, Yehuda Dominitz, expressed opposition to bringing them to Israel.[9]

There was also Israel's relationship with Ethiopia to consider. Ethiopia was part of Israel's so-called Periphery Doctrine – a policy to forge alliances with non-Arab countries in the region to counter the anti-Israel bloc of Arab states. Ethiopia was strategically important to Israel. It was a Christian-majority country (with a large Muslim minority), which bordered Arab-majority Sudan and sat across the Red Sea from Saudi Arabia and North and South Yemen. Of the countries with a Red Sea coastline, Ethiopia was the only one friendly towards Israel. Crucially, it also bordered the Bab al-Mandab Strait, the 35-kilometre-wide waterway connecting the Red Sea with the Indian Ocean. For Israel, unfettered access through the strait was vital for the import of oil as well as for trade with East Africa, Iran and the Far East.

Israel had fostered links with Ethiopia since the 1950s and did not want to do anything to antagonise Selassie. To make an issue out of its Jews risked stoking demands of their own from the array of other ethnic groups in Ethiopia, a country of such diversity as to have earned the epithet of 'museo di populi', or museum of peoples.[10] In Ethiopia itself there was no real history of emigration – the few Ethiopians who did leave the country went to study abroad but nearly all returned.[11] Among them, hardly any were Jews trying to get to Israel.

'There were very few, because the policy of Haile Selassie was "They're all my sons",' recalls Reuven Merhav, a Mossad official seconded to the Israeli embassy in Addis Ababa from 1967–69. 'He looked at [all Ethiopians] as if he was the great emperor and everyone there was under his wings, and there was no such trend. The Jews knew the Israeli government wouldn't let them in – the Rabbinical Establishment did not recognise them as Jews – and the Ethiopian government didn't want to let them out.'[12]

The advent of Begin, however, changed the trajectory. His motives can only be speculated upon, but it is arguable that he was driven not only by Zionist idealism and an egalitarian approach to Jews regardless of colour, but also by an affinity towards peoples in peril, born out of the tragedy of the Holocaust. In his first act as prime minister, for instance, Begin gave refuge to dozens of Vietnamese people fleeing the aftermath of the Vietnam War, who were picked up in boats in the Pacific Ocean by an Israeli cargo ship. Announcing his decision to the Knesset (Israeli parliament) on his inaugural day in June 1977, Begin evoked the abandonment of Jews to their fate by the nations of the world, saying: 'Today we have the Jewish state. We have not forgotten [countries' indifference]. We will behave with humanity.'[13]

Whatever his rationale, it was clearly important enough to him to make the Ethiopian Jews a priority at a time when Israel had all manner of domestic and foreign challenges to deal with.

It was an unprecedented order for the Mossad. Designed primarily for espionage, sabotage and assassination in defence of the state, the agency was not structured for such a task at that time.

However, the instruction had been issued by the Prime Minister and it was the Mossad's duty to carry it out. Begin had ordered Hofi, and Hofi commissioned one of his most experienced officers, David Kimche, to do it. Born in the leafy north-west London suburb of Hampstead, Kimche has been described as a 'true-life Israeli equivalent of John le Carré's fictional British spy, George Smiley'.[14] He was, according to agents who worked with him, an exceptional person, both professionally and personally. In particular, he knew Africa well, having spent many years there quietly fostering relations for Israel with military chiefs and heads of states (earning himself the nickname among colleagues of 'the man with the suitcase').[15]

From the outset, Kimche, who came from a strongly Zionist family, was convinced of the mission's virtue and persuaded others of it too. His philosophy, according to a senior operative close to him, was that 'if you believe in something, there is no obstacle – you will go round, you will go up, down, whatever, you will do it, and that is what Kimche relayed to everyone working for him'.[16]

By the early 1970s, Israeli projects in Ethiopia in almost every field – military, economic and technical – were extensive and pervasive.[17] In fact, a US state department official who served in Ethiopia until 1972 observed that Israelis there 'were probably more influential than the United States … If you really wanted to get to the Ethiopian government, you went through the Israelis, not the Americans'.[18] For the Jewish state, such level of involvement was key to strengthening Ethiopia against subversion by Israel's regional enemies; for Selassie, Israel was an asset to Ethiopia in its struggle against Arab and Muslim-backed secessionists in Eritrea on its northern frontier.[19]

Israeli intelligence reputedly saved Selassie himself from three coup attempts, and compared to the rest of the continent, where leaders had been toppled like dominoes in the post-Second World War period (there had been some 60 coups or attempted coups in Africa since 1946) Ethiopia had been a politically stable ally.[20]

All that was to dramatically change though in 1973, when the Arab-Israeli war led to a haemorraging of Israel's relations with African states. Through a combination of Arab pressure and pan-African solidarity, one after the other, African nations severed ties with Israel in October and November of that year.

In a shock to Israel, Ethiopia followed suit. Arab states had threatened to move the headquarters of the Organisation of African Unity (OAU), from which Selassie derived much prestige as its figurehead, from Addis Ababa, and his prime minister convinced him to choose relations with the Arab world over the Jewish state. Despite the public rupture, Selassie held out the prospect of resuming diplomatic relations – but it was not to be.[21] Less than a year later, in September 1974, he was overthrown by a group of Marxist Army officers (his position made more vulnerable, it has been suggested, by the expulsion of Israeli security advisors).[22] The historically sympathetic emperor was replaced by a radical anti-capitalist, anti-religion, pro-Soviet regime, and Ethiopia to Israel looked a lost cause. However, realities were such that the political tumult created an unexpected opportunity.

The new military junta, known as the Derg, inherited the problem of the rebellion in Eritrea and intensified efforts to crush it. Armed uprisings also broke out in other parts of the country and by the end of 1976 the regime was beset by insurgencies in all of Ethiopia's provinces. The Derg turned to Ethiopia's erstwhile ally, and in December 1975 secretly recalled the Israeli military experts ejected by Selassie.

Even without an embassy, the Mossad had continued to operate an undercover office in Addis Ababa, staffed by a single agent.[23] Publicly, it masqueraded as an agricultural development office, its real purpose to preserve a secret but solid contact with the new regime through Israel's foreign intelligence service. According to high-ranking Mossad officials, it was (officially, at least) known about only by the Ethiopian president, Mengistu Haile Mariam (who violently manoeuvred his way to become head of state in February 1977) and one or two others in the highest echelons.[24] This is questionable, though, because it is said that once when the agent was waiting for a meeting with the Ethiopian minister of defence, a Soviet general, chest full of medals, emerged from the minister's office and acknowledged the waiting man with a Russian-accented 'Shalom'.[25]

In July 1977 Ethiopia faced a new battlefront when neighbouring Somalia invaded the eastern Ogaden region, home to predominantly ethnic Somalis. Somalia and the allied Western Somali Liberation Front (WSLF) made swift territorial gains, putting the beleaguered Ethiopian forces on the back foot.

Ethiopia had previously been a recipient of US military aid, but after Jimmy Carter took office earlier that year, Washington publicly announced cuts in response to Ethiopia's woeful human rights record. Mengistu retaliated by scrapping a mutual defence assistance treaty and ordered US personnel to leave the country.[26] As a result, the US, which had been Ethiopia's biggest arms supplier, stopped sending weapons.

Stung by the loss of US military support, Mengistu called the Mossad's man in Addis Ababa for a meeting. Israeli personnel had already (in 1975) helped set up a 10,000-strong counter-insurgency division (known as Nebelbal, or Flame) to fight the Eritrean rebels, and the Jewish state was supplying crucially needed spare parts for Ethiopia's US-made weaponry.[27] Now Mengistu wanted Israel to significantly step up its military assistance.

He also wanted the Israeli Air Force (IAF) to bomb Somali positions and air-drop supplies to a brigade besieged by Eritrean insurgents.[28]

The message got back to the Mossad HQ in Tel Aviv. It was picked up by Dani, the deputy head of a department responsible for handling relations with intelligence services in the developing world.

Dani, whose brief included Ethiopia, went to discuss the issue with Kimche, the head of his division.

By now around two months had passed since Begin issued his order, and no Jews had yet been brought out of Ethiopia. Kimche spotted an opening.

'We can't give Mengistu everything he wants,' he said, 'but we can give him something – and we can ask for Ethiopian Jews in return.'

The two men went to see Hofi in his office on the eleventh floor.

Kimche proposed a meeting with Mengistu. 'We can discuss what we're prepared to give him, and what we can get in return,' he said. Hofi agreed and instructed Kimche to make the trip.

Kimche turned to Dani, 'Okay, you're coming with me.'

At that time, Dani, although having risen to a senior position, like many in the Mossad had not been involved with this kind of mission before, nor exposed to negotiations with heads of state. Born in Uruguay to French parents, he had been recruited from the Army, where he served as a paratrooper officer, to the Mossad in 1968 when the agency was looking for officers with foreign language skills. Dani spoke Spanish and French fluently, and knew several other languages. Kimche also saw in him someone who, like him, was not afraid to think outside the box, question authority and even rebel against it. For much the same reasons, Dani greatly admired Kimche and considered himself a kind of apprentice to him.

Kimche and Dani flew to Addis Ababa on an unmarked military plane. They went straight from the airport to the presidential palace – formerly Selassie's seat of power. They entered Mengistu's office, where they found the president, a translator and the Mossad's representative.

The atmosphere was businesslike as the group shook hands and sat down. As Dani took his seat, Mengistu made a remark in Amharic.

'Fidel Castro was sitting there a week ago,' said the translator, in English.

'Ah, Fidel Castro!' responded Dani. 'I grew up with Che Guevara!' he said, gesturing with a salute.[29] It was an offbeat moment, which made Mengistu laugh, breaking the ice. For the rest of the meeting, Kimche and Mengistu discussed matters, as Dani and the representative observed. (Mengistu broke off with a 'May I?' to pocket a box of Israeli matches offered by Dani to light the president's cigarette.)

The result of the talks was that Israel agreed to send consignments of small arms and ammunition and to lend pilots who would teach the Ethiopian Air Force how to make air drops to the encircled brigade. In exchange, Mengistu would allow the planes bringing in the supplies to transport back to Israel a number of Ethiopian Jews, according to a list which Israel would draw up – first and foremost relatives of some of the 300 or so who were already legally there.[30]

The person nominated to sort this out was Chaim Halachmy, who headed the office of the US-based Hebrew Immigrant Aid Society (HIAS) in Israel. Tunisian-born Halachmy had previous experience in smuggling Jews from one place to another during the North African Jewish immigration to Israel in the early 1950s. He also worked for the Jewish Agency, which had been involved with Jews in Ethiopia for some 25 years, setting up a network of Jewish schools there, teaching them, among other things, Hebrew.[31]

Isolated from world Jewry for centuries, the Ethiopian Jews had practically no knowledge of the Hebrew language or of mainstream Judaism.[32] Though the biblical foundations were the same, the Beta Israel followed a form of the religion which had not evolved with that practiced by Jews in the rest of the world, having branched off perhaps as far back as 3,000 years.

While the Jewish Agency's purpose was not to promote *aliyah* (ascent, or migration to Israel) among Ethiopian Jews, in the 1950s, at the behest of Israel's second president and Beta Israel historian, Yitzhak Ben Zvi, it brought a handful of the younger generation to Israel for education and training, in order for them to return to Ethiopia and help their community. Ben Zvi had higher hopes though. 'You are the first bridge,' he told the pioneering group of twelve in 1955. 'You are going back to prepare your brothers for immigration. You are setting out on a national mission.'[33] Impassioned as they were, his words were delivered at a time when there was no prospect of Israel allowing Ethiopian Jews to settle. Nevertheless, the programme inevitably stimulated interest among the young Ethiopian Jews in Zionism and the Jewish state, and, for the first time, the ancient longing to return became more than just a dream.

It was only two generations back that Ethiopian Jews were still living in obscurity, and they may well have disappeared out of existence in years to come were it not for the remarkable endeavours of a Polish-born Jew by the name of Dr Jacques Faitlovich.

Faitlovich had learnt about the Ethiopian Jews from his university lecturer, Frenchman Joseph Halévy, who had become the first Jewish outsider to make contact with this fabled people.[34] An expert on Ethiopia, Halévy had been sent on an adventurous mission in 1867 by the Alliance Israelite Universelle (AIU), a Jewish rights organisation, to find the mysterious black Jews and report on their conditions.

As an indication of just how detached Ethiopian Jews were from the rest of world Jewry, when Halévy first arrived in a village the community did not believe he could be Jewish too as they were convinced there were only black Jews in the world. 'I assured them that all the Falashas of Jerusalem, and in other parts of the world, were white; and that they could not be distinguished from the other inhabitants of their respective countries,' he wrote.

It was, in fact, the mention of Jerusalem, more than the revelation that other Jews existed, that excited these Ethiopian Jews.

'[It] changed as if by magic the attitude of the most incredulous,' Halévy observed. 'A burning curiosity seemed all at once to have seized the whole company.'[35]

Just a few years earlier, Ethiopian Jews had made the first attempt to walk en masse to Jerusalem. Led by an enigmatic priest, Abba Mahari, thousands of followers are said to have trekked in the direction of what Mahari believed to be the Holy Land. According to accounts, the episode ended in disaster, with many dying of starvation or exhaustion en route, and other followers drowning when they waded into a body of water which they believed was the Red Sea, and which Mahari attempted, futilely, to miraculously split with his staff.[36]

Halévy noted that the Jews he found believed the Holy Land was still ruled by the Romans, and that when he informed them that Jerusalem had lost its ancient splendour and that a mosque now stood on the site of the fallen Jewish temples, they were grief-stricken.

Despite Halévy's reports, the AIU did not take any action and interest in the Ethiopian Jews waned. The issue lay dormant for another 40 years, until the arrival of Faitlovich on the scene.

Inspired by his mentor, in 1904, Faitlovich travelled to the province of Gondar, where the majority of the Jews lived. After overcoming their suspicions of white foreigners, he spent the next year and a half living among them and learning their ways and customs. He concluded that although they were devoted to their Judaism, they were under serious threat from Christian missionaries and needed outside help if they were to survive.

While the interest in Ethiopian Jews generated by Halévy had petered out, it was the actions of Faitlovich which were to put them on the map. Understanding that their acceptance as Jews by Orthodox religious authorities was key to their future, Faitlovich managed to get some 44 prominent rabbis from across Europe, America, Egypt and Palestine to sign an open letter expressing their solidarity with the community, to whom they referred as 'our flesh and blood'.[37]

While Faitlovich's aim was to regenerate Jewish life in Ethiopia rather than encourage emigration, the letter which the rabbis put their names to reassured them of their hope that God 'will gather us from the four corners of the earth and bring us to Zion'. For the first time in the history of the Ethiopian Jews, their brethren in the diaspora embraced the notion of their return.

Over the following years and decades, Faitlovich made ten more trips to the Beta Israel, established a string of Jewish schools in their villages (and one in Addis Ababa) and set up Pro-Falasha Committees in America and Europe. It was through his activities that the Beta Israel emerged from their long period of isolation from the wider Jewish fold and were introduced to a Judaism they never knew existed.

Despite (arguably) millennia of separation, the two forms still shared fundamental beliefs. The Beta Israel kept kosher, practised circumcision and observed the Sabbath scrupulously – the backbones of mainstream Judaism. They marked the same major biblical festivals as the rest of the diaspora (but were oblivious to those which developed at a point in history after they had separated), and their Bible (known as the Orit) contained all the passages of the Hebrew Bible used by Jews the world round.[38]

Faitlovich's project continued up to the Italian Fascist invasion of Ethiopia in 1935, when it was suspended, along with contacts between Beta Israel and foreign Jewry.[39] The colonisation lasted until 1941, when Ethiopia was liberated, and Faitlovich returned the following year to resume his work.

However, he did so in the context of a different world. The Holocaust of European Jewry happened, the plight of its survivors inevitably became the focus of Jewish conscience, and while the State of Israel was created in 1948–49 as a safe haven for Jews, it did not open its gates to the Beta Israel (although the Ethiopian Jews, upon learning that it had been attacked by Arab armies, fasted for two days in grief and prayer).[40] In large part this was down to the status of the Ethiopian Jews in the eyes of Israel's Orthodox chief rabbinate (although some Orthodox rabbis did accept them as Jewish) and the state.[41] In addition, for the latter, unlike the Jewish communities in enemy Arab countries, their situation was not considered an emergency.[42]

In the early 1950s, the Jewish Agency took up Faitlovich's mantle and opened a boarding school in Asmara, employing among its teachers an Ethiopian Jew by the name of Yona Bogale. As a child in the 1920s, Bogale had been taken from his village by Faitlovich to study in Jerusalem and Europe and returned as an educator. The Jewish Agency recognised him as a leader of the Ethiopian Jewish community and co-operated with him to open schools in remote Jewish villages.

By the turn of the 1960s though, the agency's activities in Ethiopia dried up and it shut its schools. After a period of unprecedented contact, in the years that followed, apart from some aid from foreign Jewish charitable groups and efforts by activists to keep the issue of the Ethiopian Jews alive, to Israel and most of world Jewry, they did not really matter. The educators and emissaries had left and the Jews of Ethiopia became less relevant.

It would take until 1976 for Ethiopian Jews to receive outside help in a meaningful way, when a Jewish humanitarian organisation with considerable clout was allowed by the new regime to operate in Gondar.[43] The Organisation for Rehabilitation through Training (ORT) began a rural development programme, including building schools and health facilities, digging wells and financially assisting farmers. In the schools in Jewish villages, Hebrew and Judaism classes were forbidden, although ORT staff defied this, at great personal risk, teaching children Hebrew by day and adults by lantern light at night.[44]

Education had always been important to Ferede Aklum. His father Yazezow, had insisted Ferede go to school, at a time when it was not the done thing for Ethiopian Jews. It was through this exposure to learning that Ferede developed a curiosity in the world around him, reading books and educating his siblings. To those who knew him, it was no surprise that when he was unable to get to Israel in 1973, Ferede decided to become a teacher. After graduating in biology from university in Addis Ababa, and then teachers' college, he got a position at a school in Indabaguna where he rose to become headmaster. He was also elected head of the local town council, growing his status among Tigray's Jewish and non-Jewish communities. Ferede became known to Yona Bogale, and was entrusted with building the first Jewish school in the province, funded by the ORT.

Tigray, though, had become a hotbed of activity by the mainly student-led Tigray People's Liberation Front (TPLF) and violence broke out there between TPLF insurgents and government forces. Teachers were a particular target for repression and many were arrested. One of the places where the TPLF found support was in Ferede's home village of Adi Woreva, and the village was repeatedly raided by government troops. Life for Ferede became difficult. Suspected by both sides for not allying with either, he left for the remote Jewish village of Ambober in

Gondar, where he took a position at an ORT school. All the while, he continued his Zionist activities, looking for ways to get to Israel and trying to convince other Jews to do so too.

When Chaim Halachmy, who had been briefed by the Mossad, arrived in Addis Ababa in August 1977, with a list of 63 names for the first batch of Jews to be secretly transferred to Israel in exchange for small arms, the first problem was finding them. He sought help from Bogale, who in turn recruited trusted Jewish activists – among them Ferede Aklum. Bogale introduced his team to Halachmy.[45] 'These are the names,' Halachmy told them. 'I need you to bring them to me.' Aklum and his comrades managed to locate the individuals in Gondar and move them to the capital.

Israel sent a Boeing 707 (which, as it was used for military operations, had no Israeli markings), to make the swap. The mission was so highly classified that even the pilots – instructed to fly in civilian clothing and not in uniform – were not informed of its purpose. The plane flew to Addis Ababa airport, where it was guided to a remote area and unloaded of its cargo. Halachmy's group boarded, the engines revved and it took off, carrying the 'shocked but quiet' passengers, dressed in their white cotton shawls, towards the Promised Land.[46] It was a small beginning, but the deal in all its secrecy had worked. Begin was getting what he asked for: the first of the Ethiopian Jews had officially arrived.

3

THE LOST TRIBE

The transfer had been made possible by a sea-change in Israel's position on the Beta Israel.

In 1973, one of Israel's two chief rabbis, Ovadiah Yosef, the spiritual leader of Sephardi Jews, issued a watershed ruling on the Ethiopian Jews.[1] They were, he pronounced, authentic Jews 'whose immigration to Israel is to be hastened'.[2] He based his conclusion on earlier positive declarations by illustrious rabbis down the centuries who had explored the question of the community's Jewish status and had ruled that they originated from the biblical tribe of Dan.[3] Rabbi Yosef rebuffed prevailing scepticism and firmly sided with the Ethiopian Jews' claim of Israelite roots.

Dan was one of the twelve tribes which, according to biblical narrative, conquered and settled in the land of Canaan (broadly corresponding to present-day Israel and the Palestinian territories) in the 13th century BC. According to Jewish tradition, ten of the tribes, including Dan, disappeared when the land (the Kingdom of Israel, as it was then known) was invaded 500 years later. It is not known what happened to the so-called Ten Lost Tribes, and their fate has been the source of much historical speculation.

The assertion that they descend from Dan is the most widely held belief among Ethiopian Jews themselves – but it is just one of several theories, some colourful and exotic. The fact that Ethiopian Jewry's origins are shrouded in mystery has beguiled scholars and travellers through the ages.

Perhaps the narrative about where they stem from which has captured imaginations the most is the story of a romance between the Jewish King Solomon and the Queen of Sheba. The 14th-century Ethiopian chronicle known as the *Kebra Nagast* (Glory of Kings) tells of a visit by the 'Queen of Ethiopia' (elsewhere identified as Sheba) to King Solomon in Jerusalem. It describes how Solomon tricked the queen into having sexual relations with him, from which she bore a son, Menelik. The story says that years later, when Menelik visited his father, Solomon ordered the first-born sons of the High Priests who served in the Temple to accompany him back to the Kingdom of Aksum (territory corresponding to modern Ethiopia and Eritrea), the seat of the queen. The chronicle tells how Menelik stole the Ark of the Covenant, which had resided in the Temple, and took it back to Aksum, along with his entourage. For centuries, some Ethiopian Jews believed themselves to be the heirs of this retinue of holy noblemen but the community has long since dismissed this as fable.[4]

Although no one can be certain about the Beta Israel's precise beginnings, no serious scholar casts doubt on their credentials as 'proper' Jews. The issue of their authenticity is a critical one, since it predicates their right to be accepted as part of the Jewish diaspora no differently to any other Jews anywhere in the world.

*

Two years after Rabbi Yosef's declaration, Israel finally extended the Law of Return to Ethiopian Jews.[5] While in theory, the community could now settle in Israel, in practice, old obstacles remained. Ethiopia barred emigration, there was no sense of urgency in the Israeli government about the Ethiopian Jews' situation, and Israel's delicate relationship with Ethiopia, albeit under a new Marxist regime, still mattered.

Under the secret arms-for-Jews deal, a second group of 61 immigrants was flown to Israel in December 1977. (A last-minute dispute between the Israeli crew and an Ethiopian officer threatened to jeopardise the flight after the officer accused the Israelis of trying to take out one too many people.)[6]

These two transportations increased the Ethiopian Jewish community's entire population in Israel by some 40 per cent in just four months.

The pact was short-lived, brought to an abrupt end when it was exposed by one of Israel's own top officials, Foreign Minister Moshe Dayan. At a news conference in Switzerland in February 1978, Dayan admitted that Israel had been providing weapons to Ethiopia.[7] Later Dayan said he had done so to protect relations between Israel and the US. By 1978 Ethiopia had pivoted towards the Soviet Union, and Washington would, Dayan feared, view Israel's arming of a Soviet ally as a betrayal. It has also been suggested that this was a pretext and that Dayan might have sabotaged the agreement out of personal objection to aiding a brutal regime.

Either way, Mengistu was furious and ordered the immediate expulsion of all Israeli advisors. Ethiopia branded Dayan's disclosure a 'deliberate and sinister act', and while Begin publicly downplayed it as 'human error', privately he was said to be livid.[8]

Mengistu gave the Mossad representative 24 hours to leave the country. Mossad HQ sent Dani on an unmarked military plane to get him. Mengistu's military intelligence chief, who was ordered to take care of the expulsion, was apologetic, saying he had no choice. The two agents destroyed various intelligence materials and got out before the deadline.

Once again, Israel was cut off from the Ethiopian Jews. The Mossad was back to square one and had to devise a new strategy.

Around this time, conditions for Ethiopian Jews significantly worsened. On the one hand, a major source of discrimination and deprivation was removed when in 1975, as part of the Derg's reforms, they were allowed to buy plots of land to farm (for centuries Jews had been the only Ethiopians forbidden from owning land). On the other hand, it brought bloody vengeance against them from dispossessed former landowners and peasants. One such group, the Ethiopian Democratic Union (EDU) went on rampages in Jewish villages, slaughtering men, women and children, committing rapes and selling victims into slavery. Hundreds of Jews are thought to have been killed and possibly thousands forced to flee their villages from 1977 to 1979 (in a speech to the Council of Jewish Federations in New York in 1979, Yona Bogale appealed for help, warning that without it the suffering of Ethiopian Jewry was so great, the entire community could disappear in as little as five years).[9] At the same time, they were also targeted in Tigray by the militant anti-Derg Ethiopian People's Revolutionary Party (EPRP), which launched attacks on the regime and its supporters in a period known as the White Terror. Avowedly anti-Zionist, the EPRP singled out Jewish villages because of their perceived sympathies to Israel. The Jews (and more so non-Jewish Ethiopians) also suffered under the regime's backlash known as the Red Terror, which saw tens of thousands of perceived opponents of the regime killed or 'disappeared'.

Although the Jews in Ethiopia had not been subjected to state-sponsored anti-Semitism like those in Europe down the ages, they were historically stigmatised and treated with disdain by their non-Jewish neighbours. At a local level, among Ethiopian Christians, the Jews were blamed for the killing of Christ, and were associated with malevolent forces. One of their main occupations, metalworking (a trade which they pursued out of economic necessity, excluded as they were from owning land), was condemned as a form of witchcraft, and they were believed by many to transform into hyenas at night and prey on victims for their blood. They were also blamed for ills which befell neighbouring non-Jewish communities and even adverse environmental phenomena like crop failures and droughts. This was a belief perpetuated by the anti-Semitic governor of Gondar, Major Melaku Tefera, who persecuted the Jews in his province in the late 1970s and early 1980s, despite the government's assertion that Jews and other minorities were free to practise their religion.[10] Old attitudes did not change with the revolution.

While Israel could no longer operate in Ethiopia, the ORT still could and it became an invaluable source of intelligence about what was happening with the Ethiopian Jews.

The only way to know operationally if it was possible to get the Jews out was for the Mossad to get in. Through Chaim Halachmy, the Israeli secret service made contact with the ORT's project manager in Ethiopia, French-born Jean-Claude Nedjar. Nedjar was, for security reasons, the only foreigner permitted by the authorities to operate in Gondar at that time, and he knew the Jewish communities well. The ORT had unimpeded access, so Dani decided to use it as a cover and go there himself.

Nedjar was willing to help, and Dani was sent to meet him. The two men rendezvoused in Nairobi, in neighbouring Kenya, Nedjar having bluffed his way to getting an exit permit, as required by anyone wanting to leave the country.

'The Mossad wanted me to give him [Dani] all kinds of information,' Nedjar recalls. 'He needed to know from me about the places and the people in order to be able to do his job. Of course I knew why, and I told him everything I could to enable him to do this. It was a terribly dangerous place he was planning to go to. Security people were everywhere. It was forbidden to even think against the government. I remember seeing bodies in the streets and in the rivers, people dragged from their homes at night and killed. And Israel was considered the enemy. You could not as much as even send a letter there without getting arrested.'

To complicate matters, at that time no one knew exactly how many Jews there were in Ethiopia. According to a 1976 census by the British Falasha Welfare Association, there were slightly more than 28,000, but the survey was conducted under very difficult conditions and it was thought there could be many more.[11] In terms of how many people it had to plan for, the Mossad was working in the dark. It was known that Jews were concentrated in the Ethiopian Highlands of the north-west, but they were scattered across hundreds of villages, some so small they were not even mapped.

What the Mossad's mission amounted to was having to engineer a mass exodus of an unknown number of nationals of

a foreign, hostile state, people who spoke no Hebrew, were anti-
quated in their ways, barely travelled and distrusted strangers.
The challenge was monumental, as were the risks.

Dani made two exploratory trips to Ethiopia. Posing as an ORT
worker and using a non-Israeli passport, he flew from Paris to
Addis Ababa and up to Gondar. There, he was met by a young
Ethiopian Jew (facilitated by Nedjar), who took him to meet
communal leaders in some of the Jewish villages and acted as a
translator. Trusting that they would not hand him over to the
authorities, he let the locals know he was an Israeli Jew, though
not that he was from the Mossad. His second trip took him
further north still, to Tigray, landing at Aksum, close to the
Eritrean boundary.[12]

From Aksum Dani went west to Shire district, where many
of Tigray's Jewish villages are found. Through his conversations
with locals he tested their willingness to emigrate to Israel.

'In that aspect,' Dani recalls, 'they thought I was going to
take them there and then. They didn't know how – they didn't
care. As soon as they heard about the birth of Israel in 1948,
they thought for them the moment was going to come any
time now.'

Motivation was not a problem, but it was clear there would
be operational difficulties.

The two main centres of Jewish life – Gondar and Tigray
– were at least 350 kilometres apart, the inhabitants spoke different languages (by and large Amharic in Gondar, and Tigrinya
in Tigray), and there was no common leadership.

Getting around was also a problem. In Gondar, although
the villages were linked by only dirt tracks, they could still be

reached by car, while in Tigray, many places were impassable by anything other than four-by-four or donkey. Then the numbers were still uncertain too. Dani had been told by villagers that there were about 40,000 Jews in all, though this was an approximation (as it turned out in years to come, the actual figure was about 36,000). Jews also lived way beyond Gondar and Tigray too, sometimes in extremely remote settlements, and they would have to be accounted for.

Dani came to the difficult conclusion that to secretly exfiltrate a huge but uncertain number of people from within such inhospitable terrain would not be possible. He reported his findings to Kimche.

'As we both know, if you want to take people out, you have three ways to do it,' Dani told him back in HQ. 'By land, by sea or by air. By land, you need an open border, or at least a cooperative country on the other side. There's Kenya, yes, but it's at least 800 kilometres from Tigray. Gondar is not much closer, and even then you'd have to pass through areas where tribes will attack at the mere sight of a white man. Then there's the infrastructure – there isn't any. Put people on a truck, when it rains you get stuck and that's the end of it.'

Kimche listened.

'Then there's sea. Yes, Israel's got access to the Red Sea and the Red Sea comes to Ethiopia. But there's a problem. The whole area separating the Jews from the sea is occupied by insurgent movements – three Eritrean and one Tigrayan. Some of them are specifically hostile to Jews, some of them aren't, but nevertheless we're talking about getting people through a combat zone. You couldn't even get young men through there, let alone women and children – we'd be putting them in harm's way. So sea is out of the question.'

'So that leaves air?' remarked Kimche.

'Yes, we could use Hercules for this kind of operation, but you need some kind of a landing strip.* But look at northern Ethiopia – it's summits and valleys – and even if we did find somewhere to land, we'd have to be sure the ground can take the weight. We can't risk getting noticed, so we're also talking about night flights, but it's a complete battlefield – everyone's fighting each other – bandits, deserters and guerrillas. The chances are someone somewhere would spot us.'

Kimche agreed with Dani: evacuation from Ethiopia, even piecemeal, was not feasible. But abandonment was not an option either, and the prime minister's order still stood. At their weekly meetings, Begin would ask Hofi to update him on the mission to bring out the Ethiopian Jews. Hofi would tell him the Mossad was working on it.

As the Derg waged war on its political opponents, it cast its net wide. One of the names which came to its attention was that of Ferede Aklum, whom it suspected of links to the TPLF. Ferede's Zionist activism was also considered treacherous. The regime ruled under the slogan of 'Ethiopia First', and wanting to emigrate was seen as betrayal. Ferede was declared a *wombedeh* (anti-government activist) and a warrant was issued for his arrest.[13]

In July 1978, while Ferede was on a trip to Tigray, police turned up at his father-in-law's house in Teda, a Jewish village near Ambober, looking for him. They left empty-handed. When

* Hercules, or C-130, aircraft are large military transport planes designed to land on, and take off from, short runways and unprepared surfaces.

Ferede returned to the news that he was a wanted man, there was only one option: to leave. It was a heartrending prospect. Escaping inevitably meant going it alone, parting from his wife of just one year, Eneyeshe, and beloved five-month-old son, Benjamin. To stay would put them in grave danger. Ferede hugged and kissed his wife and child, then went to ground. For a week he hid in a barn full of sheep until, with the help of his father-in-law, he was able to slip away to Eneyeshe's uncle's home in Gina, some 50 kilometres to the north. Anybody sheltering a wanted man was putting themselves at great risk. Eneyeshe and her father were arrested, jailed and tortured. Discovering Ferede had gone to Gina, the police raided Eneyeshe's uncle's house. Neither man was there but they beat up everyone they found – men, women and children. With his own life at stake, Ferede had to move on, but under the regime, an authorised permit was needed to travel. Eneyeshe's uncle served in the local administration in Gina and held the forms. Without his knowledge, one of his daughters stamped and signed a pass for Ferede, which he used to make his way from one Jewish village to another. After weeks of walking and hiding, he got to Armachew, an area about 20 kilometres west of Gina, where cousins of Eneyeshe lived and gave him shelter. Anywhere Ferede stopped could only provide temporary respite. He was a fugitive and nowhere was safe. It became clear he would have to get out of the country.[14] The climate of fear, violent repression and the years-old armed conflict in Eritrea, had already led many thousands of Eritreans and latterly Ethiopians to flee westwards into Sudan.

Tens of refugee camps and unofficial encampments were now operating in grim conditions across the border in a 280 kilometres stretch between Kassala to the north, Metemma to the south, and Gedaref some 120 kilometres further west.[15]

That particular year there was a surge in refugees after the Ethiopian government launched a major offensive in Eritrea in May, doubling the numbers to some 400,000 from just twelve months earlier.[16] Officially the border was closed and emigration barred but there was no concerted attempt to stop the growing stream of people desperate to escape. For Ferede, though, it presented a potential way out. Weapons-smugglers used the border to transfer arms to rebels in Eritrea, and the people shielding Ferede decided to pay a Christian smuggler known to them to help get him across. The way was notoriously treacherous. It meant navigating mountains, passing through jungle, traversing rivers, then crossing miles of exposed, barren land. Here roaming gangs of *shiftas* (bandits) preyed on anyone they could – robbing, raping, beating and killing. There was also the danger of wild animals, and the risk of dying from starvation or thirst. Even if the forces of nature did not prevail, there was always the possibility that the smuggler would rob, sell or otherwise abandon Ferede en route.

It was late November, 1978, and Ferede and his guide set off. The smuggler kept his word, and after just five days – swift for a journey of this kind – they reached the refugee camp of Sefawa, just across the border.

Ferede was the only Jewish migrant known of in Sudan, the largest country in the African continent.[17] American activists claimed a handful were in refugee camps, but there was no firm evidence.[18] Either way, Ferede was alone. By chance, in Sefawa he came across some people he knew, Muslims from Indabaguna, but after a few days they abandoned him, suspecting him of being a Derg spy.[19] Ferede decided to move on to Gedaref, a huge refugee slum which had formed around what had been a small town, and from there to Khartoum, the capital of Sudan. The Sudanese authorities had banned refugees from living in the city or entering it without a permit, so tens of thousands had settled on its north-east edge, in a neighbourhood known as Riyadh. It was dirty, cramped and dangerous. Starving and exhausted, for over two weeks Ferede survived by begging for money and scavenging for scraps of food. By night, he slept in an old car yard. There were only two things left in his possession: his gold wedding ring, which he kept hidden in his shoe, and a notebook. The decision Ferede took next, on the face of it unremarkable, would prove to have momentous consequences. His situation desperate, Ferede sold his ring for a few US dollars and with some of the proceeds bought writing paper and a pen. In his notebook were scribbled three names and contact details: Chaim Halachmy, and the HIAS office in Geneva; and two representatives of the AAEJ activist group in New York and Nairobi.[20] Ferede wrote along the following vague lines, choosing his words with care in case they fell into the wrong hands: 'My name is Ferede Yazezow, I am in Khartoum, I ran away from Ethiopia. You know why. Send me a ticket for Europe or the USA.'[21] Ferede included a post office box number to send the ticket to, but provided no other details of his whereabouts. He sent copies of the letter by telegram to the three contacts.

At that time, Halachmy was in Tel Aviv. Ferede's telegram was received in Geneva and was passed on to him. He got on the phone to the Mossad agent who had briefed him prior to his visit to Ethiopia a year and a half earlier.

'Dani, remember when I was in Addis and I told you I met a guy who was very good, very effective?' Halachmy said. 'Well, he's now in Khartoum and he wants me to send a ticket for him to come to Israel. I'm telling you, someone should meet this guy, because if you want to …'

'Okay, I understand,' replied Dani.

Although Halachmy was not in the Mossad, he was someone whose opinion Dani respected, especially since he had experience getting Jews out of Arab countries.

Dani went to see Kimche and told him about the conversation with Halachmy.

'Chaim thinks we should make use of this guy, and you know what, I think he's right,' said Dani. 'Instead of sending a ticket, we should send someone to find him and talk to him. We're looking for ways to get Jews out of Ethiopia, right? This guy Ferede, he found a way that we didn't think that a Jew would do, but he did it. We need to find out what it means, whether it's a one-time thing or what.'

Kimche, with his vast operational experience, recognised the potential.

'I'm with you,' he told Dani. 'And I think you should be the one to go.'

For such an operation, which called for total secrecy, they would need authorisation from the head of the Mossad, so they arranged a meeting with Hofi and senior officials.

Before they went in, Kimche told Dani not to volunteer.

'If you put yourself forward, there's a chance they'll refuse.'

There were people in the meeting, including Kimche's deputy with whom Dani had a difficult relationship, who would not want him sent, either for personal reasons or because they just considered him unsuitable. Dani's own head of department would not want to lose him and was likely to be one to object.

The group convened. Some said Ferede should be flown over and rigorously questioned, but Hofi thought someone should be sent in undercover. The question was who.

Kimche wrote down some names, and Dani caught a glance. In his mind they were all completely unfit. He whispered to Kimche: 'That's crazy! These guys will never be …' – then he realised it was a tactic – the more who were ruled out, the more it would create an opening for Dani. Kimche ran through the list.

Hofi responded to each name. 'Who is this guy? … What, him? He's incompetent … No way …'

Dani's head of department looked his way, realising what was going on. He seemed like he was about to intervene. Dani scribbled a message and passed it to him.

'Please let him do it'.

The head of department looked at Dani, paused and sat back. At that time, Dani was fresh back from an assignment in Nigeria, where he had been stuck for five weeks when the authorities had closed the ports and airports because of unrest. He had not shaved before or since, and by now had a lengthy beard.

'What about this guy – *if* he shaves,' said Hofi.

'Haka [Hofi],' replied Dani, 'for this I'm willing to shave my head!'

Kimche gave his approval, and it was decided – Dani got the assignment.

Time was of the essence. They did not know how long Ferede would stay around and they could not risk him disappearing.

Dani got back in touch with Halachmy and told him the Mossad was working on it. He asked him to send a positive answer back to Ferede from Geneva, so Halachmy dispatched a telegram, addressed to Ferede's PO box in Khartoum. It said: 'Wait. Someone will come.'

Under normal circumstances, sending a Mossad agent to an enemy country in the Arab world required months of detailed planning. Concocting a cover story alone was a lengthy process, involving intensive preparation. The minutiae of every conceivable aspect had to be meticulously worked through. This time, though, they went against all the rules. Three weeks from the moment the decision was made, Dani was in the air.

4

//////////////

OUT FROM THE SHADOWS

With no formal relations between Israel and Sudan, it was not possible to fly direct to Khartoum, and certainly not with an Israeli passport from anywhere. Arriving as an Israeli would mean immediate arrest and interrogation, or worse, and trigger a serious political crisis. In addition, visitors to Sudan required a visa to get in, something unobtainable in Israel. To get round this, Dani, using a non-Israeli passport, flew first from Tel Aviv to Paris. He had a cover story but not a visa, a document which could only be issued in person by the Sudanese embassy. He walked into the building on Avenue Montaigne to get what was needed.

'So what are you going to do in Sudan?' asked a Sudanese official dealing with applications.

'I'm an anthropologist,' replied Dani. 'I do research for [identity withheld] university.'

He produced a letter of sponsorship, written in French, which read as follows:

Dear Mr ——

Your letter of December 15th informing me of your trip to Sudan interested me a lot. Among the different ethnic groups represented in this region of Africa is the Falasha tribe (there would be refugees belonging to this group in Sudan). As you well know, the origin of this group remains obscure. I would be very grateful if you could try to meet members of this tribe to learn more about it. It goes without saying that any expense incurred during your efforts will be covered by the department. Thank you in advance. Please accept, dear Mr ———, my best wishes.

It was signed in the name of the director of the Anthropology Department.

The signature was genuine. The letter was not.

Dani had some knowledge of anthropology, having taken a course in the subject at university years earlier, but not to any level of expertise. Had the official called the university to check, he would have discovered that the person in front of him was not what he was claiming to be. As it was, the official accepted the letter, took the fee and issued the visa.

Dani had his documentation and cover story, but he still had to make sure not to take any trace of Israel into Sudan. He changed into a fresh set of French-made clothes and binned the Israeli shirt and shorts he had arrived with. He kept his reliable Israeli Nimrod sandals though, but burnt off the name of the brand.

He went to Charles de Gaulle airport, from where he took a ten-hour flight to Khartoum. There he made his way to the north-west tip of the city and checked into the newly built Hilton Hotel. Overlooking the confluence of the Blue and White Niles, the hotel had quickly established a reputation as one of the finest in Africa and was the choice of international business people, diplomats and airline crews. It was also well-known as a meeting place for foreign intelligence agents, shady dealers and figures from Palestinian militant groups. To avoid his coming and goings being surveilled, Dani obtained a master key, which he got copied at a local locksmith so he could enter and leave the hotel via the service door without anyone seeing.

As no one other than Halachmy knew what Ferede looked like, the plan was for Dani to get to the central post office and simply observe his PO box, in the hope that he might come and check it.

The post office was a couple of kilometres east on Gamma Avenue, and a stone's throw from the south bank of the Blue Nile, with its tree-lined Nile Street, a legacy of the city's colonial past. Dani went to the building, adjacent to the 'People's Palace' (Nimeiri had seen fit to lose its former 'Presidential' title to make it sound more classless), and located the box with the number. He walked around, keeping an eye on the hatch, watching and waiting for anyone to approach it. Although he had dressed not to be distinctive, before long Dani was getting glances, and he could understand enough Arabic to make out comments wondering who the *khawaja* (white foreigner) hanging around was. It was too risky to stay, so he left. It was not going to be possible to monitor the box, the only clue as to who and where this Ferede was.

Dani was left to his own devices. There were tens of thousands of refugees in and around Khartoum and the chances of tracking down Ferede without anything to go on were at best remote. He started to ask around as to where the Ethiopians and Eritreans lived and was told Riyadh district. He went there and carried out some reconnaissance. Riyadh was made up of ramshackle huts where immigrants lived and traded. There was no proper infrastructure and conditions were dire but he noticed it was built in a grid-like formation, which meant raking it could be done systematically. He began, going into stores and asking if anyone knew of a Ferede Aklum, but answer after answer was 'No'. When he had finished one row he would strike it from a map he drew and move on to the next. It was a slow process and by sunset when it got too dangerous and difficult, he would pause the search and catch a taxi back to his hotel. The next morning he would return to Riyadh and pick up from where he left off. The routine continued from one day to the next, asking traders and groups on the streets, but to no avail. By the sixth day the search was looking futile. 'Do you know a guy called Ferede Aklum?' went the refrain. 'No,' invariably came the answer, or just a shake of a head or a shrug.

End of another row, crossed off the grid. One of the stores Dani tried was a wig shop. He approached the shopkeeper, who was sitting on the counter.

'Do you know a guy called Ferede Aklum?' he asked. This time, the response was different. 'Why do you ask?' came the reply.

'Because I saw his wife and I've got a message for him,' Dani answered. 'I need to deliver it personally.' Dani sensed the shopkeeper was suspicious, so he continued: 'If you see him, or someone who knows him, tell him I'll be at the Blue Nile Hotel every evening between six and eight.'

The Blue Nile was down the road from the Hilton and not somewhere frequented by Westerners. If Dani needed to be noticed, as a white man there he would stand out. He got to the hotel by six that day and took a seat on the large patio facing out towards the river.

He ordered food and paid his bill straight away, in case he needed to suddenly get up and follow his mark. Then he began to watch, observing every male who walked through for the smallest clue that they could be the elusive Ferede. That night no one came who fitted his description. The next evening Dani repeated the routine, reading a newspaper and drinking *karkade* (hibiscus tea), while furtively keeping an eye out. For a while, no one caught his attention, until one particular man entered. He appeared more Eritrean or Ethiopian than Sudanese and was wearing a shirt, trousers and sandals rather than the native *jalabiya*.[1] Dani watched as the man, carrying a copy of *Newsweek* under his arm, walked around the tables, and without as much as a glance at Dani, left. Dani stayed put. Could it have been Ferede? If it was, why didn't he stop? It was impossible to know, but by 8pm no other possible match had shown up, so he decided to call it off for the night.

The following evening, Dani returned to the hotel patio, ordered a *karkade*, paid, and sat with his drink and newspaper, surreptitiously watching out. He had been in Khartoum for over a week now, without a result. Direct communication with Israel from Sudan was not possible, so the Mossad had put an agent in a flat in Paris, ready round-the-clock for a call from Dani. The understanding was that Dani would make contact only if there was something to report, otherwise the assumption would be that everything was okay.

After a while the same man appeared as the night before, same clothes, same *Newsweek* – but this time he made eye contact. Neither man spoke. The visitor walked around the patio and left, but now Dani went after him. The two men exited onto the street, Dani walking behind.

'Ferede? … Ferede?' he called.

The man did not respond.

Dani got closer to him.

'Ferede? Are you Ferede Aklum?' he asked in English.

The man stopped as Dani caught up.

He hesitated, then replied in a cautious tone. 'Yes. Why?'

On Nile Street in Khartoum, Sudan's most populous metropolis, Dani had found his man.

'You asked for a ticket to go somewhere?' Dani said. 'Well, I'm your ticket!'

The two men shook hands, though Ferede was very suspicious. A wanted man and an illegal immigrant, as far as he knew he could have been walking into a trap. His telegram could have been intercepted and this stranger sent to pick him up. However, the guy was a white man, so the chances were he would not be working for the Sudanese secret police.

As it turned out, Ferede had never got Halachmy's response to his message.

Dani continued: 'Look, I'm French. You sent a telegram to Geneva and it came to France, to the Jewish community in Paris.'

Hinting at being Jewish was not something a Mossad agent in a country in the Arab world would ever normally do, but Dani realised he had to gain Ferede's trust. The term 'Jewish community in Paris' meant something to Ethiopian Jews because of Joseph Halévy and Jacques Faitlovich, so in their eyes French Jews in particular were bona fide.

Based on their backgrounds alone, the two men could not have been more different. One was born and raised in Africa, the other South America and Israel. One was white, the other black, the cultures they were used to being completely dissimilar. All they had in common was that they were Jewish, but that would prove to be enough.

'So you got to Sudan by walking all the way from Ethiopia?' asked Dani.

'Yes,' said Ferede.

'Do you think other Jews could come the same way?'

'It's possible,' replied Ferede, 'but it's hard. Very hard.'

'And do you know if there are any other Jews already in Sudan?'

'I don't know for sure. When I left Gondar I heard others had gone too, but I don't know who or how many. Probably just a handful.'

'Well if there are, there might be a way to get them out to Israel via Europe. Will you help me look?' asked Dani.

Get them to Israel. The words rang in Ferede's ears. Could this stranger hold the answer?

'I have to get to Israel,' Ferede said. 'My wife and baby are still in Ethiopia and I promised them I'd get them there.'

'The French Jewish community will take care of that,' said Dani. 'So will you help me?'

'I'm exhausted and I've been through a lot,' replied Ferede. 'But if you've really come this far to help us, then yes, I'll help you.'

That meeting, that evening, on the pavement across from where the Blue Nile flowed, marked the start of what would become a remarkable partnership. In time it would change not only both their lives, but those of thousands of others too.

Dani contacted the agent at the flat in Paris and informed him he had found his man.

It was February 1979, and ever-increasing numbers of refugees were trekking across the border and fanning out to camps, most heading to the area around Gedaref. If any other Jews had hidden among them and made it into Sudan, it was logical for the two men to start looking there. There was a problem, though. It would be impossible to tell Ethiopian Jewish refugees from the non-Jewish ones by looks alone, and they would not make themselves identifiable as Jews through fear of being singled out and attacked.

Gedaref was some 400 kilometres away and to get there Dani and Ferede would need a sturdy vehicle. There was practically no proper road network in Sudan, apart from the recently paved 1,200 kilometre Khartoum–Gedaref–Port Sudan highway, and to get to anywhere else meant travelling on rough dirt tracks or desert paths carved by traffic.

Foreign visitors could rent cars, but the vehicles came with an appointed driver, who could easily be in the pay of the secret police. Because of this danger, Dani headed off to the bustling market in the city centre to look for transport of his own. He spotted a four-by-four Land Rover Defender and waited for the owner.

'I need a car like this,' he said when the man approached. 'Are you willing to sell?'

The owner was taken aback but gave Dani a price – high by Sudanese standards of the time. Dani accepted and paid in cash. He had brought some US$5,000 into the country, to pay for what he needed.

The man handed over the keys and the deal was done. Dani picked up Ferede, and the Mossad agent and the fugitive set off towards Gedaref.

They had gone only about fifteen kilometres when an obstacle came into view on the road ahead. As they got closer, soldiers appeared. It was a security checkpoint, and Dani decided it would be best to act compliant.

The checkpoints were set up to try to prevent the smuggling of arms and people between the border and Khartoum and vice-versa. Most of the insurgent movements fighting in Ethiopia had bases in the area around Gedaref and Kassala, and it was a route used by slave traffickers as well.

Dani was conscious that a white man driving with a black man would give rise to suspicion. A guard manning the post gestured at Dani to halt and wind down his window.

'Papers,' demanded the guard.

Dani presented his passport – a perfectly forged document produced by the Mossad – and visa.

The guard looked at the two men in the vehicle, and examined the passport at all angles.

'Have you seen enough?' asked Dani, responding in Arabic and projecting self-assurance.

The guard handed the items back, then peered at Ferede.

'You, come with me,' he ordered.

It spelt trouble. Ethiopian refugees were known to be treated with contempt, often violently, by Sudanese security men, and Ferede was clearly not a local.

About 45 metres away stood a tent where a group of soldiers milled around. Dani sensed that things were turning dangerous. If he let Ferede go, it was likely he would not see him again, and fighting their way out against armed guards was not an option.

'No,' he intervened, 'he's not going anywhere. He's staying here.'

The guard stood firm. 'I said he's coming with me!' he demanded.

'No,' replied Dani. 'You go and get your commanding officer,' he ordered, raising his voice. 'Go and call him. Now!'

The guard turned around and started walking towards the tent. After he had put enough distance between himself and the car, Dani hit the accelerator and drove away at high speed, the engine racing.

It was a gut decision. On most missions there were textbook procedures – examining maps, plotting roadblocks and finding alternative routes were rudimentary – but here it was uncharted territory. So little was known by Israel about Sudan, which was not a first-line enemy country, that when Dani had gone to get information from military intelligence to prepare for his trip, they had provided him with just half a page. He ended up equipping himself by studying a section on Sudan in the *Encyclopaedia Britannica*. Dani, a former chief instructor, had partly written the Mossad manual for the training of new recruits, but here even his own rulebook did not apply. The assignment was defined, but not the way to go about it. Kimche knew that, and knew that the kind of person to carry it out was someone who had sharp instincts and, as he would have done, could work it out as they went along.

The incident at the checkpoint had particular significance, as it brought Dani to two conclusions. Firstly, it ruled out operating in daylight as that meant being seen. Secondly, that from then on he would not stop at roadblocks. There were nine more such checkpoints on the road to Gedaref, and Dani ran every one.

It was dark by the time they got to the town. Dani and Ferede looked for a place to spend the night and came across a *fondouk* (hostel). It was dilapidated, insanitary and overcrowded. Ferede decided to stay with Tigrayan friends from the TPLF who he knew in the camp instead, but for Dani the hostel would suffice for now. The two men agreed to rendezvous the next day by a particular tree. Dani paid for a mattress, found a space on the floor, and went to sleep. At first light he woke up, itching from head to toe. He was covered in lice. He grabbed his belongings and promptly got out. Back in the car, he headed into the outskirts and parked up by a stream. Infested, Dani rolled around on the ground, wriggling in the sand like a horse with botflies, and jumped into the water. He did it over and over again, in and out, until he had killed off the lice. After that, Dani opted to sleep in the car.

That first morning the two men met up at the agreed tree and set off to begin their search. Gedaref was by far the biggest camp in the area, but was only one of dozens, spreading out for kilometres around. More akin to shanty towns minus any sort of infrastructure, the camps were not the kind of places where newcomers could safely walk around, least of all white ones.

They agreed that only Ferede would venture in to look for Jews and Dani would wait outside.

Every moment was a risk. Asking questions and scouting around would raise suspicions. There were not only ordinary refugees there, but scattered among them were members of rebel groups, some violently opposed to each other, and all on alert for Derg spies.

Dani found this out early on. He wanted to look for Jews too, and asked Ferede how he could help.

'All you have to do is sit in a cafe. If you see an Ethiopian guy, start talking to him. Ask him where he's from. I'll tell you the areas Jews come from. If he comes from one of those areas, then ask him "What village?" and so on.'

Dani tried it on and off – sitting in cafes, waiting, casually striking up conversations – but with no success. Without staying too long in one place, he would get up and move on to another part of the camp. It was when he was walking down one of the countless alleyways that he realised something was wrong. A group of young men clutching bamboo sticks approached him from in front, blocking his path. At the same time, others closed in from behind him. Before Dani could react, the men rained blows on him, threw a sack over his head and hustled him away. He was shoved down one lane after another until he got pushed into what he sensed was a hut and forced down onto a chair. One of the men pulled the sack off his head. He surveyed the area: a table; two chairs; oil lamp hanging from the roof; and men – lots of them.

A figure stepped forward and sat down opposite him. The man locked eyes with Dani and said something to him in a language which Dani recognised as Tigrinya but did not understand.

Dani shrugged. 'English?', knowing it was most likely his interrogator would know at least some of the language.

'So, you are an Ethiopian spy, you work for the Derg,' the man declared.

'Me?' replied Dani. 'I'm French. What is "Derg"?'

Dani realised the men were members of the TPLF who thought he was looking for opponents of the regime.

'I'm an anthropologist and I'm a socialist like you. Here …' Dani pulled 50 pounds from his pocket. 'Take this, give it to your organisation. Use it to fight Mengistu. I don't give a damn about the regime.'

'But we've watched you, asking people questions in the market,' his inquisitor responded.

'It's my work. I'm studying tribes. I'm interested in all kinds of stuff – where refugees have come from, why, where they are going …'

The man sat back and beckoned his aides. They muttered in Tigrinya, then he turned back to Dani.

'You are studying tribes, huh?'

Dani nodded, unsure whether his inquisitor was convinced.

'Can you please let others know this, so when they see me they know what I'm doing?' he said to try to further assert his innocence.

'Okay, we will let you go – but be aware that we will be watching you!'

The sack was put over Dani's head again and he was led back out, through the network of passageways until a point where they pulled it off and released him with a push.

When Dani met back up with Ferede, Ferede warned him that he had heard that the TPLF were on the trail of a white man, who had been seen asking too many questions.

'It's okay, I've taken care of it,' said Dani, to Ferede's astonishment.

After that, Dani decided he and Ferede would drive up to about one kilometre from a camp boundary, where Dani would wait with the car while Ferede went to search inside.

Over days, then weeks, Dani and Ferede tried to scour the camps systematically. There were no surveys of the area to go on, no signposts or directions, and apart from the road between Gedaref and Kassala, there was not so much as a dirt track to follow. As an ex-paratrooper officer, Dani had advanced navigational skills, so he drew his own map of the camp network as they went along by using the vehicle's odometer and a compass.

Operating covertly, the two men never met up in daylight, rendezvousing only after dark at a predetermined point outside a camp. Some days they would go without meeting up at all.

After combing a camp they would retreat into the bush, where they would make a small fire to keep warm and take turns to sleep. Whoever was awake kept watch – not just for people but for animals too, the silence punctuated by the calls and roars of wildlife in the dark. For food, they ate whatever Ferede had got hold of during the day – sometimes meat from a village, sometimes whatever they could catch in the wild – from snakes to ants, which they would fry. They drank bottled water brought from Khartoum, and when that ran out they filled up from a stream. Dani used chlorine tablets to decontaminate it, but Ferede could not stomach the chemical taste so drank it neat. It was during these times that they would talk and share stories about their lives, developing a camaraderie and a deepening bond.

Ferede learnt about Dani and what Israel was like, Dani about Ferede, life in the villages, and his family.

'If I can get them to come, others will follow,' said Ferede, thinking.

'How?' asked Dani.

'I'll write a message telling them I've found the way to Jerusalem and get someone to deliver it.'

'Like who?'

'There's a merchant I know, an Ethiopian Muslim. His name's Shuffa. He goes backwards and forwards across the border. We can tell him to bring my brothers first. That way we're not risking anyone else before proving it can be done. My brothers are young and fit. If they make it and get word back, then others will see it's possible and come. My parents will come. My wife and baby will come!'

Dani agreed. It was worth trying. At the very least, it could bring Ferede his family, and could be the key to much more than that.

'Tell him if he'll do it, I'll pay him. Half now, half on his return,' said Dani.

Ferede found Shuffa and told him what he wanted him to do. He gave him the message to deliver by word-of-mouth, along with a passport photo to show Ferede's family he was alive. Ferede gave Shuffa part-payment, promising the remainder when he came back.

Shuffa went on his way, but there were many pitfalls to overcome. There would be no way of knowing if the messenger should fall foul of bandits or fighters, and even if he reached Ferede's parents, there was no guarantee his brothers would leave or make it across alive.

The immediate task in hand for Dani and Ferede was to find anyone who, like Ferede, had already come. Day by day they would move between camps, Dani mapping as they went. Ferede would go in after the sun had gone down, but invariably emerge with a shake of his head, before moving on to the next. Ferede also hired cattle smugglers to get the message to villages back in Ethiopia that the way was open to get to Israel, and that people should come.

After more than a month of looking, they had still not found any Jews.

Driving from place to place around Gedaref and not knowing how far away camps would be found, Dani had an important practicality to consider: petrol. There were no petrol stations between Khartoum and Port Sudan, and this was not the kind of area to get stuck having run out.

The only places at which to refuel were a military compound

in Gedaref and another in Kassala, 225 kilometres north. Getting the petrol was an ordeal in itself. It meant waiting in a long queue of mainly truck drivers before getting issued with a coupon for an allocated amount, then taking it to another location where an attendant would take payment and fill the vehicle with the fuel.

The Defender was running low, so, without Ferede, Dani diverted to the compound in Gedaref. Judging by the length of the line, it looked to be a three-hour wait. He parked up and joined the queue, squatting by a wall like the others, every so often shuffling along. After a while, to break the tedium, Dani took a handheld electronic game from his pocket and started to play. Such consoles were something of a novelty even in the West at that time, and were unknown in Sudan. The sight of this dishevelled sole white man fiddling with a strange device started to attract attention. Having been immersed in the game, Dani glanced up to find some fifteen faces peering back at him. Suddenly a figure in uniform emerged and walked towards him. It was a sergeant, come to see what was going on. '*Ta'al!*' ('Come!') he said, turning back. Dani got to his feet and followed. The sergeant led Dani into the main building and into an office. Seated at a desk was an individual who Dani identified as a lieutenant colonel, the sergeant's superior. He was, it transpired, the military governor.

'This guy is communicating,' the sergeant told him in Arabic, understood by Dani. He believed the game to be some kind of radio.

'Give it to me,' he said, making a move to take it.

Dani pulled the game away with a 'No'.

The governor started talking in Arabic.

'Can you speak English?' Dani asked. 'Français? Deutsch? Italiano? Español?'

The governor looked at him and paused.

'Would you please show me what you have in your hand?' he asked politely in English.

Dani complied. He produced the game and leaned in to hand it over, emitting a terrible odour. After more than a month without washing with soap or a change of clean clothes, Dani smelt foul. The governor recoiled.

'Who is this stinking guy?' he asked the sergeant in Arabic.

Grimacing, he took the game and examined it, turning it around. 'What is it? How does it work?' he asked Dani.

Dani went to lean forward again.

'No, no, no, no, no,' implored the governor, handing the game back. 'It's not for communicating. Here, take it.'

He sat back in his chair.

'Tell me, what are you doing here?' he asked.

'I'm an anthropologist,' replied Dani.

'What?'

'I'm researching the Beni-Amir tribe.'[2]

'Why are you interested in these people? They're just criminals. They get arrested all the time. Have you got a permit? This is a military area and you need a permit. I assume you've got one?'

Dani knew he required a permit, but that would mean having to get one from one of the ministries, who would ask questions, and even then take months to issue one, if at all.

'No,' he replied. 'What permit? Nobody told me anything about a permit.'

'But how could you pass all the roadblocks?' demanded the governor.

'I just went through,' said Dani, with an air of innocence. 'The soldier would wave like this' – mimicking a 'slow down' gesture with his hand – 'so I just did it back and drove through.'

The governor laughed at the thought.

'And where are you staying?' he asked.

'I've been sleeping sometimes at the Fondouk Amir …'

'What?!' the governor interjected. 'It's very dangerous there. They'll kill you. You can't stay there. I won't allow it.'

'… but most of the time in my car,' finished Dani.

The governor raised his eyebrows.

'I just go out in the car and close the windows with the mosquitoes inside, and then we sleep together – me and the mosquitoes,' he said, prompting another laugh.

The governor turned to the sergeant and spoke in Arabic.

'Take this guy to the base and let him have a shower. See if he's got a change of clothes – if not, go and get him a jalabiya from the souk. I'll come and see him this evening.'

He turned to Dani. 'Go with the sergeant. I'll come and see you tonight.'

Dani took from his tone that it was best not to refuse.

The sergeant and Dani left the building and went to his car. They set off, Dani driving, the sergeant next to him giving directions until they arrived at another compound. The base – small wooden houses with verandas – looked like a former British Army barracks from colonial times and was reminiscent of the old British-built Army quarters still in use in Israel.[3]

The sergeant led Dani in and took him straight to the showers.

'Here, go and get washed,' he said.

Dani stepped in, still fully clothed. It was a small but reinvigorating luxury. For the first time in weeks, he stood under hot water and cleaned himself with a bar of soap, the black grime from his body swirling down the plug hole.

When he was done, the sergeant showed him to a room where there were four beds.

'Take that one,' he said. 'You can rest until the governor comes.'

Dani lay down and drifted off to sleep.

After an indeterminate time, he was woken by the sound of voices. He stayed motionless, listening but with his eyes still closed.

He made out that a conversation was taking place about problems along the border. The 'sleeping' Mossad officer discovered he had been given a room with a battalion commander in charge of securing (as it turned out, not very successfully) part of the frontier with Ethiopia against refugees, along with the head of the local secret police, and the area's chief of police. Through sheer serendipity, pieces of intelligence about the influx of refugees and what the security forces were doing about it fell into Dani's lap, giving him a clearer picture of the situation.

His stay in the barracks was open-ended. That first evening, the military governor came to see him as promised and told Dani that whenever he was in Gedaref he could come and go in the day but at night he had to sleep there. The governor did not want to risk a white man being killed on his turf. The arrangement suited Dani. There was a shower, a bed and even a cook, not to mention the flow of information from his roommates. (Every so often when he was there Dani would visit the outhouse, a place where he knew he had privacy, and, using secret equipment, transmit intelligence back to headquarters.)

The morning after his first stay at the base, when Dani met up with Ferede and told him about his new accommodation, his companion was both impressed and relieved. He had only agreed to sleep in the bush for Dani's sake and it meant he could now sleep back in a bed in Gedaref. The search operation continued, only now they were less fatigued.

One night, after a tour of the camps, Dani returned to the barracks. There an officer approached him.

'The governor wants to see you in his office,' he said.

Dani made his way to the compound, knocked on his door and went in.

'Sit down,' the governor said. 'Look, I'm being asked questions about you.'

'Yes?' replied Dani.

'Tell me again, what exactly are you doing here?' the governor asked, a seriousness to his tone.

'I told you, I'm an anthropologist,' responded Dani.

'Have you got proof?'

To add credibility to his cover story, Dani had had the presence of mind to visit the Beni-Amir tribe soon after arriving in Sudan, taking photographs and making notes, and continued to go there in his free time to build up a convincing file of 'research'.

'Here,' said Dani, reaching for his logbook. 'Can you read French?'

'No,' replied the governor.

'Okay, I'll read it for you and translate into English.' Dani continued: 'On [date], sat with the chief on [name of a] hill. Asked him why they [did a particular practice]. He told me [the reason]. Asked him why the tribe [had a special custom]. He told me it was because [the reason]. Asked him why his people

went [from place X to place Y]. He told me [the reason] …'
And so on.

'My university needs to learn about these things to understand why this tribe is disappearing …'

'But they're not disappearing,' the governor interrupted,
'they're growing.'

Dani tried to think of an answer, when at that moment the
phone on the governor's desk rang and he took the call.

'Can I … is it possible to call from here to Paris?', Dani
asked him when he hung up.

'I don't know. You want me to try?' said the colonel.

Dani passed him the telephone number of the flat where
the Mossad agent was waiting.

The governor rang the telephone exchange and asked to be
connected. After a long wait he spoke again, then handed Dani
the receiver.

'Here's the number you wanted,' he said, 'there's a guy on
the other end.'

It was the first time since he had arrived in Gedaref some
two months earlier that Dani had made contact with the
Mossad. Speaking in French, he began with a coded phrase
which signalled he was okay. It was met with a sigh of relief.

The agent in Paris started rapid-firing questions.

'Where have you been? What's been happening? People are
worried!' Then he asked: 'So, did you find any merchandise?'

'No, not yet,' replied Dani.

'And what do you expect? asked the man in Paris.

'I don't know,' said Dani. 'It will take as long as it takes. I'm
looking every day.'

Then the man said: 'Dad wants to see you urgently.' In other
words, a senior boss.

Dani knew he did not mean Kimche. Dave would not have been concerned about the radio silence.

'But I've hardly started,' said Dani, sternly.

'It doesn't matter,' said the other agent, 'Dad wants you back.'

'So tell him I said "no". I'm not coming.'

'You've got no choice,' the man replied.

'No choice' meant the order must have come from the chief of the Mossad himself, Yitzhak Hofi. To disobey him would automatically result in a dishonourable discharge, a line that even Dani was not prepared to cross.

'Okay. Tell him I'll come,' he conceded.

The conversation wound up, the colonel let him go and Dani went back to the base. That night he rendezvoused with Ferede and told him what had happened.

'What?' said Ferede with alarm. 'But what about me?'

'You keep looking for Jews,' said Dani.

'But what if you don't come back?'

'I will come back!' Dani said.

'And if you don't?'

'If I tell you I'm coming back, I'm coming back,' Dani assured him. 'Whatever happens, I'm not going to abandon you.'

In fact, Dani had decided not to return to Israel at all, but to lead the Mossad chiefs into believing he was.

He drove to Khartoum and caught a flight to Paris. There, he should have switched passports and flown on to Israel, but Dani had other plans. He needed to get to the Israeli embassy in the heart of the eighth arrondissement, the city centre district where the Champs Elysées connects the Arc de Triomphe and the Place de la Concorde. It was also home to more than twenty embassies, fertile ground for the Direction de la Surveillance du Territoire (DST), the domestic intelligence agency, who surveilled all comings and goings. For operational reasons Dani had to keep under the radar, so after nightfall he donned a peaked cap and glasses with plano lenses to disguise his appearance and went to the Israeli embassy building. Knowing where the French intelligence agency's cameras were trained, he kept his head down and went inside.

Using an encrypted line, he messaged Kimche, trying to convince him of the need to stay in Sudan. Questions and answers followed but with no agreement.

Dani got on a secure phone line to HQ and talked to Kimche directly.

'What's going on?' Dani asked. 'You want me to come back? It's too soon!'

Kimche, his voice electronically distorted, responded: 'If it was up to me, I'd say carry on, but Hofi wants you back to discuss it. He wants to assess the situation and for you to be there.'

Dani knew that if he went back to Israel there was a strong chance that he would not be allowed to return to Sudan, and he could not let that happen.

He told Kimche he was convinced they would soon find Jews – in camps or with the arrival of Ferede's brothers. He had also promised Ferede he would go back, he said, and he would not betray his trust.

'Dave, do whatever you have to do but please, just get me another month.'

There was a pause.

Kimche resumed: 'Haka wants to speak to you.'

The Mossad chief came on the line, his voice scrambled.

'Dani, we need to evaluate the mission. I want you to brief us all here, then we decide where to go with this. So far there are no concrete results.'

Dani told Hofi that he and Ferede were working together, combing the camps. If there were Jews there, he said, they would find them. To stop now would put it all in jeopardy.

'All I'm asking for is a month,' said Dani.

The line went quiet, then Hofi continued: 'You've got a week.'

This was the Middle East, where deals are made by bartering, so Dani pushed his luck.

'Can we say two weeks?' he countered.

Hofi hesitated.

'Okay, two weeks – not a day more. And I have your word for it. I don't want you to stay a day longer – unless you find Jews.'

Dani had got an extension, but with it a deadline. With no time to spare, he got the next flight back to Khartoum.

At their last meeting, Dani had told Ferede to give him a week then go to a particular tree on the edge of Gedaref every evening at 6am and wait for him. When he returned, he said, he would meet him there.

Dani went back to Gedaref and as daylight faded went to find the tree. In the distance, he saw Ferede – but he was not alone. He was walking with two people, and their body language suggested they were at ease.

Dani set off towards them, approaching them from behind. Realising they had not noticed him, he decided to surprise Ferede. He caught up with him and put two fingers in his back.

'Hands up!' he ordered.

Ferede swung round, flinging his outstretched arm. Dani instinctively ducked as it swept over his head.

'Never do that to me again!' blurted Ferede. 'I thought you were the police!'

'Okay! Okay!' said Dani apologetically.

It was an unnerving introduction for the two men with Ferede. While Dani was away, he had discovered them in the camp. They were emaciated – walking frames of skin and bones, one maimed from a beating by a Sudanese soldier – but it was the breakthrough Dani and Ferede had been hoping for. After three months of fruitless searching, Ferede had finally found his first two Ethiopian Jews. More than that, it meant there could be others in hiding in the camps too.

'This is Daniel,' said Ferede. 'The one I told you about.'

The two gaunt men shook Dani's hand. One of them spoke in Tigrinya and Ferede translated.

'He says: "We heard you can get us to Jerusalem? Is that true?"'

'Yes,' replied Dani. 'We can get you there. Do you know if there are more Jews here?'

'Yes, for sure,' answered one of the men.

'Can you bring them to us?'

'We can try.'

Ferede and the two haggard figures went back into the slums while Dani waited. Before long they re-emerged. They were not alone. The group of three had become six.

They greeted one another, then one of the men spoke.

'There's a Jewish girl. She came with us but she was kidnapped by some Sudanese. Please, you have to help us get her back,' he said.

'Tell me what you know,' replied Dani.

The girl, the man explained, was about sixteen years old. He had information that she was being held in a particular village not too far away, but that was all.

Dani knew how to prepare rescue operations but freeing a captive was not part of this assignment, and if anything went wrong, it could scupper the entire mission.

'I know someone who might be able to help,' said Ferede.

The man he had in mind was an Ethiopian smuggler who had been living in Sudan for a long time and spoke Arabic like a native.

Dani told him to make contact and they would all reconvene.

They dispersed and later met up again at a certain time and place, with Ferede and the smuggler.

Dani told the man to go to the village and gather intelligence about it – what was there, the layout of the houses, ways in and out, and where the girl was being held.

The man went, leading a cow as pretence, and, some hours later, returned. The group gathered around. With a stick, the man drew a map of the place in the sand. The village consisted of about fifteen to twenty huts and most of the inhabitants appeared to be nomads. He had also found the Ethiopian girl, who was being sexually abused by her captor.

'I can get her out,' said the smuggler, 'but I need one more person to help me.'

Ferede volunteered but Dani overruled him. He could not take the chance.

One of the other, fitter Ethiopians stepped forward. 'I'll do it,' he said. 'Let's wait till they've gone to sleep, then I'll sneak in, hit the guy over the head, grab the girl and run.'

'Okay,' said Dani. 'Let's do it.'

That night the two men disappeared. When they returned later on, they had the girl.

The six had now become seven.

The girl was in a dreadful condition from her ordeal, physically and mentally. They took her back to Gedaref and got her to a safe place.

It was one thing to now be finding Jews, but Dani did not yet have a plan for how to get them out.

The case of the girl made him realise they could not be kept in Gedaref for long because of the increasing risk of someone finding out. They were going to have to be moved, and operationally it made sense to relocate them to Khartoum.

Ferede started looking for secure places there, and happened to run into an Ethiopian Christian woman he knew from Tigray. He asked her for help and she told him of refugee hostels, where guests paid per bed.

Dani and Ferede took the five men and the girl and drove them from Gedaref to Khartoum. They put them in one of the lodgings and Dani bought them a room to themselves. He told them not to make a sound nor go outside, saying he would come back and take care of their needs.

It had been about five months since Ferede had escaped from Gondar and his family had heard nothing more. One rumour had reached them that he had been captured by government forces and killed, and even though there was no proof, they feared the worst.

His sister, Abeju, was at home in Adi Woreva when a stranger appeared at her door. Ferede's mother, Avrehet, was also there, visiting at the time. The man introduced himself as Shuffa the merchant and said he had come with a message from someone important in Sudan.

'Is this your son, Ferede?' he asked, pulling the passport photo from his pocket.

Avrehet saw Ferede's face and burst into tears, throwing her arms around Shuffa.

'Yes! Yes!' she exclaimed, trembling with joy. 'Did you see him with your own eyes?' she asked, firing questions at Shuffa. 'How does he look? How did you meet him? What's he doing?'

Shuffa replied: 'He told me to tell you he's safe and well and that he's in contact with Israel. He said to tell you that I must bring Leul, Addis [Ferede's brothers] and Negusseh [Abeju's brother-in-law] back to Sudan. He said you must make sure they have provisions for the journey and not to hesitate.'

Having not known about her son's fate for so long, Avrehet was now being asked to send two more of her children the same way. She called the family together (Yazezow, her husband, had been sent to Shire by the regime and was not allowed to leave) and told them she placed her faith in Ferede.

'I'll get my boys ready,' she told Shuffa. 'They'll go with my blessing. Nothing will happen to them because it's God's will.'

The brothers accepted their mother's wish dutifully. Addis, who was only twelve, had never as much as been away from home before, and expected the trip to take just a few days.

With only the belongings they could carry, and rations of food and water, the boys met up with Negusseh and Shuffa the following day. He briefed them and gave them jalabiyas (typically worn by Muslims) to wear so they would not be identified as Jews, then the group set off on foot.

It was a gruelling journey. They walked mainly by night, guided by the light of the moon. They kept out of sight by day, avoiding rebels and government soldiers. For long stretches they did not see a living soul, at other times they had to run from non-Jewish villagers attempting to attack them.

After about a week they reached the village of Golij just before the border with Sudan. From there they took transport to Gedaref, where Shuffa led them to a shop. It was owned by a friend of Ferede. The man gave them food and told them to wait while he went off to Khartoum to look for him. Several hours later the man came back, telling them he had found their brother. After three days, Ferede appeared in Gedaref, and the group embraced in an emotional reunion.

The boys, Negusseh and Ferede talked excitedly and shared news of life back home and how it was in Sudan. Ferede reassured them he would get them to Jerusalem, but stressed that it had to be done in complete secrecy. He told them they could not talk about it to anyone, nor let on that they were Jews.

Shuffa had delivered and got the rest of his payment. He had proven his trustworthiness and as far as Ferede was concerned, having done it once he could do it again. Ferede asked Shuffa to go back and tell his family that the brothers and Negusseh had arrived safely, and that they should follow. He gave him a colour photograph of the four of them together to show as proof, and said he would pay him well. Shuffa agreed and set off on the journey for a second time.[4]

The family lay low in Gedaref, and days later Dani arrived and took them by car to Khartoum. There Leul, Addis and Negusseh were hidden in a safe place arranged by Ferede, and, apart from being taken to be photographed for a passport, were told not to leave. By now, other Jews had been discovered, sporadically, in the camps and a system was developing. Ferede would lead them out at night to a place where Dani would be waiting. He would brief them and then drive them to Khartoum, where they would be secretly housed in hostels, prepared by Ferede in advance. As more came, Ferede spread them out. By May, the six had become 32. Half had been moved to Khartoum, and half were still in Gedaref. They had all put their trust in Dani and his promise that he would get them to Israel. Not only were their lives at stake, but if he failed them, word would get around that the 'secret route' to the Promised Land was just a fallacy, and no more Jews would come forward.

5

CRACKING THE CONUNDRUM

Taking a room at the Hilton while he was in Khartoum, Dani contemplated what to do. The Jews were going to have to pass as non-Jews and be flown out. The problem was that they had no papers, and even if they managed to get through Khartoum Airport and onto a flight without being caught they would have to go to a third country first and then change planes. That meant an extra layer of transit rules to navigate without any official documentation. Credentials could be faked, but that carried risks, and would take too much time. He needed to 'prove' their legitimacy, but the question was how.

It was around that time, one morning, that Dani went to fetch his car from the hotel car park. On his way he caught sight of a large motorbike parked there. Dani was a veteran motorbike owner and in all the months he had been in Sudan, he had not seen a single one. He went to take a closer look.

'You like it?' came a voice in heavily French-accented English.

Dani turned around to find a man walking over to him.

'Yes, I like it very much,' he replied in French. 'I ride bikes back home.'

'You want to take it for a spin?' asked the man.

'Sure,' responded Dani eagerly.

'Here,' said the man reaching into his pocket. 'Go for it', throwing Dani a set of keys.

Dani did not wait to discuss. He smiled appreciatively, climbed on and fired up the engine. It was an unexpected treat. He steered the bike out of the hotel and set off down the road. He kept going, until the road ended and the ground became desert. He continued for about fifteen kilometres before turning back and riding through Omdurman, past the Hamed al-Nil mosque, where he liked to go to watch Whirling Dervishes perform their famous spinning ritual. Dani had not been on a bike for months. The last time was when he was stuck on the mission in Lagos and with time on his hands bought a Norton motorcycle and rode 1,000 kilometres across the savanna to observe Tuareg nomads in Kano. Now there was that same exhilarating feeling, riding unencumbered out of the city limits and back again.

'That was beautiful, thank you!' he said to the man as he pulled up, and they started to talk.

The man introduced himself as 'Jean-Michel'.

'So, what are you doing here?' he asked Dani.

'I'm an anthropologist,' Dani replied. 'I'm researching some of the tribes out in the desert. What about you?'

'Well I was a lawyer – I'm from Belgium, and I used to work in Brussels, but I grew tired of it and thought it wasn't really for me. So I went to work for the UNHCR [United Nations High Commissioner for Refugees]. I wanted to spend some time in a hard place and do some *real* work, so they sent me to Khartoum!'

Jean-Michel, it turned out, was responsible for relocating refugees to countries which had agreed to take quotas.

Dani and Jean-Michel became friendly and in the days that

followed would stop to talk when they would see one another in the hotel. In the evenings they would go for a drink at the bar or shoot some pool. Jean-Michel would ask Dani about his research, Dani would ask Jean-Michel about his job, especially the mechanics of getting refugees out of Sudan.

He learnt that if there were, say, 1,000 Somalis in a camp, Jean-Michel would contact embassies – US, Canada, UK, Germany and others – to see how many they would be prepared to accept as refugees. Once numbers were agreed, he would provide them with a list of names, ages and nationalities, and purchase airline tickets. The embassies would stamp requests for passports (known as Convention Travel Documents, effectively a passport for refugees), which Jean-Michel would collect and take to the offices of the Commissioner for Refugees at the Interior Ministry, where he would obtain the passports and exit visas.

It occurred to Dani that this could be the solution he was looking for.

He regarded Jean-Michel as a sincere person and someone he genuinely liked. It was possible, he thought, that the Belgian could help.

One day when they were talking, Dani tested the water.

'There's something I want to tell you,' he said.

'Hmm?' said Jean-Michel.

'I'm Jewish, and I'm letting you know this because I've discovered there are Jewish refugees in the camps.'

'What do you mean "Jewish refugees"?'

'I mean African Jews.'

'What do you mean "African Jews"?'

'Ethiopian Jews.'

'What do you mean "Ethiopian Jews"?'

'There are Ethiopian Jews,' said Dani. 'They're Ethiopian, they look like any other Ethiopian and they're Jewish. Just like I look like any other white guy, but I'm Jewish. So they're black and Jewish, and I'm white and Jewish.'

'Excuse me, but I never knew there were black Jews!' replied Jean-Michel.

'Okay, so you learnt something,' said Dani. 'The Jewish community in Paris asked me to see what I could do for them. They want to bring them to France.'

He could see from Jean-Michel's expression that the Belgian realised what Dani was getting at.

'I understand what you mean,' said Jean-Michel. 'You're asking if I can relocate these people to France?'

Dani gestured in hope.

'In principle I would, but I'm afraid I can't. This is an Arab country and my boss is Egyptian – how can I ... I mean, those are Jews ... if I get caught ... I'd lose my job and might even go to prison. I'm not worried about myself but my wife is pregnant ...'

'Okay! Okay!' interrupted Dani. 'So look, I'm not asking you to take any action, but will you just do one thing? Next time you go to get passports from the Interior Ministry, let me come with you.'

Jean-Michel thought. 'I couldn't say you were from the UNHCR, because that would be lying.'

'You wouldn't have to,' said Dani. 'Don't say anything about me. If they ask, I'll tell them I'm an anthropologist interested in ethnic minorities, and I'm studying why these Ethiopians come here and want to go to Europe, et cetera.'

'Let me think about it,' replied Jean-Michel.

Without waiting for an answer, once he was on his own, Dani sent a message to Kimche.

'I need you to organise all the friendly embassies you can in Khartoum. Tell them that if a guy answering to the name "Antoine" brings a list of names to be relocated – in Germany, Holland, France, wherever – that they don't ask any questions, they just stamp their approval. The rest I'll take care of.'

Kimche went to work. Since taking charge of the Mossad's foreign liaison work just a few years earlier, Kimche had revolutionised the way in which intelligence agencies cooperated with one another, and was held in high esteem by friendly agencies around the world. He secured the help of his counterparts among the Germans, Austrians, Swiss, Dutch, Greeks and French, and sent word back to Dani that it was a 'go'.

Dani had to get the 32 refugees out but the plan on the table was risky and untested. He knew if he got caught, he would face very harsh treatment, with a real possibility of being tortured or killed. The refugees would also be found out and taken away, and it would be a catastrophe not just for the Mossad but the whole Israeli state. Dani, though, had enough confidence. He would be doing it himself, and if he pulled it off, it could be repeated, again and again.

He got from Ferede the names of the sixteen in hiding in Khartoum and went to the Greek embassy, where he submitted the list. The embassies' intelligence organisations had instructed their foreign ministries to authorise their diplomats in Khartoum to stamp passport requests from 'Antoine', and within a few hours Dani collected the list, now officially approved for emigration to Greece. The intelligence agencies knew the requests were false, but the diplomats did not. They did not know the refugees were Jewish, nor that 'Antoine' was Dani from the Mossad, and there were no questions asked.

Dani met up with Jean-Michel again and asked him what his answer was. He said if Dani kept to his word, and never claimed to belong to the UN, then 'okay'.

The next piece had fallen into place.

Jean-Michel took Dani to the offices of the Commissioner for Refugees. They went to the first floor, Jean-Michel knocked on a door and, not waiting for an answer, walked in.

'*Marhaba* [Hi],' he said, and without another word, gave the senior official there the list of names.

The official counted the names then fetched the corresponding number of blank, light blue passports from a metal cabinet.

With a '*Shukran, ma'a salam* [Thanks, bye]', Jean-Michel left with Dani and queued up at a second office. When their turn came, Jean-Michel handed over passport photos and the passports, and the clerk inserted the pictures and filled in the names by hand.

Then they joined a queue at a third office, where another clerk stamped the completed passports with exit visas. Dani watched the procedure closely and stayed quiet, but made sure the senior official and clerks saw his face.

He repeated the process with Jean-Michel twice more that week. Each time the routine was the same. Jean-Michel never asked Dani exactly what he was planning, but if he assumed Dani was after passports for Jewish refugees, then he turned a blind eye.

After the third visit, Dani waited two days, before attempting it himself.

He collected Ferede and drove back to the offices. Ferede was worried that the escapade would not work. He had been doubtful from the moment Dani had mentioned it, suggesting it would be better to just make forgeries, something Dani was opposed to.

They parked and sat in the car, tense. The plan was for Ferede to wait outside. Dani took deep breaths and readied himself.

'Good luck,' said Ferede.

Dani gave a nod, climbed out and went into the building.

He walked up to the first floor and repeated identically Jean-Michel's routine. Dani knocked on the first door and let himself in.

'*Marhaba*,' he said. The senior official behind the desk did not respond. Dani handed him the list of sixteen names, and without saying a word, the official took the paper and started counting.

He went to the cabinet, counted out sixteen blank passports and gave them to Dani.

'*Shukran, ma'a salam*,' he said, and moved on to the second office. Dani queued, then handed over the passports and photos of the refugees taken earlier. The clerk put them in and wrote in the names by hand. Once completed, Dani went to the third office. There he queued and inched his way forward until it was his turn. He presented the documents and watched as, one by one, they were stamped with exit visas.

With his task completed, Dani walked down and out and back to the car.

'Ferede!' he exclaimed, gripping his partner by the arms, 'We have it! We have a system!'

Ferede breathed a sigh of relief.

Dani went to a European airline office and bought sixteen tickets. He then went to the hostels and briefed the Jews on what to do at the airport – a bewildering prospect for the unworldly villagers. There were many refugees flying out of Khartoum, so they would not look out of place. All they needed to do was to say they were Ethiopians who were being relocated to Greece. They made their own way to the airport, followed by Dani and Ferede who watched them from afar until they passed through border control and disappeared from view.

That month – May, 1979 – the first sixteen, including Addis, Leul and Negusseh, were flown out to Athens and from there to Tel Aviv. The second group of sixteen went the same way two months later.

Dani and Ferede had done it. Initiative, risk and subterfuge had delivered a result. It was a great accomplishment, but also just the start. Apart from Ferede's brothers and Negusseh, the Jews who had come to Sudan so far had done so randomly and not as part of a movement. They had also come only from Tigray; in Gondar, where the vast majority of Ethiopian Jews lived, no one yet knew about the route.

Ferede decided he would have to go to back to Ethiopia to spread the word himself.

Dani was under orders not to go there while he was on assignment in Sudan, but his recalcitrant streak – a characteristic which Kimche knew the job actually called for – kicked in.

'Good idea,' he said. 'We should do it.'

'No, not you,' replied Ferede. 'It's better if I work there alone.' It was his way of saying Dani might not do as he was told, and could endanger the trip.

'Look, there is no way you are going there and I am staying waiting for you – I'm not your wife!' Dani said.

Ferede relented. The two men took the Defender and drove to the border, pulling up in a field. Dani used branches to hide the car and they crossed the border on foot. The vehicle was not the only thing they had to conceal – as a white man, Dani would get spotted straight away, so he took some charcoal and covered himself from head to foot with black dust.

They walked at night and stayed out of sight during the day. After a two-night trek they reached a Jewish village near Wolkait on the boundary of Gondar and Tigray in the far north-west. They met the village elders and Ferede explained to them that they had come from Sudan. Dani hung back, without saying a word. The elders looked at him curiously. Ferede beckoned Dani, licked a finger and wiped a stripe of black dust off his face.

'He's a white Jew,' said Ferede, to much curiosity. He told the elders about the route into Sudan and how from there it was possible to get to Israel.

'You've got to tell people,' he said. 'Spread the word, get the message out to other villages. Tell people to come. I've done it and so can everyone else.'

He gave instructions for anyone who came, to look for him at specific places in Gedaref market, and that from there they would take care of them.

Dani and Ferede stayed in the village until the next day, then at night began the long walk back to the field where they had left their car. They uncovered the vehicle and headed back into Sudan to carry on the search.

Having worked together for several months, Ferede searching the camps, finding Jews, smuggling them to hideouts – and risking his life in the process – Dani strongly felt that Ferede ought to be recognised as a Mossad agent and thereby entitled to a salary. After all, they were doing the same work, only Dani was getting paid, and Ferede was not. He put the request to HQ, who agreed – on condition that Ferede go to Israel for a month and complete an official training course.

As former chief instructor, Dani knew what was involved and objected. It would set them back weeks, as without Ferede, Dani could not carry on the job. 'What are you going to teach him?' he asked, facetiously. 'How to know if he's being followed? This isn't Milan. This is Africa. He can teach *you!*'

HQ was insistent, but without documentation the first task was to make sure Ferede could not only get out of Sudan, but also get back in again. Dani bought him a ticket to Zurich and Ferede left Sudan with an Ethiopian passport provided by the Mossad and an official exit visa. He was met at Zurich by a Mossad agent, who brought him an Israeli passport, without which, having come from Sudan, he would likely have been barred from an El Al (Israel's national airline) flight on security grounds (the same did not apply to the groups of refugees, whose arrival the Israeli authorities were prepared for and for whom normal security procedures were waived; as he was working for the Mossad, Ferede travelled as a 'regular' visitor, under the radar of even Israeli officials themselves). From Zurich he flew to Tel Aviv, where, for the first time in his life, Ferede Aklum stepped onto Israeli soil. It was an extraordinary and emotional moment for him, the realisation of a lifelong ambition. As a child, Ferede had listened in wonder to his father's stories of the mystical Land of Jerusalem; while the ground where he now was might not have been made of gold as he had once believed, it did not matter. There, where he stood on the sun-beaten tarmac at Ben Gurion Airport, Ferede Aklum had fulfilled a dream.

As it happened, Ferede's stay turned out to be shorter than expected. Within a week, Dani got a message from HQ. They conceded there was nothing Ferede was gaining from the course after all, and they were sending him back, a Mossad agent on a salary. He returned to Sudan, getting back into the country on a forged entry visa and with a letter declaring he was working as a translator. Both documents were courtesy of the Mossad.

Following the interruption, the two men resumed their work.

The number of Ethiopian Jews who had so far been found in Sudan and smuggled out to Israel, while significant in itself, was a tiny proportion of Ethiopia's Jewish population.

That all changed after Shuffa the merchant arrived back in Tigray around the beginning of June 1979, with the photograph of Ferede, his two brothers and Negusseh. He found Ferede's mother and gave her the picture, along with a note.

'You will learn as the young people learnt,' it said, a coded way of appealing to her to leave in the same way as they had done.

Shmuel Yilma, a nephew of Ferede who was there, recalls a scene of rejoicing and excitement. His grandmother Avrehet, he says, was reduced to tears, torn over what to do. She came to a swift decision.

'I have to join my children while there's still life in me,' she said. 'Otherwise I can't carry on.'

Yilma's father asked her how she proposed to do that.

'We'll all go. Men, women and children. Everyone,' she replied. 'We'll do what Ferede asks and follow them.'

Others there objected, dismissing the idea as madness. Avrehet was not young, they said – how did she think she was going to survive such a journey?

Avrehet was stubborn. For days and weeks she did not change her mind. A few months later a letter arrived. It was from Negusseh in Israel.

'The merchandise has reached its destination,' it said. 'If you do not buy more goods, it will be too late – you'll miss the opportunity.'[1]

The family got together to decide what to do. The atmosphere was different. Avrehet declared she would leave immediately. Some chose to go with her. Others said they would follow on later.

Avrehet had already gathered information from traders about the route and what was in store. She assembled a group of fourteen people, comprising one of her daughters, her daughter's family and two families of friends. The group included young children, one of whom was just three months old. Avrehet's two other daughters stayed behind. Yazezow said he would also go after he had organised the sale of his house and land. Avrehet's group left at night, so as not to alert any non-Jewish villagers to their departure. They left behind almost everything they owned. 'To go to Jerusalem,' Avrehet said, 'it is enough to have the clothes you stand up in.'[2]

People did not know what to make of Avrehet's decision. Was it brave, or foolhardy? Was she leading deluded souls to their doom, or indeed along a path to the land of milk and honey? Was it a chance worth taking, or wiser to stay where they were? There was anxiety and uncertainty among the villagers in the days that followed, fuelled by rumours that Avrehet had been killed, or even eaten by wild animals. The first piece of concrete information came from a group of merchants, who told villagers they had seen her along the way. The fact that she was alive was enough for some, and a second small group from the village decided to do as Avrehet had done, and her sons before her, and followed on. The departures became the subject of obsessive conversations, and the idea started to gain momentum. Three months after Avrehet's group had gone, another (including Negusseh's family) upped and left, slipping away quietly in the middle of a family wedding, using it as a distraction, and after that a group of eighteen. Each left in secret, leaving behind anything they could not quickly sell, and setting off at night without so much as waking loved ones to say goodbye, should any disturbance attract the attention of Christian neighbours.

Word started to spread, from Jew to Jew and village to village, that some of the community had secretly left for the Land of Jerusalem. One of those who heard about it was Zehava Gedamo, then a young girl.

'People started to tell us that many people were walking to Jerusalem. This was a distant dream for us. Someone dreams all day, and when the dream comes true he doesn't believe it, and then he starts to dream again. [I] took [my] mother's hand and thought to [myself]: "We're going to Jerusalem. Everyone is going there, and now we are too. We are going to Jerusalem, which is all golden, even the earth and the stones, and there is always a rainbow and a golden halo above its sky. It doesn't matter that we're leaving our homes – we're going to a better place, in fact – to the best place in the world."'[3]

Indeed, there was a widespread assumption among them that it was not to Sudan that they were walking, but to the Holy City itself.

After centuries of longing, it was felt that the hour of redemption had finally come. Abba Mahari, the Beta Israel holy man, had valiantly tried and failed to lead his followers to Jerusalem in the mid-19th century, so the story went, but he had headed north-east. The way out, it transpired, was west, and this time the Ethiopian Jews had the State of Israel to help. In 1979, just 32 had made it out, while by the end of 1980 the number had soared to about 800, all smuggled through Khartoum Airport.[4]

Benny Ghoshen was five and a half years old when he was collected from his bed by his parents late one night at their home in Adi Woreva. They had chosen Saturday night as departure time, as the Sabbath, when there was no contact between Jewish and Christian neighbours, had just concluded. They crept out of the village in a group of thirteen – the smallest children and elderly people carried on donkeys – and made their way down a valley to the Tekeze River. They went hastily, covering the 25 kilometres to the river in a day and a half. Benny's parents had had to make the agonising decision that for the sake of their youngest children they would have to go without two of their older sons – one aged sixteen, who had been forced into the TPLF, and another aged eighteen, who was working elsewhere as a teacher.

At the river they converged with Jews who had come from other villages as part of a plan to go en masse, until there were about 400 people walking together. They crossed the river, wading through on foot, or by horse or donkey. Some of the youngest children fell off into the water and had to be saved from drowning, but everyone eventually made it to the other side. After days and nights of more journeying – moving only after dark so as not to be seen – the group arrived at the Wolkait mountain range. With the rugged escarpments rising thousands of feet above them, the tired throng began its long and difficult ascent. The crossing took days, stopping when it was light and carrying on at night. The terrain transformed, from lush and verdant to arid and barren, where it became a matter of survival. Provisions of water were running so low that they started to ration portions to three bottle caps a day for children, and just one for adults. What little food they had left was also divided into morsels.

Weaker people in the group fell ill, and some died. Benny, who had been walking barefoot on scorching sand, was suffering from exhaustion, so was put on the back of a donkey. As they continued, the animals suddenly went wild and started to stampede. They had seen a small pool of water and, dying of thirst, charged towards it. As Benny's donkey ran, he was struck by the branch of a tree and fell off. He lay where he landed, showing no signs of life. Members of the group checked him but were convinced he was dead, another tragic casualty of the brutal trek. They decided to bury him and dug a grave, but the Jewish custom of ritual purity was so strictly observed by the Beta Israel that even in the desert they would not put a body in the ground unclean. With water from the pool, they started to wash him, whereupon Benny began to move. To the shock of everyone, the boy started crying. He had been knocked unconscious but the water brought him round. Picking him up, the group carried on, and a few days later they reached the border town of Humera. It was too dangerous to cross in daylight, as they would get caught by Derg soldiers. Accounts from Jews who made it to the border only to fall into the hands of Ethiopian patrols tell of beatings, torture and rape. They would be arrested for trying to leave the country illegally, get sent back to where they started and slung into jail. Benny's group managed to get across under cover of darkness and headed to Gedaref.

Three months after leaving their village, they finally arrived at the camp. Within days, Benny's family were smuggled out and driven to Khartoum. Ferede got them passports and they were put on a flight to Marseille. There they switched to an El Al plane, and on 25 May 1980 they landed in Israel. As a child, Benny did not know what an aeroplane was, and would playfully throw stones at the sky whenever one flew overhead. By the age of 30, he was a major in the Israeli Air Force.[5]

The Jews who trekked from their villages in the Ethiopian Highlands to Sudan left behind not only the places where their ancestors had dwelt for centuries, but also their way of life. No one knew just how perilous the journey would be. Some thought it would take only hours. For many it took months. The way was merciless. They were stalked by hunger and thirst, preyed on by wild animals, struck by illness and disease, and robbed, murdered or abducted by bandits. At least 1,560 are known to have perished en route and in the camps in Sudan.[6] Around 50 disappeared (some of whom might still be alive in Sudan or elsewhere).[7]

After the first groups were successfully smuggled out of Sudan, and knowing word had been sent back to the Jewish villages of northern Ethiopia that a way to Jerusalem was open, Dani realised the system of hiding Jews around hostels could not cope if numbers swelled. Also, the more spread out they were kept, the more chance there was of them being discovered. A better way had to be found.

Dani drove around the capital, looking for solutions. In an upmarket district on the edges of the urban sprawl he came across compounds of houses, surrounded by three-metre-high stone walls. From the street, only the roofs were visible. Some of the properties looked empty. He went to a real estate agent in the city and asked for a place to rent. He explained he was an anthropologist and had people coming to study with him. He said he needed somewhere away from the city centre, without distractions or neighbours, preferably with a courtyard and somewhere to park his car. Perhaps somewhere on the outskirts to make it easier logistically for field trips. The agent offered to take Dani to have a look, so they set off, Dani leading him back to the area he had seen.

'How about these?' he asked.

'They're available,' said the agent.

'Fine, I'll take one,' said Dani, and they went back to the office.

It was 100 pounds a month, and Dani paid six months in advance.

The compound acted as a safe house, and from then on, Dani and Ferede placed groups of newly found Jews there, out of sight and sound. Eventually, as the number of Jews expanded, Dani rented a second compound about a kilometre away. Between the two places they could hide dozens at a time, sometimes as many as 70 in each house.

The Jews were under strict instructions not to make any noise nor leave the property, apart from one person appointed from each dwelling who was allowed to stock up once a day at a nearby grocery shop. They understood, and for the whole time they were there, they, and even their children, stayed totally quiet, sometimes for several days and nights.

The system – precarious as it was – was holding up. Night after night Ferede would scour the camps, and let Dani know whenever he found Jews. Dani would collect them from a meeting point at a *wadi* (valley) or dry river-bed, load them onto the Land Rover and drive them to the safe house in Khartoum, arriving at 2 or 3am. (On nights where soldiers at checkpoints were seen near the road rather than sleeping in their tent he would turn off and loop through the desert, navigating by compass and the stars.) The following day, with the list of names, he would obtain approval for passports from the embassies, buy airline tickets and get the papers and blank passports from the Interior Ministry, the slowest part of the process because of the queues. The group due to go would get briefed by Ferede on what to say and do at the airport, then they would make their way there, watched by Ferede and Dani from a distance until they were through. From there, they would fly to a destination in Europe, where they would be met by a representative of the Jewish Agency or the Mossad, transferred straight on to an El Al plane and flown off to Israel. Stories abound of new arrivals kissing the ground at Ben Gurion airport, with one elderly immigrant even ingesting mouthfuls of soil in fulfilment of a vow upon reaching the Holy Land.[8]

One day Ferede pointed out to Dani that they could speed things up if they did not have to wait so long at the ministry.

'Every time you have to queue for an hour until the second guy is free, then another hour for the third guy.

'Why don't we just fill in the passports ourselves?'

Dani had seen that Ferede had elegant handwriting and anything that would help cut corners was, he thought, a good idea.

The next time they went to get the refugees' documents, Ferede accompanied Dani into the building. He waited while Dani collected blank passports from the senior official, then, bypassing the second office, both men joined the queue for the last room in the system. When their turn came, they went inside. Before the clerk did anything, Ferede shouted '*Far! Far!*' ('Rat!') and pointed under the furniture. The clerk jumped up to look for the creature, and while he was distracted, Dani quickly picked up a visa stamp from his desk and put it in his pocket. The two men slipped out and left the building. Now with all the tools they needed at their disposal, they could replicate the entire process themselves, thereby reducing the amount of time they had to spend at the ministry.

Soon after that, Ferede came up with another efficiency. In his view, passports were being wasted by just using one per person, meaning they kept having to go back to the ministry each time there was a new group of refugees needing to be moved out.

'Let's try and do a family passport,' he suggested. No such thing had been done before anywhere in the world, and doing so now would be taking a big chance.

Dani admired Ferede's creativity and initiative. 'He was like me, in black,' he would later say, describing him as born for the role.

They gathered five unrelated Ethiopian Jews – a man and a woman, two children of other parents and an orphan – and photographed them together. Ferede invented names for the family and wrote them in one passport.

They took the group to the airport, and Dani stayed with them as they showed the passport to the border guard.

'What's this?' the guard asked, looking at the photo.

'Don't worry,' replied Dani. 'You know there's a paper short-age, so we've got to be sparing with the passports because every bit of paper comes from trees and there just aren't enough of them. You'll be seeing a lot more passports like this from now on.'

The guard did not question it, nor ask Dani who he was, but stamped the document and let the five through.

From then on, Dani and Ferede used the same method every time, entering 'families' into single passports, getting them through the airport border control without incident.

On one occasion they took out a group of fifteen – the highest number for a single 'family'. The faces crammed onto the photograph were so small they were barely identifiable. The record-setting photograph would later be exhibited in the Mossad's private museum in Tel Aviv.

6

'I'M IN PRISON'

As a single, white man spending a long time in Sudan, Dani had to lower his profile, and one way was to act as 'normal' as possible and do what other Europeans did.

To enhance his cover, he began to socialise with other members of the French expat community in the city, and at the Hilton he got friendly with airline personnel stopping over. Two young Frenchmen who piloted President Nimeiri's private plane were permanent residents of the hotel. They were called on only occasionally and spent most of their time by the pool or trying to charm newly arrived air hostesses. Dani got to know them and the three would often hang out together, going to bars and meeting women.

For Dani, forming relationships was part of the facade of blending in. One was with the sister of an Italian diplomat. Her brother was an expert crocodile hunter, who would be called on by villagers to dispose of man-eaters preying on fishermen. He would take Dani on these crocodile hunts, where they would lie on the river banks at night until the warmth of the rising sun drew the crocodiles out, whereupon the Italian would kill them with a high-velocity rifle. His sister's best friend was the daughter of a wealthy, influential ethnic Armenian businessman and after Dani's relationship with the Italian woman ended, he started to date her friend. Dani would get invited to the family mansion for dinners and won the approval of her father. The man viewed Dani as a potential son-in-law and took him into his confidence. He would often talk to Dani about his business, once even sending him to carry out a major transaction abroad on his behalf (Dani obliged so as not to create any tensions).

The father introduced Dani to important people, among them President Nimeiri's brother Mustafa and senior officials in the military. Dani would sometimes play Mustafa at tennis on a court at his girlfriend's father's home, throwing games to let him win.

One evening at the house, the Armenian businessman brought Dani to meet one of his visitors, the director of the University of Khartoum.

'I understand you're researching our tribes,' the director said to Dani.

'That's right,' he replied.

'You know, I'm Sudanese and I don't know that much about them. My students don't either. Would you be willing to give a lecture at the university?'

Dani kept up the front and complied. Subsequently, appearing as 'an invited lecturer' in front of 200 students, as well as the director and the head of the history department, the Mossad agent spun his theories about why the semi-nomadic way of life was slowly disappearing. The students took notes and his hosts complimented him afterwards on his talk.

It was one of several times where his cover was tested. On another occasion, Dani was called by the wife of a French couple he had got to know in Khartoum.

'Tonight, you have to come to dinner,' she instructed him, 'I'm having some friends over and I've got a surprise for you.'

Dani accepted, and during the evening the woman brought over a guest, whom she introduced as 'another French anthropologist'.

Dani's blood ran cold. At that moment, he expected to be caught out.

After exchanging pleasantries, the man started: 'So, tell me, what are you doing exactly?'

'Oh, I'm researching the Beni-Amir tribe,' replied Dani.

'Interesting,' replied the man. 'Tell me about it.'

'Listen,' said Dani, thinking on his feet. 'I've just come back from the field. I'm fed up with these guys. I haven't been able to see them or talk to them. Tonight, let's talk about something else. What's going on in France? What's happening with Marseille football team?'

After a brief discussion off-topic, Dani said: 'Tomorrow morning, be my guest at the Hilton Hotel, 8am. We'll have breakfast and I'll tell you everything you want to know.'

The anthropologist accepted.

The following morning Dani slipped out of the hotel at 7.30am, leaving a note saying: 'Sorry, I had to go. Something came up. Leave me your telephone number, and next time I'm in Paris I'll give you a call, we'll have lunch and we'll talk.'

That was the last he heard from Dani.

The incident with the anthropologist was not the only moment which was too close for comfort.

One night, Dani and his girlfriend were out with friends at a discotheque at the Meridien Hotel. As they were all chatting, the subject of Israel came up.

'These fucking Jews!' spat Dani's girlfriend.

He was perturbed but kept his composure.

'What do you mean?' he asked. 'The Jews and you

Armenians have got a lot in common. The Germans tried to exterminate the Jews and the Turks tried to exterminate you. You too are persecuted, you should be more …'

'No, we're not like them. We're Christians and they killed Jesus!' the woman replied.

With that, the relationship fizzled out.

By early 1980, the Mossad's mission was bearing fruit but it was fraught with danger, which increased as the number of Jews getting to Sudan grew. Dani and Ferede had been working together for about twelve months when one day in February they went back to the government offices to collect more passports.

Ferede, a heavy smoker, got out of the car for a cigarette, and Dani went inside. He knocked on the door of the passport office, but there was nobody there, so he turned around and left. As Dani came out he stopped in his tracks. He saw across the road Ferede being dragged by his collar towards another car. The man who had him was in civilian clothing but Dani realised he was undercover police.

'Hey,' he shouted in broken Arabic, running after them. 'Leave him, he's working with me!'

'*Ruh min hoon!*' ('Get out of here!') the policeman shouted back at Dani, pushing Ferede into the car.

He drove off, so Dani jumped into the Defender and followed.

The unmarked car carrying Ferede drove to the police headquarters. A guard raised the barrier to let it in, with Dani in pursuit. The policeman hauled Ferede out of the car and pushed him inside the building and into a room. Manhandling his frightened prey, he shoved Ferede onto a chair and left the room. Ferede was alone and helpless. He knew what the Sudanese thought of Ethiopians like him, and he was terrified as to what lay in wait. He had been plucked off the street, something he had always dreaded might happen, and now he was at the mercy of people who could do whatever they wanted. As panicked thoughts ran through his head, the door opened causing Ferede's wide eyes to dart towards it.

To his great relief, in walked Dani. Ferede let out a long breath, as if to say 'Thank God'.

'What happened?' Dani asked his companion, sitting down next to him.

Ferede explained that on the way to the police station, the officer had said to him hintingly: 'If you help me, I'll help you.' Ferede said he offered 50 Sudanese pounds, whereupon the officer told him: 'Now I'm arresting you for attempted bribery.'

As the two men discussed their predicament, a senior officer – an imposing figure of a man – entered.

'A refugee without a passport, bribing a policeman,' he declared in Arabic. 'Come here!'

Ferede approached a desk where the senior officer had sat down.

'I'm sorry, I can't understand Arabic …'

Whack! Whack!

The officer slapped Ferede across the head, sending him reeling. Dani jumped up.

'Why did you hit him?' he snapped.

'*Ruh min hoon*,' the officer growled back, pushing Dani against the wall.

'I'm not going anywhere without him!' Dani, regaining his balance, responded in English.

'No?' answered the officer, also in English. He called in the sergeant.

'Lock them both up!'

The sergeant gripped Dani and Ferede and hauled them off to a cell. There he unlocked and opened the door. A foul smell seeped out as he pushed the two men inside. The room was small – about five by fifteen metres – crowded and windowless. It was dimly lit by a single low amp bulb, just enough for Dani to make out faces peering in their direction. He and Ferede stood there silently, scanning their surroundings. Dani counted nineteen other inmates, sitting or standing all the way round the walls. There were filthy mattresses on the floor but not enough space to lie down without crossing limbs with someone else.

The prisoners appeared to Dani more like creatures than humans and his priority was to protect Ferede and get them both out.

Trained as he was in combat techniques, Dani thought that he might be able to take care of himself in there, but he knew once Ferede was identified as an Ethiopian he would be victimised straight away.

He took Ferede and moved into a corner. 'Do as I do,' he told him.

With his back against the wall, Dani squatted. Ferede did the same.

Dani took out a packet of cigarettes, intending to try and mask the stench, as well as helping him think. But as he did so a hand came out of the dark and snatched the box.

'Hey!' said Dani in the direction of the culprit. 'One for me!'

The hand reappeared, holding out a single cigarette.

Dani squinted into the gloom. He looked for the person who had his cigarettes, and spotted a tall figure holding the box. This, he calculated, was the boss of the cell.

'*Ta'al!*' ('Come!') Dani called to him.

The man stared back.

'*Ta'al!*' repeated Dani, in a friendly tone.

The man cautiously approached.

'I have money,' said Dani in Arabic. 'Go to the guard. Tell him to get bread, bottled water and cartons of cigarettes.'

Dani gave him ten Sudanese pounds, a considerable amount.

The man, who said his name was Bassem, took the money and called the guard. He told him what he wanted and gave him the payment.

Later on, the guard came back, handed over the goods and took some for himself.

Dani turned to Bassem. 'I don't know how long we're going to be here, but as long as we are, you'll have a supply of cigarettes, bread and water – on one condition,' he told him. 'You are responsible for our security.'

Whether or not Bassem cared, or would use it to assert control in the cell, Dani hoped his 'arrangement' would work if it came to it.

The first night, Dani and Ferede decided to take it in turns to sleep or keep guard, like they had done in the bush.

As they sat at one end of the room, they could make out goings on at the other. An inmate had taken hold of a second man and had him pinned down, stripped from below the waist. The man underneath was shouting, then screaming. The first inmate shouted something back and repeatedly punched him in the head until the screaming subsided into groans.

Dani and Ferede felt sickened.

'I have to stop them,' said Dani quietly.

'Are you crazy?' whispered Ferede back. 'What do you think will happen? You won't stop it and then they'll just turn on us!'

Dani already knew that but had to hear it said. He stayed where he was.

'Ferede,' he said, 'I'm telling you now, one thing is for sure – we came in here as virgins and we're going to leave this place as virgins!'

That night, neither man slept.

Hour after hour, they sat propped up against the wall, as the screams of young men being raped carried through the dark. It was difficult to tell when night became day, so little light crept in. Nor when night returned, apart from the sound of the screaming again.

It was on the second night when Dani fell asleep that he was woken up by Ferede.

'Look!' he said, pointing at two men moving towards them on all fours.

Dani bent his knee and readied his foot. As the first man got close enough, Dani planted his foot in his face and pushed him away.

'Bassem!' he shouted. 'Bassem!'

Bassem appeared, pulled the men away and kicked them about.

After that, no one else bothered Dani or Ferede.

It became clear that the prison authorities were in no hurry to deal with them, and as day became night again, and with it came the screaming, their incarceration wore on. They were let out for only half an hour a day to exercise in the courtyard, which Dani used to look for opportunities to escape. The courtyard was surrounded by a wall which he could have scaled, and a back entrance which although it was manned could have been dealt with by a bribe. While Dani himself could have got out, the problem lay in how to spring Ferede. He decided it was too high risk, but as long as Ferede was not going anywhere, neither would he.

Physically and psychologically, the imprisonment wore away at them. They were on a constant state of alert, both day and night, stuck in a cramped, stinking cell surrounded by violent criminals and knowing that protection from Bassem was not something to be relied upon. No one on the outside knew they were there, and as far as they were aware they could be left to rot. They lost weight, refusing to eat most of the putrid prison food which was served up, surviving on only bread and soup, and bottled water bought from the guards.

Several days had passed when the door of the cell opened up. A guard appeared, pointed at Dani, and said the commander of the police station wanted to see him.

'Bassem,' Dani called, nodding towards Ferede, signalling to the man to look after him while he was gone.

The guard took Dani to the commander's office.

'What are you doing here?' the commander asked him. 'Why are you here? You can go.'

'I'm with my employee,' said Dani, 'and I'm not leaving without him. I know him and his family, and in my country we have a code of honour not to abandon people. Why are you holding him?'

'He tried to bribe a Sudanese officer,' replied the commander.

'He was trying to buy his freedom, this was not bribery,' Dani said.

'That's for a judge to decide,' the commander replied. 'Either he'll go to prison for a long time or he'll be thrown out over the border.'

Dani refused to leave without Ferede, and was returned to the cell.

On one of the exercise breaks in the yard, Dani caught sight of the police officer who had arrested Ferede, talking to someone Dani recognised. It was the driver of Jean-Michel's Egyptian boss, Ibrahim, the chief of the UNHCR in Khartoum. Dani had seen him at Jean-Michel's house and the two had talked.

'Hussein!' called Dani, catching his attention.

'Mr Daniel!' Hussein replied, coming over. 'What are you doing here?'

'I'm in prison. It's a long story but I shouldn't be here. It's a mistake. Can you get your boss to come?'

Hussein said he would try.

Dani returned to the cell but was later called back to the room of the large officer who had hit and pushed him and Ferede.

Ibrahim was there, talking to the officer as Dani came in. While speaking, the Egyptian walked over to the officer and perched on a corner of the desk.

'Get your dirty ass off my table!' bellowed the officer. 'Get the fuck away – and take that French guy with you!' gesturing to them to get out of the room.

Ibrahim backed off in shock and made his exit, followed by Dani.

'I really apologise,' said Dani, 'the guy's a barbarian!'

'It's okay,' said Ibrahim. 'But why are you here?'

'My guy was arrested. He's Ethiopian and he's my translator. We work together. He's a good man. Can you help get him out?'

'Ethiopian?' replied Ibrahim. 'No chance. They'll never let him go. Find someone else. I can't do anything. Forget about him.'

'No,' said Dani. 'Then tell your driver. He knows people here. Maybe he can help.'

The driver was waiting with his boss's Mercedes, and the Egyptian sent him inside.

'Hussein, who was this police guy you were talking to?' Dani asked him.

'He's my cousin. Why?' replied Hussein.

'I want you to persuade him to get the bribery charge against Ferede dropped,' said Dani. 'Tell him I'll pay, no matter what.'

Hussein said he would see what he could do.

Dani went back into the cell and told Ferede what had happened. He did not hear anything more for the next two days. Some ten nights and days had passed, and by now Dani was starting to get concerned about Mossad HQ. Sooner or later the agency would wonder if something had happened to him and they would send an agent to look for him. Dani wanted to avoid that at all cost, as there was no knowing where it could lead.

On the eleventh day, Dani was called out of the cell again.

'Your Ethiopian is going to be judged,' said the guard.

Dani was taken to an office, where the judge was sitting.

'The complaint has been withdrawn,' he told Dani. 'But the Ethiopian has to pay for the food and water he was given in prison. That comes to 300 pounds.'

Dani paid the money – as well as another 300 Sudanese pounds demanded by the officer who withdrew the charge – and got the release papers signed.

Ferede was brought out of the cell, without knowing why, and led to Dani.

'We're out,' Dani told him. 'Let's go.'

They were words Ferede had almost given up hoping to hear, but he did not even care to question what had happened. He had lived through days and nights of stress and fear and just wanted to get away. Exhausted, filthy and stinking, the two men walked out of the police station and back into daylight and freedom. Dani's training had prepared him for coping with capture, but the brutality of the night-time assaults, and the screaming which accompanied them, resurfaced in his night-mares for many years to come.

The detention of an agent was considered a very serious event by the Mossad, and although it was mandatory to report such an incident to HQ, Dani weighed up doing so. He was well aware that if he let Tel Aviv know, both he and Ferede would be pulled out of the country. He decided to sit on it for the sake of the mission. His judgment was right. One of his former most senior bosses said that if he had known at the time, he would have got the operation aborted without ques-tion. Nobody would have allowed an operative who had been arrested in an enemy country in the Arab world to continue doing intelligence work there, the former boss said.

The episode had cost Dani and Ferede nearly two weeks, but it could have been much worse. Despite what he had been through – and knowing the same could happen to him again – Ferede never considered quitting and the pair went back to work.

To begin with, when they were finding Jews in small numbers, Dani and Ferede would transport them to Khartoum in the Defender, by night. As numbers grew, they needed a bigger vehicle, so Dani leased a Toyota Land Cruiser pickup from a local importer. With this they could ferry up to 35 people (depending on the number of children) at once, in the front and back, though most of the time they took groups of about ten. The downside was that the cargo bed was exposed, meaning it was difficult to hide what – or who – they were carrying when it came to passing through checkpoints. When they approached a roadblock, Dani would bang with his elbow on the cabin window behind, as a signal to one of the Jews acting as a look-out to tell everyone in the back to lie flat and cover themselves with blankets he had 'borrowed' from the Hilton. Seeing nothing odd, soldiers, often bored and tired, invariably waved the vehicle through.

On one occasion, they had just passed a roadblock (considered one of the most risky due to its position at the foot of a bridge across a canal) with a near-full cargo in the back, and two Ethiopian Jewish women upfront – one elderly, the other young and pregnant – when the older woman gestured for them to stop, uttering something in Tigrinya.

'Okay,' said Ferede, turning to Dani. 'She's going to give birth!'

Dani had no choice but to pull over and let the Jews down from the back. It completely broke with protocol; short of a life or death situation, he never stopped between Gedaref and Khartoum. Now the Jews were clambering off the pickup and standing together within earshot of the guards on the other side of the bridge. Dani and Ferede carefully helped the woman who was in labour out of the cabin and over to the group of Jews, signalling for everyone to stay absolutely quiet. Some of the Jews dug a hole in the ground with their hands, as others passed them their *shamas*, or shawls, to use as cushioning. The females in the group gently manoeuvred the young woman, in her pain, into position over the hole, where she lowered herself until she squatted. In the silence of the night, as Dani watched for any sign of movement on the bridge, the woman gave birth without making a sound.

Forty-five minutes after their emergency stop, Dani, Ferede and the passengers quietly reboarded the vehicle, and drove off, leaving as five in the cabin, not four.

Eight days later, Dani and Ferede went to visit the mother and baby in the safehouse in Khartoum. The baby's father approached Dani and asked him if he would perform the *brit milah* (circumcision ritual).

'Thank you, but I can't do that,' he replied. 'My professional training did not include circumcision …'

Ferede laughed.

'Do you want to be a grandfather?' Dani asked the man. He nodded.

'Then please, don't give the job to me – I might cut off more than I'm meant to!'

The man understood. Due to the circumstances, the baby was circumcised in Israel well after the customary eight days, a rare occurrence in Beta Israel society.[1]

When their stocks of blank passports ran low, Dani would return to the Interior Ministry with lists of names to get fresh ones. That was nearly jeopardised in early summer 1980 when it was the turn of the next group of 25 refugees to leave.

Dani called the Swissair office and asked to buy them seats.

'I have an empty plane going,' said the ticket agent. 'You can fill it up if you want.'

At that time there were 74 people in the safe houses, and it occurred to Dani that he could send them all at once – more than twice the number that had ever been sent at any one time before.

He got the list of names from Ferede and the stamp from the Swiss embassy, and went to the Interior Ministry. He had never presented so many names in one go – 30 was about the most – so as an inducement he brought a bottle of Courvoisier cognac, concealed in a plastic bag, and put it on the table at the same time.

The list of names had always only filled one side of paper, but now it stretched to three.

The official ignored the bottle and took the list.

'Whoa! *Ma hdha?*' ('What is this?') he asked angrily. 'This is too many! It's not allowed!' he snapped.

It was out of the ordinary, and if the official linked Dani with Jean-Michel and called the UNHCR to complain, it would become clear Dani was an imposter.

The official went to the metal cabinet and handed over just 30 passports.

Dani thanked him and promptly left. He called Jean-Michel.

'If you get a call from our mutual friend at the Interior Ministry and he asks you about me and passports, you can tell him what you like, but please let me know, because if he phones, I'm leaving Sudan,' he told him.

With the 30 passports, Dani and Ferede took out all 74 anyway, using group photos. They were the only passengers on the plane. Effectively, it was an entirely Mossad flight.

Jean-Michel never heard from the official and Dani returned to picking up passports, but with just single-page lists.

*

Smuggling Jews without getting caught at any stage of the process was down to a combination of professionalism and luck. There was only one system – taking them clandestinely to the safe houses in the middle of the night – and if that was discovered, the operation would be finished.

Refugees were not allowed to travel to Khartoum without special authorisation, or through the UNHCR which arranged permits for those accepted for resettlement abroad to get from the camps to Khartoum airport, from where they would relocate to a third country. In Gedaref, this was organised by a local Sudanese UNHCR worker, who would issue select groups of refugees with travel passes stamped by the agency. When they travelled by truck to Khartoum, they would show it at checkpoints and be waved through. Dani thought if the Jews could secretly become part of this system, then it would serve as a second, safer, way out.

The risk, though, lay with them being exposed by non-Jews in the same transportation. If they were discovered, they would be arrested, pass or no pass.

The local Sudanese UN worker could not be involved in the plan, because if he knew they were Jews there was a chance he would refuse to cooperate or even turn them in himself.

Dani went to talk to Jean-Michel. He told him that conditions in Gedaref were getting so bad, the UNHCR ought to have someone senior there.

Jean-Michel was hesitant, concerned about the security situation, but after a while headquarters in Geneva created a sub-office in Gedaref and sent staff to man it – first a New Zealander and then a Frenchman.

Dani made sure he got to know them both. As compatriots, he and the Frenchman, 'Philippe', struck up an instant rapport. Dani asked Philippe about the 'pass' system and told him there were some people he would also like to transport out. Philippe did not ask any questions. 'Just send them to me,' he said.

Dani told Philippe that from time to time, a list of names requiring exit would be brought to him by one of the refugees (in practice, Ferede), and not the Sudanese local. From then on, in the summer of 1980, groups of wretched Jewish refugees surreptitiously became part of the UN's passage out.

While Dani respected Philippe, he suspected that he was more than just a UNHCR worker. Dani thought he might also be an agent of the French secret service – and, it turned out, Philippe wondered the same of Dani too. Before he returned to France the following year, Philippe invited Dani for a beer at his home in Khartoum.

'Okay,' said Philippe. 'Cards on the table. Which department [of French intelligence]?'

'What do you mean?' replied Dani. 'I'm not from any. Why, are you?'

'Of course I am!' said Philippe. 'Come on … why have they sent you as well?'

'Look, I'm not,' answered Dani, 'I'm just who I said I am, an anthropologist.'

Philippe accepted Dani's story.

Several years later, when Dani was based in a city in Europe, he discovered that Philippe was also there at the time. He called him, and the two met up.

'You guessed right,' Dani told him. 'I was not an anthropologist, but I was not a French spy either – I was an Israeli spy, only I was there smuggling out Ethiopian Jews to Israel.'

Philippe reacted with amused surprise, and expressed his admiration for what the Israelis had done. Because of its proximity to the Gedaref camp, another Mossad agent who joined the operation used to stay at Philippe's house there, posing as a relief agency worker. Philippe never knew who he really was.

Every time the safe houses in Khartoum had space after Jews hidden there were flown out, Ferede (and later other Ethiopian-born Israeli Mossad agents who succeeded him in that role) would rendezvous with a trusted contact in the camp, from what was known as The Committee, a handful of older and more able male Jewish refugees who had been chosen to take care of Jewish life there. The Committee Men could operate inside the camps where the Mossad could not and were the lifeline between the refugees and the intelligence agency. Ferede would tell a Committee Man how many Jews were needed for the next trip and pass him cash from Dani to distribute among Jews in the camp according to their needs (large amounts were smuggled into the country by various means, including hidden under false bases inside chocolate boxes). The Committee would pick which Jews should be on the forthcoming evacuation – normally prioritising the elderly, women and children, though the responsibility was sometimes abused by a minority in return for favours – and give the list of names to Ferede (or his successors in that role), who would deliver it to the New Zealander or Philippe. The Committee Men would also tell one of the evacuees the address of the safe house in Khartoum with instructions to memorise it. It was all carried out with such secrecy that, to try to prevent leaks, the Committee Men themselves were not informed of an operation more than a day in advance, and to begin with Jews on their list would only be told that the following night they would be 'travelling'. Even though it was not spelt out, they understood the destination was Jerusalem. Twenty-four hours turned out to be too much notice because they would prepare festive meals, sell their tents and spend too much time gathering their belongings, so later they were given no warning at all and just told on the spot that they were leaving.[2] One Committee Man was caught by other members having passed information to the authorities. Word got back to Dani that the rest of the Committee wanted to kill him, but he forbade it, instead ordering that the man be put on the next flight out and ensuring he would be dealt with in Israel.

The Mossad's 'legitimate' daytime UNHCR pass system was carried out in parallel with the night-time smuggling operation until, in August 1980, an incident occurred, serious enough to scupper the entire operation.

Time came for the Committee to prepare a list of names, which was then collected by Ferede, who obtained a pass for them from Philippe. The Jews who had come from Gedaref and nearby camps boarded the truck, which set off for Khartoum. When it came to a roadblock, the driver stopped to show the passes to the soldiers.

At that moment, one of the non-Jewish refugees jumped up. '*Inahum Yahud! Inahum Yahud!*' ('They're Jews!') he shouted in Arabic, pointing at the Jewish passengers.

The soldiers ordered the Jews down, shouting and shoving and hitting them. They let the women and children back on, but it was only one of the men who knew where they were going to in Khartoum. The truck left, leaving all the men behind. The soldiers roughed them up and found that one among them knew the address of the safe house. They took him away and tortured him – pulling out his fingernails and beating him on the soles of his feet – until he gave up the information.[3] No one else was aware of what had happened at the checkpoint.

Dani and Ferede had gone to Port Sudan, where thousands of refugees had settled, after Ferede said he had heard there might be Jews there. When they did not find any, they decided to fly back to Khartoum and visit the hideouts, to check on the occupants and bring them money and supplies. They drove to the first of the two compounds, pulled up and, in accordance with operational rules, left the car engine running. They climbed out, leaving the doors ajar. Dani knocked at the entrance to the courtyard, using an agreed code of raps, and waited. Normally, one of the occupants would sleep outside next to the courtyard door, in case of visitors. This time, no one answered. Dani sensed something was wrong. Without saying a word, he signalled to Ferede that they should get back to the car. As they neared the vehicle, the courtyard door opened and two armed Sudanese (unidentified, but likely belonging to the domestic intelligence agency) jumped out, pistols drawn. One grabbed Dani and thrust his gun against his nose, but Dani brushed it away.

'United Nations! United Nations!' Dani said loudly. '*Haram!*'

Surprised, the man released his grip.

Dani gave a salute and with a '*M'a salam*' turned and continued walking, convinced he was about to be shot in the back.

Ferede had got into the car on the passenger's side unseen, crouching down in the footwell. Dani climbed in, and with the door still open, slammed the vehicle into gear and took off, the figures of the two men – guns still pointed at them – shrinking in his rear-view mirror.

After they were out of sight, Dani pulled over. Ferede was shaken.

'We have to go and see what's going on at the second house,' Dani told him. 'But this time we're not knocking at the door – and you're staying here.'

Dani walked in the darkness to the second compound. He climbed over a wall and looked inside. There was the Jewish lookout, sleeping behind the compound door. Dani quietly jumped down, crept over to him and put his hand on his mouth.

The man woke up with a start.

'Shh!' whispered Dani.

'*Daniel, lo la'lechet el habayit ha'sheni!*' ('Don't go to the other house!') the man whispered back in Hebrew as Dani removed his hand.

He explained that one of the household had met his counterpart from the other compound at the grocery store that morning, and been told that if he saw Dani and Ferede, to warn them not to come to the house because there were two men with weapons waiting there with a picture of Ferede (obtained from a file from when he had registered himself as a refugee in Gedaref).[4]

The incident meant that as a Mossad agent, Ferede was now burned. Dani knew he had to be quickly removed from Sudan. However, he was on a 'wanted' list and his picture would likely be held at every border crossing and airport.

Dani thought. He had good relations with several airlines – Swissair, Lufthansa, Air France, KLM, Olympic Airways and Alitalia – having bought a lot of seats to fly the Jews out (spreading the ticket purchases between the airlines so they would not wonder what so many so often were for).

His best connection was with a female Swissair agent, an Arab Christian called Suzanne, to whom he would occasionally bring chocolates to keep her friendly.

Normally tickets had to be purchased at least 24 hours in advance but he could not afford to wait. It was also the middle of the night. Dani knew where Suzanne lived, having once given her a lift home.

He drove with Ferede back into the city, but first he would have to find a place for his companion to hide. 'How about here?' Ferede suggested. They had parked under a tall tree.

'We're in Africa. Here is a tree. We Africans came down from trees, right? That's what you think. So I'm going to wait for you up a tree!'

To Dani's amusement, Ferede proceeded to climb until he was high up, where he sat on a branch, waiting.

Dani drove to the Swissair agent's house and knocked repeatedly on the door. After a while a man in a nightcap and jalabiya, and holding a candle, opened up.

He looked at Dani quizzically and started saying something in Arabic.

Dani interrupted. 'Do you speak English?'

'Yes,' said the man.

'I'm sorry to disturb you so late,' said Dani, 'but I need to talk to your daughter.'

Emerging from behind him out of the darkness was Suzanne.

'Mr Daniel!' she said, in surprise. 'What's going on?'

'It's an emergency,' Dani replied. 'One of my guys I'm relocating, he has tuberculosis. He's having an attack. I've managed to get him a place in a sanatorium in Switzerland, but I need to get him on the first flight in the morning. I need you to come and open the office, now. I'm going to buy a row of three – I don't want anyone sitting next to him.'

'I never go to the office in the middle of the night,' replied Suzanne.

'Please,' implored Dani. 'If this guy dies, I don't want it on my conscience. You neither.'

Suzanne's father intervened.

'Okay, okay,' he said. 'We shall all go.'

Suzanne, her father and two brothers followed Dani to the Swissair office, where she unlocked the door and let them in.

She printed three tickets and gave them to Dani.

'There's something else,' he said. 'There's a VIP gate at the side of the airport. It's where ministers or officials go straight in without having to pass customs. When I come with my guy, I want you to get us in through there. I don't want to take him through the airport because he's coughing and won't be able to answer questions. I want to take him straight onto the plane. He can sit at the back. Someone will be waiting to collect him at Geneva.'

'But I don't know how to do it!' replied Suzanne.

'I'll tell you what to do,' Dani said. 'There's a soldier who's always standing there. Here's 50 pounds. Just tell him: "There's a very important guy coming in a few hours. He'll be in a car. When he flashes you, just let him through." That's it. And give him the money.'

Suzanne was hesitant.

'I'm not sure. I'm afraid,' she said.

Her father turned to her. 'You can do it, Suzanne,' he said. 'I'm telling you, do it.'

Dani went back to collect Ferede from the tree, and from there drove to the airport to coincide with the flight.

He approached the VIP gate, slowed to a stop and flashed his lights. He waited.

The barrier lifted and he drove through. Suzanne had done the job. Dani pulled up near the plane and helped Ferede out of the car.

'Ferede, you're going to cough your soul up until you've taken off,' he told him. 'Then you can relax.'

Dani put an arm around Ferede and draped Ferede's arm across his shoulders. Ferede coughed fiercely as Dani hauled him up the passenger steps. Waiting there were Suzanne and two air hostesses wearing surgical masks. Dani and Ferede hugged and kissed each other on the cheek three times. The air hostesses looked aghast at the sight of such open embrace of a diseased man.

In the eighteen months they had been working together, the pair had become as close as brothers. Between them, they had smuggled up to 600 Jews to Israel from Sudan, and paved the way for the huge number yet to come.

Ferede got his wish to settle in Israel, along with his mother (who made it to Sudan and arrived in Israel in January 1980), father, sisters, brothers, first and second wives, and his son, Benjamin.

For the next three decades, he campaigned tirelessly for the rights of the Ethiopian Jews within Israel, and returned to clandestine work under the AAEJ to help smuggle Jews from Ethiopia to Kenya, and on to Israel.

Ferede Aklum passed away on a trip to Addis Ababa in 2009. As soon as Dani heard he had died, he informed the then Mossad director Meir Dagan. His body was brought back to Israel, at the Mossad's expense.

Ferede Aklum was buried at a cemetery in the Israeli city of Beersheba. Heads and former heads of the Mossad, along with thousands of Ethiopian Israelis, attended his funeral. He was – and remains – to them, a national hero.

Ferede's abrupt removal meant a proper replacement had to be found because of his critical part in the operation. The person chosen was an Ethiopian Israeli, Zimna Berhane. Zimna had been a prominent campaigner for the right of Ethiopian Jews to settle in Israel and after the first groups arrived in 1977 he had helped with their absorption. He was recruited specifically for this mission and was dispatched to Sudan as a prepared Mossad agent.

Like Ferede, Zimna and the other hand-picked Ethiopian Israeli Jews (Danny Yasmani and Ezra Tezazou) who succeeded him in that role were the Mossad's 'mouths and ears' in the camps, in the words of an agent who worked hand-in-hand with Zimna. They were the only ones who had the ability to speak Amharic and Tigrinya, and to tell Ethiopians apart from the Eritrean, Somali or Djiboutian refugees. They were on the front line and were the critical link between the Mossad and the Committee Men, blending in among the refugees and at risk of being caught by the secret police, who lurked there undercover.

Shortly after Zimna had joined the operation, the team expanded from two to three. Dani brought in an agent by the name of Marcel, whom he appointed his deputy commander in the field. Both South American-born, Dani and Marcel knew each other from the corridors at headquarters, where Marcel had half-jokingly volunteered to join Dani's mysterious 'African experience'. One week after their conversation, Marcel was in Khartoum.

Just three weeks later, Dani was called back to Tel Aviv, leaving Marcel and Zimna to continue smuggling the Jews out of Sudan in his absence.

At HQ, with the operation now becoming serious business, there was a meeting of heads of Mossad departments to decide how best to proceed with the mission. Dave Kimche had left the Mossad that spring and was succeeded by the man who had been his deputy, much to Dani's dismay.

Using maps and aerial photographs, Dani talked through the logistics, explaining the positioning of the camps, the routes in and out, the rugged topography of the Ethiopian Highlands and the flatlands of Sudan.

One of the department heads slapped his hand on a map, and mis-reading the distance, told Dani he should be going from A to B instead.

Anxious to get back to the field, Dani's patience ran out.

'Look, if you don't understand scales, don't put your fat finger on the map – just shut up and sit where you are!'

Dani's newly appointed division head jumped in. 'Don't talk like that to someone your senior in my presence!'

'Why?' Dani retorted. 'You think you're any better than him? You don't understand anything either!'

He stood up brusquely, knocking his chair backwards. 'You might be a head of division on paper, but don't fool yourself,' Dani told him. 'I'm going back to Sudan. I know I do not have back-up from headquarters and no one here to talk to, but it's fine, I'll manage!'

He stormed out, slamming the door, causing a glass picture frame hung on the other side to fall off and smash.

One of the department heads who was friendly with Dani came out after him.

'Dani, you can't talk like this,' he said. 'You'll get yourself fired!'

'I'm fed up,' said Dani. 'I can't work with guys like that. Maybe *you* can, but *I* can't. I'd rather speak my mind and get on with the job.'

An hour later, Dani was called to Hofi's office. He knew it was for a reprimand over what had happened and that he could be kicked out on the spot.

'Whatever you might think, this is a hierarchical organisation,' Hofi told him, 'and you cannot treat a guy like this who is three levels above you!'

Dani had great respect for Hofi. Like Dani, he had been a paratrooper and had gone on to become chief of the brigade. His active service stretched back to the days before Israel was formed and he had fought or led in every major campaign and war.

'I know,' said Dani, 'but even you couldn't take orders from a guy like this. You're his superior, so maybe you can work with him, but I can't. Just tell me now if I've still got my job or not – because I need to go back to Sudan, tomorrow.'

'Okay,' Hofi replied. 'Go back to Sudan – but if I find someone to replace you, expect to be fired.'

Dani had held on by the skin of his teeth. He thanked Hofi and left.

The next day he flew back to Khartoum.

Soon after, Hofi decided that, owing to the scope and complexity of the Sudan operation, it should be moved from foreign liaison and brought under another division whose purpose was more focused on this kind of activity in enemy territory.

Hofi appointed Efraim Halevy, a senior Mossad figure of almost twenty years' experience (including in many parts of Africa) to assume direct control of the operation at HQ. Hofi promoted Halevy to head and relaunch a then-dormant division which had previously orchestrated the secret evacuation of almost 100,000 Jews to Israel from Morocco in the early 1960s.[5] As part of this restructuring, Halevy instructed Dani to set up within the reconstituted division a department entirely devoted to the evacuation of the Ethiopian Jews. While Halevy became its overall commander, Dani remained commander in the field, as well as now taking on the function of department head – a double role without precedent in the Mossad.

7

THE BUILDINGS WITH THE RED TILED ROOFS

Towards the end of 1980, Dani further expanded his team, recruiting two more operatives – Shlomo Pomeranz, a neurosurgeon at Hadassah Hospital in Jerusalem who spoke flawless English; and Uri, German-born and himself a former child refugee of the Kindertransport who had grown up in London before settling in Israel.[1] Uri was already a Mossad agent, and Shlomo was being trained for another mission when Dani persuaded Shlomo's deputy division chief to let him move across.

The two men were brought in to help run the transfer of the Jews from the camps to Khartoum and their concealment in the safe houses. It was becoming clear, though, that the clandestine transportations, which only had the capacity to move as many as the Toyota pickup could manage, would not be satisfactory in the long term.

On another visit to HQ, Dani told Halevy they were going to have to look for other solutions.

'I've been thinking about the sea,' Dani said. 'Sudan is not like Ethiopia. If we can evacuate people by the Red Sea and have a boat coming in, then we can do things on a larger scale.'

Halevy gave him the green light to examine it as an option.

As an officer in the paratroopers, Dani had experience of joint operations with the Shayetet 13, an elite Navy commando unit, Israel's equivalent to US Navy SEALs. From this he had some idea about the kind of coastline that would be required for a maritime evacuation, but he needed the opinion of specialists. He was on friendly terms with the deputy head of the Special Operations division in the Mossad, Shlomo Gal. They had worked together on missions in Europe in the wake of the 1972 Munich Olympics massacre of eleven Israeli athletes by members of the Palestinian Black September group. Back then, the Mossad was tracking down and killing those involved. Dani went to see Gal and explained the situation.

'Do you have anyone under your command who used to be in the Shayetet?' Dani asked him.

'Yes,' replied Gal.

'Well, I need one. Loan him to me.'

'Sure,' said Gal. 'There's a French guy, Yoni. He's very experienced, but I have to warn you, he doesn't like being told what to do.'

Dani called 'Yoni' for an interview. They sat across a table from one another.

Yoni began: 'My understanding is I'm going to be in charge.'

'You're going to be in charge?' replied Dani. 'Who told you that?'

'Any place I go, I'm in charge,' answered Yoni.

'Well, not this time,' replied Dani. 'This time *you're* not going to be in charge – *I* am.'

'Who are you?' Yoni asked Dani, deprecatingly. 'What have you done?'

'Enough to be sitting on this side of the table interviewing *you*,' answered Dani. 'I am not obliged to tell you *anything* about me, okay? But you're obliged to listen. You can say you don't want the job and walk, but I've got a feeling you're bored and you'll like this. It's more than you're doing at the moment. But, you have to decide now – and I'm not going to tell you anything about it until I know you want it. So, swallow your pride and choose.'

Yoni considered the options for only a moment.

'Okay,' he said.

With that, he was in.

Dani briefed him on the mission and they went to talk to the Navy about what was required. In the meantime, the office constructed a cover story for Yoni.

A few weeks later, Yoni, travelling on a European passport, flew into Khartoum. He was met by Dani in the Land Cruiser, and they started the long journey to Port Sudan. It was late and they drove into the night, which, on Sudan's unlit, unmarked roads, was itself an ordeal. Even if smaller vehicles used head-lights, truck drivers did not, in the belief that it would use less fuel. Articulated trucks would suddenly loom up, causing crashes not only with other vehicles, but also animals, leaving the roads littered with corpses as big as camels. At one point Dani slammed into the remains of a donkey, sending the pickup into a ditch.

'What the hell …?' blurted Yoni.

'It was nothing. Go back to sleep,' replied Dani as he revved the vehicle, steering it back onto the road.

It was daybreak when they arrived at the coast. At Shayetet HQ, Yoni had seen on a map of Sudan a series of coves there – possible landing points for naval craft – running up to the

Egyptian border, so they started to explore. They headed north from Port Sudan, when after about an hour and a half Dani felt the vehicle getting sluggish as the terrain started to change.

'Quicksand?' Yoni asked.

'I don't know,' said Dani, trying to control the car.

'Go left,' said Yoni.

Dani turned leftwards.

'No, no, no – right, go right!'

Dani swerved back.

'No, left … no, right! Right!'

The car suddenly regained traction and shot upwards as the ground became steep, before coming to an abrupt stop.

The vehicle had ended up perched on the top of a sand dune, all four wheels off the ground. The only thing to do was to dig the car down to a point where it could get a grip and be able to move again.

They had no shovels so Dani and Yoni broke glass bottles they had with them in the pickup and with the shards began scooping away at the sand. They had run out of water, and in the heat of the day, by the time they had finished they were both exhausted. They restarted the vehicle and carried on driving, passing by a lagoon.

'And then we saw something that looked to us like a mirage,' recalls Dani. 'Buildings with red tiled roofs – but we're in Sudan, this is not Europe.'

They took a right-hand turn off the track, and headed towards the site in the distance. They drove for about a kilometre and a half off-road, negotiating their way across sand until they were almost at the sea. Dani pulled up in front of a large single-storey Mediterranean-style structure set between identical putty coloured villas, side by side. They were on a small peninsula, isolated for miles around. As they sat in the car wondering about where they had arrived, a figure, more than six foot tall, stepped out. The two men got out of the car to speak to him.

He told them he was a *ghafir* (caretaker) who now looked after the place. Talking in Arabic, he explained that it had been a holiday village but it had closed some two years earlier, after the previous owners – an Italian company – pulled out. The ghafir, whose name was Abu Medina, had worked there at the time.

'What's it called?' asked Dani, also in Arabic.

'Arous,' replied Abu Medina.

Dani asked him if they could have a look around and Abu Medina took them inside. They walked into the lobby area of the main building, where there was a portrait of Nimeiri – in uniform, rows of military ribbons on his chest – peering down from above the reception desk. Behind was a large dining room with some 21 tables and a bar, surrounded by pointed archways giving unobstructed views of the sea on one side, and the natural beauty of the Red Sea Hills rising on the other. The dining room was served by a kitchen, which at first sight looked well-equipped. There was a freezer, two ovens, eight gas hob burners and two chip-making machines. However, they found none of them were working and were all beyond repair. Outside, flanking the main building on each side was a neat string of fifteen chalets with arched porchways, situated about 150 metres from the beach. Each comprised two adjacent double bedrooms (there was still bedding, towels and linen, some in their original packaging) and bathrooms. There were also four Boston Whaler-style fibreglass boats, outboard motors and other pieces of aquatic equipment lying there, evidently untouched for a long time. Yoni checked them over. All but one of the boats had holes in them.

Whoever had built the complex in such a remote location had tried to solve the problem of electricity by installing two large German Magirus Deutz generators. Dani and Yoni tested them but they did not work either.

There were also two 5,000-litre tankers used for bringing fresh water, and a cistern for storing it in. Considering it had been deserted, the property itself was not in bad shape, Dani thought.

'Who's in charge?' he asked Abu Medina.

'Colonel Mohammed Mahgoub,' the ghafir replied, 'at the Ministry of Tourism in Khartoum.'

The implications dawned on both Dani and Yoni. If they could get hold of this place, they thought, they could use it as a base from which to operate, under a perfect cover.

'With a thing like that,' Dani later said of it, 'the sky's the limit!'

They thanked Abu Medina and headed back to the road.

While the village had the potential to be a headquarters for agents in the field, it was not part of their thinking that it would serve as the secret transit point for the Jews. For that, they would need somewhere nearby. They went about sixteen kilometres further north and came to Marsa Awatir (Awatir Cove), which Yoni thought might be technically suitable for a transport ship to dock at night, lower a platform and take Jews on board from the beach. Knowing they would have to check depths themselves, Yoni had brought two diving cylinders from Port Sudan. Dani had never dived before, so, with just a tank and a mask, he had an impromptu introductory lesson right there. Yoni gave him a large rock to hold, to weigh him down.

They descended about six metres, and when Dani broke into a panic, Yoni calmed him down and took a measurement with a depth gauge. Once Dani had got the hang of it, they came back up. One of the masks broke, so Yoni went to sit on the side.

'You carry on,' he said to Dani, 'but don't go far.'

Dani went back under the water, and immediately got caught by a current and carried out further than he should have. He reappeared half an hour later, exhausted, having had to swim on his back, cylinders balanced on his front.

Leaving the sea, they returned to the vehicle and loaded the gear.

'I'm going to speak to this Mahgoub,' Dani said. 'Let's go to Port Sudan. We can leave the car there and fly back to Khartoum.'

Port Sudan was about 86 kilometres south. They had not gone far when they got a puncture. They changed the tyre and carried on, but just a few hundred metres more, a second tyre blew. It was already dusk, and with no other cars around they decided to sleep in their vehicle for the night and deal with the problem in the morning. Dani lay down in the open back, zipped up to his neck in a sleeping bag, Yoni in the cabin. Neither got much sleep. Yoni was bitten by mosquitoes all night, Dani disturbed by the '*slap … slap … slap*' of him swatting them on his skin. When Dani did drop off he was awoken by the big snout of a camel, which had plodded up to the car and leaned over the side panel, grunting into his face. He managed to pull an arm out of his cocoon and push his inquisitive visitor away.

Come daybreak, they were stuck for what to do. There was no second spare tyre and it was a long walk to Port Sudan. Yoni then had an idea. He still had the two cylinders, and using what was left in one of them, managed to inflate the flat tyre enough for them to get going and stay mobile until they eventually trundled into the town. There they left the car and flew to Khartoum. Yoni went back to the Hilton, and Dani went to the Ministry of Tourism to find Mahgoub.

He had to wait a long time until he was finally called into his office.

Colonel Mohammed Mahgoub was sitting at a desk.

'Who are you?' he asked Dani.

'I'm an anthropologist. I've been here about one and a half years. I'm writing my paper about the tribes but I've also got to make some money. I've seen your holiday village up in Arous, and I think there's a good business opportunity there.'

'Go on,' said Mahgoub.

'Well, I'm an experienced diver and I'm sure I could bring professionals and tourists here,' Dani replied.

Mahgoub looked interested.

'Do you have a company?' he asked.

'Yes, of course I have a company,' Dani answered.

'Okay, we charge $500,000 a year to lease you the village.'

'Half a million?' replied Dani, in surprise. 'It's not worth anywhere near that. When was the last time you went there!'

'About a year ago.'

'Look, if I take that thing I have to invest *at least* $150,000, just to get those buildings back into shape, and then there's all the engines and equipment, and boats. I can't pay more than $200,000 a year.'

'Not possible. I've had better offers. I could sign tomorrow for at least $250,000.'

'Okay, I'll go up to $250,000,' said Dani, 'but that's it.'

Mahgoub grumbled.

'Okay,' he said.

They shook hands and signed a piece of paper confirming the price of the lease.

The Mossad had built an unrivalled reputation for inventiveness, but for all its ingenuity and long record of using ruses, that moment marked the beginning of one of the most extraordinary of all. Nothing like it had been attempted before. What was planned was nothing short of the covert takeover of a small village by secret agents behind enemy lines. Even more remarkable, with all the risks it would entail, it was not for the purpose of espionage but for a humanitarian cause. By their very nature, spy agencies were not set up for this kind of endeavour. In the history of intelligence organisations, the Mossad would become the first.

Arous village had been born out of the dream of an enterprising pair of Italian twins, Angelo and Alfredo Castiglioni. The brothers, from Milan, were accomplished archaeologists, anthropologists, and documentary film-makers, who travelled extensively throughout Africa. They spent a lot of time in Sudan, where they would study the tribes of the Upper White Nile and the Nubian Desert.

By the early 1970s, when Europeans, with Italians at the forefront, were developing a strong interest in deep-sea diving, the twins identified in Sudan's Red Sea coast – home to spectacular marine life and pristine beaches – a commercial opportunity. Its underwater enchantment had been popularised in the 1950s and 60s by pioneering oceanographers Hans Haas and Jacques Cousteau, who captured its unique splendour in films such as the black-and-white *Under the Red Sea*, and then in the Technicolor *World Without Sun*. The impact the latter in particular had on perceptions of that spot of the Red Sea is clear from a review by one of America's most influential film critics, Bosley Crowther, upon its release. Crowther hailed Cousteau's production as a 'handsome color picture [of] eerie visions of skin divers clad in silver suits gliding through translucent waters into caverns beneath the sea, brilliant and magical glimpses of all sorts of fantastic fish and surrealistic compositions of plant-like animals and underwater growths'.[2]

For all its allure, for the Castiglionis it was an extremely adventurous undertaking. At that time, the coast north of Port Sudan – inhabited by Beja tribespeople – was completely undeveloped. The brothers looked for a place with a good beach and lagoon, and found it in Arous.

They had a contact in an influential Sudanese businessman called Abdo Allateef Abu Regala, who had links to the president. Abu Regala, who made his money from transportation, construction and the import of ice, brought the twins' idea to Nimeiri. The president approved and as a result, the Italian Sudanese Tourism Company was formed. The Castiglionis were awarded the contract to build the village, with 40 per cent of whatever they made going to them, 50 per cent to the president and 10 per cent to Abu Regala.

The village was constructed by Sudanese builders under the direction of Italian experts. Basic materials were bought locally, while special fittings and decorations were brought in from Italy. The generators were imported but no one could get them working, so Angelo sent over an electrician who solved the problem.[3] The tankers were bought to fill up with potable water brought in by ship to Port Sudan once a week. The resort took a year and a half to build and was opened in 1974.

Inauguration day was a grand affair. Nimeiri himself was guest of honour, along with a raft of dignitaries and celebrities. They included Italian princess and socialite Ira von Fürstenberg, a doyen of gossip magazines; renowned underwater photographer Roberto Merlo; actresses Milla Sannoner and Carole André; Prince Carlo Giovannelli, well-known as an influential figure in Italian high-society; and Gil Cagné, who found fame as a makeup artist to the stars.

According to Angelo Castiglioni, Roberto Merlo invited Nimeiri to go for a dive, to show him the beauty under the sea. Merlo, Nimeiri and presidential bodyguards set off in one boat, the Castiglionis in another. Merlo and Nimeiri dived into the water. At some point, Merlo found a rare black coral which he wanted to show the president. As he drew his knife to cut it, the bodyguards – thinking he was about to stab Nimeiri – dived in fully clothed, grabbed Merlo and wrestled the knife off him.

'Arous,' Angelo recalls, 'was a place for people who loved deep-sea diving. Italians normally went to Sardinia or Sicily, but the fish [at Arous] were much bigger than in the Mediterranean. We offered something that was different and new.'

The Castiglionis founded a travel agency called Vento di Terre Lontane (Wind of Far Lands) to market Arous and the venture took off. Angelo says the resort was nearly always full. Guests flew in from Europe to Khartoum, then took a small plane to Port Sudan. They were collected by hotel staff in a four-by-four jeep and driven to the village.

The staff were local Sudanese, while the boss was an experienced Italian hotel manager.

The resort operated successfully for several years but ran into trouble when the Sudanese partners discovered how much the manager was being paid. They strongly objected and got him replaced by a succession of Sudanese. After that, standards went downhill, guests started coming back home unhappy and bookings declined. The resort was no longer the vision the Castiglionis had set out to achieve.

'For us, it had mainly one purpose,' says Angelo, '– to do a good project with good results and have good feedback. That was always more important than the business part.'

By 1977, the brothers decided it was unsustainable and pulled out. It carried on for a while without them, but in 1978, the resort shut.[4]

If Mahgoub knew any of this, he did not tell Dani. It was enough that he had walked into his office wanting to take the village off his hands.

At that time, there were no other shore-based diving operations, only some Swiss, Italian and German tour companies with ships that would bring clients down to the coast and anchor at sea. The only fixed sites where divers stayed were a lighthouse platform on Sanganeb reef or a scaffolding structure further south at Towartit, erected years earlier by Cambridge scientists to study the destructive effects of crown-of-thorns starfish on the corals. The two makeshift bases were used by a UK tourist agency called Explore Beyond, which would send small groups of divers there.

'At the time it was all a bit Wild West in terms of tourist operations out there,' recalls Alex Double, who worked for the company from 1978 to 1980.

'There was nothing on the mainland. Arous was the only resort-type place but it was never functional when I was there. We used to go there occasionally because we would dive up that way, but there was only ever skeleton staff there looking after it, never any tourists.'

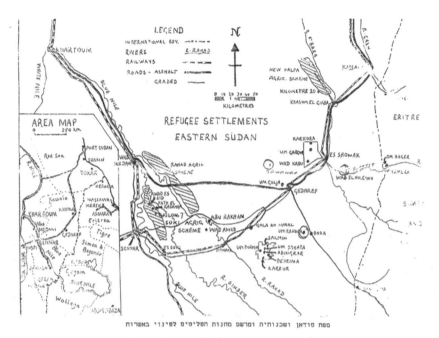

1. Mossad map of refugee camps in Sudan,
based on hand-drawing by Dani (1979).

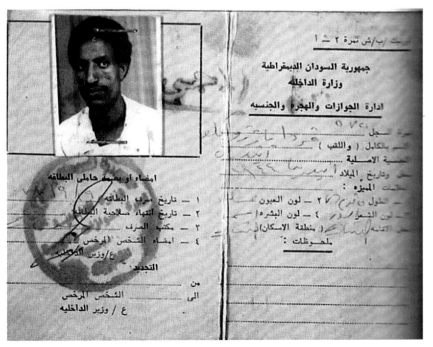

2. Identification document issued to Ferede Aklum in Sudan.
©Naftali Aklum.

3. Ethiopian Jewish woman (1983).
©Associated Producers.

4. Dani with Land Rover carrying smuggled Ethiopian Jews
– Ferede Aklum is on right-hand side, without head-covering.

5. Sudanese President Nimeiri (c) at inauguration of Arous village in 1974; Italian socialite Princess Ira von Furstenberg (l); Alfredo Castiglioni (2nd r); Sudanese businessman Abu Regala (r).

6. Arous diving resort chalets, early 1980s.

7. Sticker with Arous village logo – produced by Mossad.

8. Toyota pickup at Arous, with diving gear in rear,
including folded Zodiac MkIII (back left), one of two bought in Paris.

9. INS *Bat Galim* military landing craft used to transport Ethiopian Jews,
in port in Haifa.

10. Mossad agents with Ethiopian Jewish refugees during smuggling operation.

11. Israeli Navy commandos and Mossad agents
push out a dinghy carrying smuggled Ethiopian Jews.

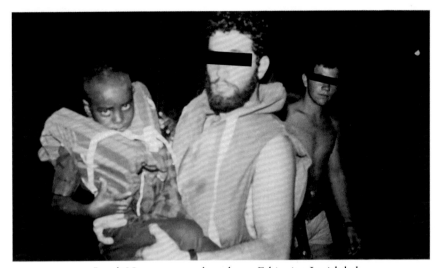

12. Israeli Navy commandos take an Ethiopian Jewish baby
smuggled out by Mossad agents.

13. Mossad agents celebrate after first naval evacuation.

TODAY

My very dear Friend

I will be brief. The escapade of last week
was highly praised by the PM at his weekly cabinet meeting.
I was told by an idependant eyewitness that there were genuine
tears in many eyes when the story was told. I was asked to
pass to you and team the highest regard and appreciation of
PM. I am happy to be the conduit of this item.

14. Letter sent from Efraim Halevy to Dani in 1982, telling of
the Israeli prime minister's delight at the result of a successful naval operation.

15. Arous resort brochure.

(Photos by courtesy of Mutad Neumann and others)

Getting there

From Europe
Regular service to Khartoum from Amsterdam (KLM), Athens (Sudan Airways), (Egyptair), Frankfurt (Lufthansa), Geneva (Swissair), London (British Airways/Sudan Airways), Paris (Air France), Rome (Sudan Airways), Zurich (Swissair).
At Khartoum, Sudan Airways provides a daily commuter flight to Port Sudan.
Note: Special excursion fares available for groups of more than 6.

Temperatures (maximum)

	Day	Night
November – March	24 °C	12 °C
October and April	27 °C	15 °C
May – September	35 °C	25 °C

Humidity is high in summer, but there is always a pleasant breeze off the sea.

From the Sudan region
Regular flights from Jeddah and Khartoum by Sudan Airways

Visas
Visas are required for all overseas visitors. Tourist visas are given at airport of entry, if previously arranged with the Sudan Tourist Corporation, or Navco Aviation Co, Geneva, Switzerland.

Booking:

arous

or Navco Aviation Co, S.A. 7, rue des Alpes, 1201 Genève, Switzerland, Telex 2775 SERV GH

arous

ON THE RED SEA

The diving and desert recreation centre of Sudan

16. *(right)* Arous resort brochure (front).

17. *(far right)* Arous resort brochure (back).

AROUS VILLAGE

RED SEA COAST – SUDAN

<u>PRICE LIST</u>

1983/1984-1

ALL PRICES IN U.S. DOLLARS   <u>US$</u>   <u>US$</u>

ROOMS:	SINGLE OCCUPANCY		FULL BOARD	75	HALF BOARD	65
	DOUBLE "	PER PERSON " "	60	" "	50
(ALL WITH	TRIPLE "	" " " "	40	" "	30
SHOWER/W.C.)	CHILD BELOW 12 YEARS IN PARENTS' ROOM	" "	30	" "	20
	" " 3 " " "	FREE		FREE

RESTAURANT:	BREAKFAST	5
	LUNCH OR DINNER	10

SPORTS:	WATER-SKI	10 per 15 mins
	WIND-SURFER	5 " 60 "
	BOAT TRIP (INCL. SHUFTASCOPES)	30 (several hours)

DIVING:	MASK AND SNORKEL	FREE
	FINS	3 per item
	CYLINDER	6 " "
	REGULATOR	4 " "
	BUOYANCY VEST – ADVANCED BACK PACK	5 " "
	" " – SIMPLE	3 " "
	WET SUIT	3 " "
	WEIGHT BELT	1 " "
	KNIFE	1 " "
	DEPTH GUAGE	1 " "
	INTRODUCTORY DIVE INCL. EQPT WITH GUIDE	30 " "

TOURS:	DAY TRIP TO ARBAAD OASIS	30 per vehicle (up to 5 persons)
	DAY TRIP TO SOUAKIN PORT	50 per vehicle (up to 5 persons)

N.B.: i. FOR INCLUSIVE TOUR DIVERS, PRICE OF ROOM INCLUDES 2 DIVES
       PER DAY PLUS AIR-REFILL.

      ii. DIVERS MUST POSSESS VALID DIVING LICENCES.

18. Arous village price list.

19. Mossad agent posing as diving instructor with tourists.

20. A Mossad agent stands in front of a bedroom with a '13' and a trident symbol on the door; cryptic allusions to the Israeli naval commando unit.

21. Mohammed Mahgoub (wearing an Arous village T-shirt),
with Mossad agents and a Zodiac dinghy in the background.

22. Guests relax in Arous. The telescope (bought by Dani as a gift for Yola)
was used by guests, and by the agents for keeping an eye on smugglers.

23. Mossad agents having breakfast in Arous diving resort.

24. Rubi windsurfing on Red Sea coast of holiday resort.

25. Two Mossad agents (right) with guests at Arous village.

26. Guests relax at Arous village.

27. Dani larks about in holiday resort at Christmas 1982.

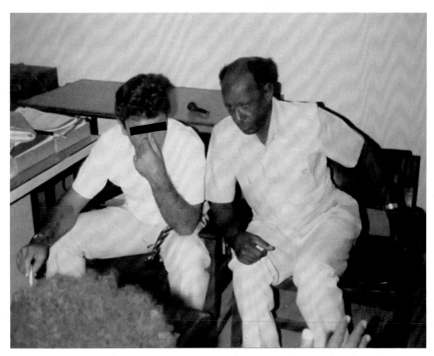

28. Dani with Tourism Corporation director Mohammed Mahgoub, who leased the village to the operatives.

29. Page from Dani's passport showing Sudanese entry visa stamp prior to his final operation.

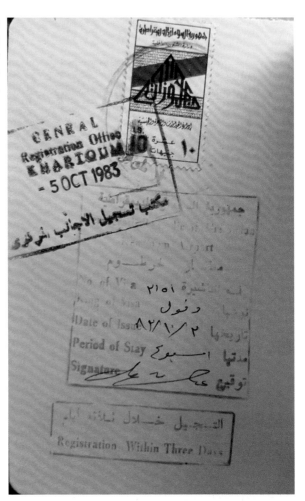

30. Licence plate from Sudanese vehicles in which Mossad agents escaped – uncensored inscription reads 'April 85 Sad Sunset – Piece of Cake – Many Thanks'.

31. Jerusalem memorial to Ethiopian Jews who died on way to Sudan.

32. Israeli soldiers at Jerusalem memorial to Ethiopian Jews
who died on way to Sudan.

The difficult operating conditions meant it was never really viable, and the company eventually went bankrupt. One of the biggest problems was getting the clients across to Port Sudan from Khartoum. Sudan Airways, the only domestic carrier, was notoriously unreliable, and was even known to fly from Khartoum and back again without bothering to land in Port Sudan, still with its passengers on board.

Now that he had come up with the idea, before he could put it to HQ Dani had to establish whether a maritime operation was even possible. That was a decision for the Navy, and if it came to the conclusion that landing at the beaches in Sudan was impractical, the plan for the village and a seaborne evacuation would have to be reconsidered.

Dani flew back to Israel with Yoni and went to see what the head of the Shayetet, Lieutenant Colonel Ami Ayalon, thought of it. Although he knew Ayalon from when he had previously participated in combined operations, Dani had concerns that Ayalon would say the Shayetet's commandos were too busy on active service to be diverted to this kind of mission.

At their meeting in his office at the unit's headquarters in Atlit on Israel's northern coast, any doubts Dani had about how Ayalon would respond were quickly dispelled.

'He was immediately enthusiastic,' Dani recalls. 'Straight away he said, "We'll do it!" He was the first. He cleared the way. When he heard it was the Ethiopian Jews, for him it was a mission of the highest importance, and it was a question of not "if" but "how".'

Bolstered by Ayalon's support, Dani was equipped to inform Halevy about the discovery of the village and how it could be a valuable asset. Halevy recognised its potential and the two men presented the idea to Hofi. The Mossad chief listened with interest. Nothing was without risks, but it was through taking risks that the Mossad had become the organisation it was. Hofi was convinced by what he heard and gave his approval.

Dani telephoned Ayalon.

'Ami, it's a go,' he said. 'Let's get this thing moving!'

From that point, a momentum started to build.

Ayalon arranged for Dani and Marcel, Dani's deputy, to brief the commander-in-chief of the Navy, Rear Admiral Zeev Almog (himself a former commander of the Shayetet) and officers from Navy Intelligence. If the plan was going to proceed as a joint operation between the Mossad and the Navy, it required Almog's authorisation, as it had done Hofi's. Evacuating civilians clandestinely by sea from an enemy country was something the Navy had never done before but it was clear at the meeting that Almog, like Ayalon, was not only in favour but considered it a moral duty. Almog suggested that if refugees were going to be taken out from the beach, one possible way would be by a landing craft with a ramp. Almog mentioned a boat called the INS *Bat Galim*, which was due to be decommissioned. Its crew was experienced in landing and picking up troops on a beach surrounded by coral reefs, having trained extensively on Sanafir Island (captured by Israel from Egypt in 1967) at the mouth of the Gulf of Aqaba. Almog gave his approval for the joint operation and cleared Dani and Marcel to go and brief the commander of the *Bat Galim*, Major Ilan Buchris.

At his base, the Red Sea Naval Command Center at Sharm el-Sheikh in the Sinai Peninsula (then occupied by Israel), Buchris received orders from Navy HQ for an unspecified mission in Sudan. They told him he was required to go on a dry run with two missile boats and some fifteen to twenty Shayetet commandos to survey a section of the coast to see how a naval operation could be carried out there. Dani and Marcel paid him a visit and briefed him on the specifics of the coves, the Sudanese Navy and the smuggling activities in that area. They also revealed to him the reason for the mission – to evacuate Ethiopian Jews and bring them back to Israel on the *Bat Galim*. For a boat about to be sunk, it was suddenly given a new and important lease of life.

Dani and Yoni flew back to Port Sudan, and in October, 1980, the two missile boats set sail. It took around a day for the convoy to travel the more than 500 nautical miles down the Red Sea, past Egypt and towards Port Sudan, stopping at a point off Marsa Awatir. The crew waited until night-time for a signal from the shore. Then it came – the flashing of a car's headlights, beckoning them to come. Under cover of darkness, Shayetet frogmen slipped into the sea and swam silently to the cove. They emerged from the water without making a sound, communicating in gestures, senses heightened as they crept onto enemy land. Suddenly, out of nowhere, the stillness was pierced by the blare of music, stopping the commandos in their tracks. Not only was it music, but to their bafflement, it was Hebrew music.

'Who brought a radio? Who brought a radio?' their commander, Lieutenant Colonel Ran Galinka, demanded to know.

The commandos glanced at one another looking for answers; then the sound of laughing could be heard. It was coming from the vehicle which had flashed its lights at the boats. Standing there were Dani and Yoni. They were playing Galei Tzahal (Israeli Army Radio) from a transistor radio which had been modified to also serve as a secret communication device, after discovering that they could pick up Israeli stations at nighttime. Galinka was not impressed by the prank, though Dani and Yoni were highly entertained.

The frogmen checked the depths and the reef formations along the stretch of coast, and concluded that a landing craft could not get nearer than the outer reef, which formed a barrier about fifteen kilometres from the shore. They mapped the area and where the corals made it more difficult for heavy-duty dinghies (known as Zodiacs) to penetrate, about fourteen kilometres further south (at a cove called Marsa Fijab), they set up radar echo reflectors to help the boats navigate their way through if they decided to operate there. When the mission was complete, Buchris and the commandos left and sailed back to Israel.

Dani and Yoni followed and the first sets of plans were drawn up for a land and sea operation. They were approved by both Hofi and Almog, but the scheme hit the buffers. One of the Mossad division heads argued that if something was to go wrong, or the secret leaked, it might harm Israel's delicate position in the Middle East, and the operation was put on hold.

It was a frustrating setback, and one which met with strong opposition from those wanting to push ahead.

Dani went back to Sudan to oversee the continuing smuggling operation from Gedaref through Khartoum airport. During the course of his stay at the military guesthouse a year and a half earlier, he had struck up a friendship with the head of the secret police in Gedaref, one of the three security officials who shared his room. Since then, the officer, Mohammed, had moved into a private house and Dani paid him one of his occasional visits.

Dani informed Mohammed he had finished his research as an anthropologist and that now he was going into business. He told him about the village and how he planned to re-open it.

'What?' Mohammed reacted in surprise. 'You're going to Arous? Then you'll have to meet my brother, Liwa [Major General] Youssef Hussein Ahmed – he's the head of the Navy and also in charge of the Army along the coast from Ethiopia to Egypt.'

'Beautiful,' replied Dani. 'We're going to be neighbours!'

'I will have to tell him about you,' said Mohammed.

He then wrote a letter to his brother, sealed it in an envelope and gave it to Dani.

'Here, take this and give it to him,' Mohammed said, handing it over.

Dani did not know what he had written, and worried that it might be a trap, possibly a warning to his brother that Dani was a double agent. On a subsequent trip back to Israel he got the Mossad to open it without leaving a trace and he checked its contents. Mohammed had in fact been effusive in his praise for Dani and had urged the major general to offer him his help.

Once he was back in Sudan, Dani visited Liwa Youssef at the Navy headquarters in Flamingo Bay, just north of Port Sudan. He introduced himself and handed him the letter from Mohammed. Youssef was welcoming and told Dani to come back again when the village was in development.

In the meantime, with no operation happening, Dani kept stalling Colonel Mahgoub over the lease. When Dani had signed a gentleman's agreement for the village, he had presented himself as the representative of a (non-existent) tourist company but for the plan to work the Israelis needed to operate as legitimately as possible. Halevy contacted a prominent

Sudanese-born Swiss Jewish businessman, and asked him for help. Dani flew to Geneva to meet him and the businessman obliged, handing over ownership of a shelf company called Navco.[5] Dani was made its director general, and as part of the pretence, the Mossad opened a Navco office in Geneva, staffed by an agent who sat at a desk, manning a phone.

Dani told Mahgoub Navco was 'studying the plans' for the village, but he realised the longer he did not seal the deal, the greater the chance Mahgoub might give up on him, or release the resort to someone else. He did not want to lose it because of what he considered a bad decision by someone in another division of the Mossad whom he did not hold any respect for anyway.

In April, 1981, Dani called the colonel and informed him that he was going to come with some experts from Navco to prepare a feasibility study, and if it worked out as expected, he would sign the contract for Arous.

Although Dani had done many things in the field, creating a Club Med-style resort had not been one of them. He needed advice on setting it up and getting it to a level where it could accept guests. Ultimately it was going to have to operate as a hotel where tourists and the Sudanese authorities did not realise what was really going on right under their noses.

On a return trip to Israel, Dani went to speak to Yoni.

'There's a guy I know,' said Yoni. 'He'll tell us what to do.'

The two men took a trip down to the Sinai. The vast desert peninsula had been captured by the Israelis in the Six Day War after Egyptian forces were routed there. Israelis had since built homes and towns along Sinai's coasts, but under the 1979 Egypt-Israel peace treaty, Israel had agreed to withdraw within three years.

One of the towns, about 70 kilometres from Israel's southern frontier, was an agricultural settlement and resort called Neviot (known as Nuweiba in Arabic), where Israelis would hang out to escape the stresses and strains of ordinary life. There was a Hawaiian-style holiday village with bungalows and straw beach huts there, which, in the desert and by the sea, struck Dani as remarkably similar to Arous. It also had a diving club.

Yoni knew the manager, fellow ex-Shayetet 13 commando 'Noam', and introduced him to Dani. Noam had been born in Egypt and had lived at Neviot for eight years. He spoke several languages, including Arabic, fluently. He also knew how to run a diving resort.

The three men had a conversation, and Noam agreed to help.

Dani and Yoni flew back to Khartoum, this time with Noam, who was also under cover. They took a connecting flight to Port Sudan, collected the car and drove up to Arous. Colonel Mahgoub had agreed to meet them there to discuss plans, and came with his assistant, Abu Rabia.

The group spent three days at the village, doing a survey, taking an inventory and coming up with ideas. Noam drew up a 27-page plan of what it would take to completely overhaul the resort – from repairs, renovations and rewiring to fully kitting it out, even down to the provision of coffee cups, ashtrays and yellow serviettes. The projected cost came to USD\$1,087,500.

Eating, sleeping and spending time together in the relaxed atmosphere meant the Israelis, Mahgoub and Abu Rabia got to know each other on a more personal level.

On one of the evenings they were sitting around a table in the dining room, drinking whisky and cognac and talking. As always on Mossad missions, there was a cardinal rule to never speak a word of Hebrew. One slip-up into the mother tongue could not only expose an entire operation, but could be enough to get people killed. (When he was lodging at the officers' quarters in Gedaref, Dani played on this to wind up his adversary, Kimche's then-deputy. 'I'm sleeping in a room with three Sudanese officers – one police, one Army and one security – and I know for a fact, because my wife told me, that I talk in my sleep,' he told him. 'I just wonder in which language? I hope it's not Hebrew!' The deputy flew into a panic, wanting Dani to sleep in the office the whole night and be tested with listening devices.)

Dani, Yoni and Noam spoke among themselves in French, and conversed with Mahgoub in English, which Mahgoub translated into Arabic for Abu Rabia. Dani, Yoni and Noam played the game, talking nonsense in French and telling Mahgoub something completely different in English, which Mahgoub would explain to Abu Rabia in Arabic. All the while, the alcohol flowed.

During one exchange, Noam asked Mahgoub: 'Colonel, on the way here, I wanted a Coca-Cola but I could not get one anywhere. Why's that?'

'Because the Israelis in Rama Jan have a big factory of Coca-Cola, and there is the Arab boycott,' he replied.[6] 'So, we drink only Pepsi.' The irony of the situation was not lost on the Israelis around the table.

At the end of the evening, Mahgoub and Abu Rabia went to their rooms and the Israelis to one of theirs. Someone among them had brought a cassette of an iconic Israeli comedy group, HaGashash HaHiver, which, being in Hebrew, was a violation in operational terms. They put it on a cassette player and listened to it through headphones, laughing out loud to the sketches. Suddenly the door swung open and Mahgoub was standing there, half-drunk with his shirt hanging out.

'What's so funny?' he asked. 'Tell me, I want to join in!'

The group covered up, saying they were just laughing at a story one of them had told, and sent him back to his room.

At the end of the three days, they went back to Khartoum. Noam departed and Dani signed the contract with Mahgoub. The tourist village was now in the hands of the Israelis.

When Dani and Yoni had been briefed by the Israeli Navy months earlier, it had asked them to carry out a reconnaissance of the Sudanese Navy, about which Israel had almost no intelligence. The two men went back to Port Sudan and rented a boat with a captain and a small crew, asking to 'see the coast'. Flamingo Bay, where the Sudanese Navy was based, was situated just north of the civilian harbour from where they cast off. As they passed the site, Dani distracted the crew by asking innocuous questions while Yoni went inside the cabin and snapped pictures with a camera fitted with a zoom lens. He photographed all the Navy's ships and installations that could be seen from the sea. Dani and Yoni went back to Israel and passed the information to Navy HQ.

By now it had been six months since the first planned seaborne evacuation had been shelved, and as a result of the growing number of Jews flowing into the camps and pressure on Hofi from Halevy's division, the operation was unfrozen and preparations got under way again. This time, the holiday village was part of it and was going to be tested for real. For something so audacious, Dani was going to need a formidable team: agents who could operate as resort staff by day, and smuggle people through the desert by night.

8

'NOT ISRAELIS ANYMORE'

Dani had two criteria. First and foremost, recruits would need native fluency in a second language – ideally be foreign-born – so they could operate under assumed identities. Secondly, some would need to fill roles as diving instructors, with a requisite level of proficiency that would convince even professional divers who might come to stay at the village. If they already belonged to the Mossad, all the better. If not, they would need to be trained up, officially or unofficially.

Yoni knew the head diving instructor at Neviot, Shmulik, and took Dani to meet him. Shmulik was born in Morocco, was conversant in several languages and had a flair for accents. He could speak English impeccably, was ex-Shayetet and had a no-nonsense professionalism about him. Dani hired him on the spot.

Neviot was natural habitat for the kind of people Dani was after. The divers there were exceptionally skilled and came from military backgrounds.

Just one day earlier, an Army officer had appeared there in a state of urgency, specifically looking for two of Neviot's diving instructors – Rubi and Asher.

'We have no time,' the officer told them. 'Grab your diving gear, you're coming with me. It's just for 24 hours, and we'll explain everything.'

Rubi and Asher were former Shayetet commandos. They were driven north at speed to Etzion airbase, near Eilat, and transferred to a Bell helicopter, with pilots at the ready. All they were told was that it was for a maritime rescue mission. After several hours without being called into action, however, they were stood down and taken back to Neviot. Only later did they learn that on that day, 7 June 1981, a squadron of Israeli fighter planes had taken off from Etzion and bombed the Osirak nuclear reactor in Iraq in a top-secret operation. Rubi and Asher's job, had they been required, was to have been to rescue any pilots brought down over water.

When they returned to Neviot, they went to have a drink at the bar. As they were sitting there, Rubi noticed Noam – at a table with Yoni and a third man – pointing at him. Noam called Rubi over. The third man at the table was Dani.

'I heard that you speak Italian,' said Dani. '*Per favore, parliamo italiano.*'

Dani explained that he was looking for certain people to carry out a two-week job for the Jewish Agency to bring to Israel some Jews from Africa. They would, he said, be brought from the beaches. He said he needed recruits who could dive, had language skills and act convincingly under assumed identities without having to be professional spies. Rubi had been born in Israel but was taken to Italy as a baby by his mother. By the time she brought him back at the age of three, he was bilingual.

He was also charismatic and genial, with an innate ability to connect with people. He had worked as a diving instructor in the resorts in Sinai – Sharm el-Sheikh, Dahab and Neviot – since 1974, and had earned a reputation as one of the best, as well as a decent living (his nickname was Beckenbauer, one of the highest paid footballers in the world). By 1981, though, the good times were coming to an end. Israel had only a year left in Sinai, and the future for everyone there was in doubt. For Rubi, Dani's proposition could not have come at a better time.

All Rubi wanted to know was when he would begin.

There was a third instructor too, whom the others all recommended – a New Zealander called 'William'. He was not Jewish, and while he might have been considered an unusual pick for this kind of mission, it provided an ideal cover. He was also regarded by his colleagues as a very talented and trustworthy man. Dani had a conversation with William, and he volunteered his services.

Dani did not mention anything about Ethiopia or Sudan, but he said enough for Rubi to join the dots.

Rubi stepped away to go to his room. He returned a short time after, holding a book, which he handed to Dani.

On the burgundy cover was a picture of a Kes (an Ethiopian Jewish spiritual leader) in a white turban and robe, praying from a Bible. It was called *Achim Shechorim* – Black Brothers. The book was an account of an Israeli anthropologist, Yael Kahana, who had travelled to Ethiopia in the 1970s and lived among the Beta Israel for a year. It had been given to Rubi by his father, who had been an advisor to President Ben Zvi, and who spoke Amharic. Rubi's uncle, Carlo Alberto Viterbo, also had history with Ethiopian Jewry. A prominent member of the Italian Jewish community, in 1936 Viterbo had been sent to make contact with the Ethiopian Jews, then living under the newly formed, Fascist-ruled Italian East Africa. His mission was brought to an end with the Fascists' promulgation of anti-Semitic laws in 1938.

Dani laughed at Rubi's astuteness. Black brothers. That was how Dani considered the Ethiopian Jews. It was how Begin saw them; and it was what the rabbis declared them, as expressed in their historic open letter, engineered by Jacques Faitlovich, decades earlier. While Rubi's book title may have influenced his thinking, Dani decided to coin the name of the mission Operation Brothers, based on this feeling of fraternity, especially towards Ferede.

'Okay,' he said, 'people will be in touch. Noam will be the liaison.'

To get accepted onto the team, Rubi, Shmulik and William would first have to be rigorously tested by the Mossad. None of them knew they were being recruited by the intelligence agency, though Rubi had an assumption.

They, along with a fourth diving instructor, were told to go to an address in Tel Aviv for interviews and psychological examinations. Once there, the first thing they had to do was to complete a detailed questionnaire.

'Place of birth', it stated.

Rubi thought he would play around.

'Born and raised in KGB,' he wrote in response. He completed the form and handed it in. Minutes later an official came in, red faced and angry.

'What is this?' he asked Rubi. 'What is this "KGB"?'

'Kibbutz Givat Brenner,' he replied.*

'Don't you dare make jokes with us! This is a serious matter!'

All the candidates were separated and, one by one, put through psychoanalysis.

The examiner reported back to Dani.

'They are not fit for the job,' he advised. 'They're too individualistic and aren't right for the discipline of the Mossad.'

---

* A kibbutz is an Israeli collective settlement, often agricultural.

'That's why I want them,' said Dani, 'because they're different.'

The Mossad carried out exhaustive background checks on the four men, one of whom did not pass. The three others were then placed on a course, to test their aptitude for working undercover. They were issued with false documents and put through a series of simulated exercises on the streets, under the covert observation of trainers who made notes on their performance. At one point, Rubi was instructed to join a tour group leaving from a hotel in Tel Aviv. The tour bus stopped off at various destinations, and after a while Rubi was told to change his appearance. The bus went by Rehovot and pulled into an area with orchards, plant nurseries and factories. It was Kibbutz Givat Brenner. Rubi, wearing a cowboy hat and sunglasses, went inside with the group. They joined a talk about the kibbutz, presented by a kibbutz member who knew Rubi. He had to avoid being noticed. One of the helpers serving coffee was also someone Rubi knew well, a girl he had gone to school with. He kept his head down and acted as inconspicuously as someone in a cowboy hat could, managing not to get spotted.

Someone then brought him a note: he was to leave the group and get into a car waiting for him outside. In it, it said, he would find communication equipment. He went to the vehicle, picked up binoculars and a two-way radio, and was driven five kilometres away to an airbase at Tel Nof, central Israel. His instructions were to take the equipment, and without being seen, report once an hour on how many planes had arrived, how many had taken off, the types of aircraft and their markings. By now it was night-time, and he took up position on a hill, watching activity through the binoculars and reporting his observations. As he did so, he started to hear voices. They were getting closer, and he began to make out that they were coming from people looking for him. Rubi left the hill and sneaked back to the car. He found the keys and turned on the ignition, then, with the lights off, drove to the kibbutz cemetery. He pulled into an avocado grove next to it and quietly nipped into the graveyard. Hiding among the plots, he continued reporting on aircraft activity for the rest of the night. Whoever was sent to find him did not bother looking there.

At the end of the course, Dani told Rubi he wanted to put him in charge of communications to begin with, but not to tell the others, nor of his suspicions that it was a job for the Mossad. The less they knew, he thought, the better.

The group went back to Neviot and carried on their normal lives, waiting for further instructions.

To carry out a secret maritime evacuation of the Ethiopian Jews required a period of preparation and complex planning by the Navy and the Mossad. While the Mossad team was in a state of readiness, the Navy's timetable was more restrictive. It was also decided that, for maximum obscurity, operations would take place only in the phase of a new moon – technically, moonless nights. This meant a window of a few days once a month.

Dani held an initial discussion with Ayalon's successor as commander of the Shayetet, Colonel Uzi Livnat, and they settled on a fresh date for the first seaborne operation: 12 November 1981.

With this and future operations, the calendar was the only certainty. Other factors of critical importance were unpredictable. The weather alone could disrupt the best-laid plans. Storms or torrential rain would mean having to postpone a mission at short notice, and consequently missing the crucial moonless nights.

Another consideration was the activity of the Sudanese secret police. Some nights they would have a heavier presence inside and outside the refugee camps than others. If the Committee Men felt it was too risky, an operation would be suspended on the basis of that alone.

For the Mossad too, the mission was about to become more onerous. Naval evacuations meant the Jews would have to be smuggled much further than from Gedaref to Khartoum. Overland from the camps to the coast was a distance of about 900 kilometres. The plan called for them to be picked up from outside the camps after dusk by Dani and the team who had come from the village at Arous, then driven through the night to a daytime hiding place until sunset, and then for a further four hours to the cove. There, the Jews would be transferred into the boats and whisked some 25 kilometres across the water to the *Bat Galim*. The ship would then sail with its passengers back to Sharm el-Sheikh, where the Jews would be taken off, put on planes and flown another 200 kilometres north to Eilat.

From the start, plans for every operation followed a mandatory procedure, known as *Nohal Krav* (Order of Battle), carried out in parallel by the Mossad and the Navy. Dani wrote the order for the Mossad. It covered every eventuality, from multiple retreat plans to what to do in the event of the loss of a second spare tyre on a vehicle. On the Mossad's side, the plan had to pass through levels of hierarchy before being signed off by the agency's chief. On the side of the Navy, it had to get the approval of the commander-in-chief. Once the operational orders were passed, the commander of the Navy, Admiral Almog, would chair a joint meeting at the Navy's headquarters, underground

at the Kirya (HQ of the Israel Defence Forces, or IDF) in Tel
Aviv. There would be the chief of the Shayetet, the head of
Naval intelligence, and other senior Navy officers. Representing
the Mossad would be Dani and his deputy, Marcel.

At the meeting, the team would go through the plans
in minute detail, using maps and aerial photographs, plotting the positions of every asset and person, moment by
moment. Dani would also hold a separate meeting with the
commander of the Shayetet unit being deployed as part of
the operation. This was particularly important because here
they would work out understandings as to who would be in
charge where. Responsibility was split between land and sea.
From the shoreline inwards, Dani would be in charge, and from
the same point outwards, the Shayetet commander would have
authority. That way, there would be no misunderstandings in
mid-operation when a moment's hesitation could mean life
or death. Once the overall Mossad-Navy plan was agreed, it
would go to the IDF's Chief of Operations for approval, then
the deputy chief of staff, and then the chief of staff himself,
and finally the minister of defence: any activity happening on
enemy territory had to get the go-ahead from the latter two.
The minister of defence would examine the plan at a meeting
with a senior official from Mossad HQ and Dani, as well as the
head of the Navy, the chief of the Shayetet, the chief of Military
Intelligence and the head of the Air Force (which would be
providing cover for the Navy).

At the time of the first planned operation, the defence
minister was Israeli military titan Ariel Sharon. He listened to
presentations from Dani and the head of the Shayetet, both of
whom explained everything in detail. Sharon, who had built
a reputation as a brilliant strategist, pointed to the village of

Arous on a map and asked his chief of Military Intelligence: 'Yehoshua, what do you think about it?'

'Well, it's a good place,' the intelligence chief replied, rather vacantly.

'Yes, I know it's a good place,' responded Sharon. 'But *why* is it a good place?'

No one around the table appeared to understand where Sharon was heading.

'What do we have on the Sinai peninsula which we have to return to Egypt and we have to evacuate which is very important to us?'

It suddenly clicked with Dani. What Sharon wanted was the village as a listening position for the Red Sea area to take the place of the listening station that Israel was having to evacuate in the Sinai, which was extremely valuable for intelligence gathering.

Dani whispered to Hofi's representative who was sitting next to him. 'He wants to steal the village from us for different purposes, and then we'll lose our base. You need to say something.'

'No, I'll tell Hofi,' the representative said, 'and we'll see what he can do.'

'Are you crazy?' Dani replied. 'If he now decides that the village is going to Army intelligence, it's lost!'

Finally, without getting the answer he was looking for, Sharon said to the intelligence chief: 'Yehoshua, can we find a place more ideal for a listening station than this one?'

At that moment everyone understood. Dani shifted agitatedly in his chair, catching Sharon's attention.

'Young man,' Sharon said to him, 'you have something to say?'

Dani had never met Sharon before, but spoke up.

'Yes, I think it's the wrong decision from our point of view. I understand why you like this place, but we worked more than a year to prepare ourselves, and the whole operation now to evacuate Jews rests upon being able to run this village. This is our cover, this is the thing that gives us the ability to travel all around the country. If you take the village from us now, we have more than 3,000 Jews in the camps and it will take us at least another year to change our cover and look for something else.'

Sharon looked at him.

'Okay, okay. I understand.' Then he said: 'I approve the operation.'

After that, Sharon presented the plan to Begin for his authorisation, and Begin gave the go-ahead.

It was the end of the summer when Marcel called the three recruits. He told them to go to a flat in north Tel Aviv for an important meeting. A fourth recruit, South African-born Louis, also ex-Shayetet, and enlisted by Dani, joined them. There were seven people there waiting for them: Dani, the four instructors who had trained the men, Halevy and the chief of the Mossad himself, Yitzhak Hofi.

'Okay,' said Dani, 'we're going to tell you a bit more about your mission. You can say "no" at any time and ask for out.'

Hofi and Halevy explained to them that what they were being asked to do was to smuggle people. They were upfront, spelling out how it was the most difficult and dangerous kind of smuggling – more so than drugs, money or weapons – and that it was taking place in Sudan. They told them the people being smuggled were Ethiopian Jews, and that they would be saving many lives.

As commander, Dani then went into the specifics, explaining how they would operate, and telling them about the diving resort and what they would be doing there. He told them that they would be given alternative identities and cover stories, and that before anything happened, they would be sent to their assumed country of origin to get to know the home towns where they supposedly came from. If they were quizzed about it in Sudan, by authorities or even in conversation with guests, they needed to be able to talk about their backstory convincingly.

None of the four backed out. On the contrary, for the professional divers, living undercover at a diving village up the coast from Port Sudan seemed like the opportunity of a lifetime.

Shmulik, William, Rubi and Louis were handed files containing details of their aliases and fictitious backgrounds. All were presented as nationals of the same European country. Rubi was disappointed that it was not Italy, although according to his cover story he grew up in Florence. William's and Louis' profiles cast them as having been born in their genuine countries of origin but having emigrated to the unnamed European country. Shmulik's story was that he was born in Cyprus but lived in the unnamed country where his wife actually came from.

Within days, under their real names and using their Israeli passports, the four men flew from Israel to the designated country, posing as tourists.

They were each sent to a different location to reconnoitre the area and get to know its buildings, landmarks, schools and roads. Later, when they were back in Israel, Rubi and Shmulik were sent to a workshop in the fishing port of Jaffa to learn how to make repairs to fibreglass boats.

By October 1981, the team was ready to go to Sudan.

'The decision to carry out an operation like this was unique,' says a former top Mossad figure, who had oversight of the mission at the highest level. In the history of the organisation, there was, in his view, 'no parallel at all'.

It was 'diametrically contrary to the modus operandi of the Mossad', he says. 'First, it necessitated exposure of Mossad people in an enemy country to large numbers of people who were unidentified, who were unknown and who could at any given moment be approached by the local authorities and recruited by them to try to use them as conduits to our people.

'Normally when you're carrying out an operation in an enemy land, you have a cover and for the purposes of your cover you have contacts – maybe – with people on the ground, but you do not intentionally expose yourself to hundreds, and virtually thousands, of people you have never seen before; and you have no way of vetting them, of finding out whether they are trustworthy, and you take immense risks by so doing.

'Secondly, training people to operate in an enemy country is not a simple matter – it's not something that you do haphazardly or with a quick going through a number of things for a week or two. It takes months and months to train people for this kind of activity.

'But, given the fact that we were under this pressure because of the necessity to evacuate the Jews, we had to train them almost in an improvised way.

'There was a lot of hostility in the Mossad about this, because sending people to an enemy country is a threat. In a normal country, it they get into trouble or even jailed, you have all kinds of ways and means of releasing them. Here the danger was they would not come back – ever – except in a bodybag. But either you take the risk or you don't take the risk, and not doing it was not an option.'

In the meantime, Dani and Yoni went on a shopping expedition in Paris for equipment for the village. They went to a well-known outdoor activities store called Au Vieux Campeur where they spent $50,000 on aquatic gear, including wetsuits, diving cylinders, compressors, regulators, buoyancy vests and masks. They also bought two Zodiac MkIII dinghies (the Mossad accounts department had a lot of questions for Dani when he gave them the receipts). In Israel, the Mossad's technology division took two more diving cylinders identical to the ones bought in Paris and fitted them with false bases in which to hide communication kit. They sent the modified cylinders to Paris, where an agent put them with the equipment bought in the shop, together with night-vision goggles and Motorola walkie-talkies. Dani scheduled the consignment on a flight to Khartoum and went back to Tel Aviv. He was at HQ, waiting for word of its arrival, when he checked the status of the flight – and saw it had landed in Cairo on a stop-over. He had not banked on that, and had to inform a commander of the operation at the top of his division. If Egyptian airport officials discovered what was inside, they would impound the cargo and raise the alarm. Dani and the commander waited tensely. An hour passed, but the plane did not leave Cairo. The commander grew concerned that the equipment had been uncovered. Dani worried, knowing that a simple laxity could end up compromising the entire operation. Two hours went by, but the plane had still not left. Three hours. Four. Then, to their great relief, it took off, completing its journey.

Dani left Israel for Khartoum, and around the same time Shmulik, Rubi, William, Yoni and Louis flew to a European city. They checked into a hotel, where one of the four instructors arrived to give them their counterfeit passports, and other prepared papers. He also checked their belongings to make sure there was nothing written in Hebrew (they had been given money to buy new clothes in the city they were in) and searched their pockets, suitcases and toiletries for anything with Israeli markings. They were all declared clean.

'Now you are not Israelis anymore,' he told them.

The group flew down to Khartoum and checked into the Hilton, where they waited for the equipment from Paris to arrive and for vehicles to be arranged.

Dani organised the hire of two trucks – an International Harvester Scout and a Japanese Hino – from the same local businessman, 'Ramian', who had supplied the Toyota pickup, and the team were joined in Khartoum by Efraim Halevy, the commander of the operation at HQ. They collected the boxes of equipment from the airport, loaded them onto the trucks and set off in convoy on the long, circuitous road to Port Sudan. Dani and Halevy stopped at Gedaref to meet representatives from the Committee and the rest of the group carried on to Kassala, where they went shopping at the souk for souvenirs. It was, after all, only a two-week trip, and they wanted to take something back to remember it by. For Rubi, trinkets did not suffice: he bought carpets, swords and an ivory rhino. Dani and Halevy rejoined them, and the convoy continued another 600 kilometres to the port. After the best part of a day on the road, they took a break and stayed overnight in the Red Sea Hotel, a colonial throwback, with its red leather couches, ceiling fans and waiters in long jalabiyas carrying trays of tea. The hotel was owned by the Government Tourism Corporation, which that night was not aware it had seven Mossad agents sleeping in its rooms.

The next morning, the team bought supplies of drinking water and tinned food, and a harpoon, and headed up the coast to Arous. After about 70 kilometres they turned off where the red tiled roofs came into view on the far side of the lagoon, and carried on, rocked and jostled, across the sand until they arrived at the village.

It was late afternoon. Abu Medina, the caretaker, was there. Dani greeted him warmly, told him he had brought his businesspeople to see the place, and they all went inside.

Dani showed the group the interior then took them out to the beach. He explained where they were in relation to the coves: on the south side of the village, Marsa Arous, and about four kilometres to the north, Marsa Fijab. Beyond that, Marsa Awatir, where they were set to carry out the first naval operation in two days' time.

Rubi stood and looked around, marvelling. It was a picture of serenity, the glistening sea calm, blue and crystal clear, save for mottled patches of coral.

'Dani,' he said, 'I'm willing to stay as long as needed!'

There was no time to rest, though. The team had to set up straight away to be ready to make the first pick-up. The divers in the group geared up and went into the sea to study the reef formation and depths, then patched up the fibreglass boats and fitted new motors. They had brought a small generator with them, which Shmulik, an amateur mechanic, got going, while

Dani and Rubi rigged up the communications equipment. They sent a message to HQ to say they had arrived and got coded confirmation back.

Before daylight faded, Rubi, Shmulik and Abu Medina took a boat out and went to catch some fish with the harpoon. That night the team ate well – the fresh fish, seasoned with garlic, olive oil and herbs, and baked in foil on an open fire, was just how they cooked it on the beach at Neviot.

In the morning Halevy wished the group luck and departed, heading back to Israel.

9

'WE WILL CATCH THEM'

By this time, the *Bat Galim*, with a 40-strong crew and 30 Shayetet commandos, had left Sharm el-Sheikh and was making its way down the Red Sea. It had been transformed into a floating shelter, specially fitted with amenities for (officially, at least) 200 evacuees. Folding beds, chemical toilets, showers, crates of babies' milk, toys, blankets and more had been put on board. Two areas had been sectioned off and turned into clinics. Also on the ship were twelve Zodiac MkVs and two fully armed Snunit attack craft, which could be rapidly deployed if the Zodiacs came under fire. Everything had been hidden in crates and concealed under tarpaulin so that it could not be photographed in the ship's open hold from above. As an additional dissimulation measure, and to elude the Soviet intelligence ships prowling around, the *Bat Galim* was repainted grey and white and with seven stars marked on the side, to resemble a civilian vessel.

The *Bat Galim* saw a return to the operation by Zimna Berhane, who had gone back to Israel burnt out after eight months of eating, sleeping and operating in the diabolical conditions of Gedaref.[1] Zimna was brought on board to act as a translator for the Ethiopian Jews, as he had experience with them unlike anyone else.

Such was the level of secrecy that it was not until a few hours after they had set sail that, for the first time, Buchris informed his crew exactly what the mission was and what would happen.

There was one Mossad agent on board the *Bat Galim*, a senior figure from Dani's department, David Ben Uziel, who had volunteered to join the operation from HQ. Uziel had a renowned reputation within the Mossad, where he was known by the nickname Tarzan. He had earned the moniker at the age of fourteen when he jumped into a river to save a drowning friend. The act of bravery prompted a boy watching from the side to remark that: 'Only in Tarzan films do you see something like that!' The nickname had stuck ever since. Tarzan had had an illustrious career in the service of the state, beginning as a twelve-year-old volunteer courier for the Etzel. After Israeli independence, he served under Ariel Sharon in Unit 101, a commando squad which carried out reprisal raids against Palestinian *fedayeen* guerillas in the Jordanian-occupied West Bank and the Egyptian-occupied Gaza Strip. He fought as a paratrooper in the 1956 Sinai campaign and in 1965 was sent to Ethiopia to train a special unit in the imperial Army as part of Israel's burgeoning ties with the country. Tarzan was an Afrophile and had acquired more experience of southern Sudan than perhaps any other Israeli. Upon joining the Mossad in 1968, he was dispatched there by Efraim Halevy, the architect of the Mossad's activities in south Sudan, to build up a separatist guerrilla movement known as the *Anya-Nya* (snake venom in the Madi language) which was fighting against control from Khartoum in the north. Tarzan trained its troops and led them on sabotage missions against the forces of the central government, blowing up bridges, sinking supply ships and walking hundreds of kilometres with them on foot. The theory was that if the Sudanese Army could be tied down, it would be less likely to send reinforcements to the Suez Canal where Sudan was helping Egypt against Israel in the War of Attrition.[2] (Tarzan came to be revered by the South Sudanese and was later bestowed with the rank of lieutenant general by a presidential decree for his 'immense contribution to the liberation' of the country from the north.[3])

According to orders, Tarzan was the only one on the *Bat Galim* allowed to talk directly to Dani on shore, in English and using language which would not arouse the suspicions of anyone listening in on ship-to-shore communications.

After sailing for two days, the ship turned to starboard, came to a stop and dropped anchor. In the distance beyond the tropical waters, just too far for the vessel to be seen, lay the coast of Sudan, at a point about 70 kilometres north of the port. Earlier that morning, sometime around sunrise, Dani told the workers at the resort that his team, bar Yoni, had to go on a trip for a couple of days to collect supplies. The group then set off from the village in a convoy of vehicles – a Land Cruiser in front, the International truck in the middle and another Land Cruiser behind. Yoni was to keep an eye on the resort but his operational function was to check Awatir Cove just before the agents returned with the Jews, to make sure it was clear of Bedouin who sometimes wandered through the area. At that point, according to the plan, Dani and his team would be descending through the Red Sea Hills with the refugees hidden in the back of the trucks. Yoni would radio Dani to proceed, and Dani would make first contact with the *Bat Galim*. If Awatir had unwanted visitors, Dani would switch to Plan B and instruct the Shayetet to divert to Marsa Fijab instead. After a year of anticipation, it was all finally under way. In the vehicles the team was focused, senses heightened and thinking of the responsibility which rested on its shoulders. It was a long journey, but adrenaline kept them alert. As it was daytime, and with no smuggled passengers on board, there was no reason to jump checkpoints along the route; the vehicles stopped at each one, Dani casually answering questions as to who they were and where they were going ('tourist company representatives working for the government') or they were simply waved on. After twelve hours on the road the team arrived at the rendezvous point at a quarry outside Gedaref, parked where they could not be seen, and waited. When dusk descended, a figure appeared in the fading light. It was a Committee Man, showing up as previously instructed, to get the go-ahead to round up the Jews in the camp. It was a moonless night – *chelema* ('darkness' in Amharic), as the Committee Men would call it. While the Committee members were the older generation, a second-level group made up of youths, called *Berare* ('Escapees'), carried out the most dangerous task. It was their job on the night of evacuation to find where the Jews were sleeping, wake them up, gather them together, smuggle them out of the camp and lead them to where Dani and his men were standing by.

Takele Mekonen was sixteen when he was recruited as a Berare. He had walked to Sudan with friends from his boarding school in the village of Weynea, about sixteen kilometres south-east of Gondar city. The students thought it would take two weeks but in fact it took them a month, ending up in Um Raquba, a camp about 40 kilometres south-east of Gedaref. He was picked by the Committee to be a Berare because he could speak some English, and ended up working undercover for a year and a half.

'The Mossad just couldn't go round from camp to camp, because of the Sudanese security, so they decided we had to work with them because we were black and we knew the community and we could organise everything,' he recalls.

'[At night] white Israelis would come to a meeting point about three kilometres outside the camp. The Berare would bring Jews there from other camps too. We rented a car with a driver, paid him with the money we got [from the Mossad] and told him we were picking up some refugees. We never let on we were Jews. If they knew we were Jews, they would have killed us.

'When there were no operations, some of the refugees cried, saying the Mossad had abandoned us, but I told them not to worry, that they'd come back. And they did.'

On the night of the first pick-up, the Berare led scores of men, women and children – including those who were sick, elderly, babies, or pregnant – out of Gedaref, in total silence, leading them on foot to the quarry. Jews who had them wore their whitest garments as if it was a holy day (it was a practice the Mossad tried to dissuade due to the fact that wearing white made the Jews stand out). The Israelis carried out a headcount and quickly loaded them onto the truck, before setting off back for the coast. Evacuees were often completely alone, separated from family and friends, including children sent for their own safety by their parents who stayed behind.

They did not know the white men were Mossad, just that they were being taken to the Promised Land.

It was a long and difficult journey, too far to complete in one night. Despite the discomfort and fear, the Jews crammed in the back of the truck, as instructed, never made a sound. Agents who took part in the operations would later comment on how astonished they were at this – they said they never heard crying or shouts, not even from the smallest infants, kept quiet by their mothers.

After travelling about three-quarters of the way to Port Sudan, at a point beyond the flatlands where the Red Sea Hills gave cover, the convoy pulled off the road and drove a few kilometres into the desert until they came to a wadi (a place they would later nickname *Nakeb al-Yahud*, or Valley of the Jews). There they would wait out the day. They let the Jews off the truck to stretch and rest, but as soon as the passengers climbed down they crouched and kissed the ground, thinking they were now in Jerusalem. The agents gave them pieces of food and cartons of drink and saw to their needs. Secret footage filmed there (it is unclear when, but the scene was similar each time) shows Ethiopians sitting in the shade, resting, eating and praying, with agents milling around. Children squat playing in the sand, while others chase each other round a tree. Older men sit expressionless but women are seen smiling. After nightfall, the Jews were put back onto the truck and they carried on, up through the hills and down towards the coast. As soon as he was able to get reception on their descent, Dani radioed the *Bat Galim*, giving it confirmation that the pick-up had happened and informing the ship of the team's position. Then further on when they passed Port Sudan, with about an hour and a half to go, Dani radioed the ship again. Here he informed them of the number of Jews on board the truck so the commandos knew how many Zodiacs to unload, and gave the go-ahead for the boats to be put to sea, a process which could take more than an hour. The two teams' arrivals had to be synchronised to reduce to the bare minimum the length of time exposed at the cove.

Although the plan was to carry out the first operation from Marsa Awatir, the tide had come in and as the International trundled past Marsa Arous it got stuck in the mud. The more Dani, who was driving, tried to gain traction, the more the vehicle got bogged down by the weight of the passengers. The paralysis of the truck was costing the team precious time, so Dani radioed the Zodiacs, which were already on their way to Marsa Awatir, and diverted them to the cove where the truck was stranded. The agents were going to have to take the Jews out from right next to the village, sneaking them past within sight of where Abu Medina and other workers were sleeping. If they got woken up and wondered what was going on, it could end up getting back to the authorities who would come to investigate.

The team let the refugees down from the truck and led them quietly across the beach to the water's edge. It was a stormy night and the sea was being whipped up by the wind, the waves crashing onto the shore. Out in the dark swell and cutting through the noise came the buzz of the Zodiac engines, approaching fast. The drivers cut their motors and the boats slowed to a stop as they ran aground on the sand. The commandos jumped out and Dani and his men went to meet them. The Shayetet commander, Major Dudu Shik, was from Rubi's kibbutz and they greeted each other like old friends. Dani's team, rejoined by Yoni, hurriedly transferred the Jews into the Zodiacs, which filled to their limit, so they loaded the remainder into the village's fibreglass boats. The motors were started and one after the other the boats set off for the ship.

On board each fibreglass were two agents – one piloting and the other watching over the refugees huddled in the back. That night, the turbulence caused everyone to get flung around. The fibreglass boats were lashed by waves up to four-and-a-half metres high, and taking in water, they started to sink. Dani, who was on one of the boats, radioed the Zodiacs to turn back and help. Amid the ferocious conditions, the commandos and the agents transferred the passengers from the fibreglass boats to the dinghies – Jews, young and old, lifted or stepping from one jostling vessel to the other. It was a terrifying experience for the Ethiopians, who had never even seen the sea before, let alone been on a boat. Overloaded, the Zodiacs carried on towards the ship, followed by Dani's team in the now-lightened fibreglass crafts. As the dinghies ploughed through the waves, the passengers getting thrown up and down, a woman lost her grip and went flailing overboard, plunging into the pitch black water. Within a split-second, one of the commandos lunged over the back of the boat and made a grab for her, managing to grasp some part of her before she vanished. Holding on he pulled back, hauling the drenched woman out of the water and back into the dinghy. 'The man had reflexes like a cat!' Dani would later recall. Had it not been for his swift action, the Ethiopian Jewess – a black woman disappearing into a black sea on a black night – would have drowned. (The woman eventually made it to Israel. She went on to have a daughter, Aviva, who, years later, had the opportunity of meeting the commando and thanking him for saving her mother's life).

When the dinghies finally made it to the *Bat Galim* the crew had to get the people on board. Because of the bad weather, Buchris had planned to hoist the boats up to the deck of the ship using cradles rather than open the ramp. However, considering the ship was about 21 metres high, he decided it was too risky – he did not want to take the chance of the frightened Ethiopians climbing or falling out. Instead, he took the decision to open the ship's bow doors, something normally done only in calm water. Buchris lowered the ramp onto the sea and the Zodiacs were piloted in. The Jews were helped off one by one, and seeing the bright light of the hold, crouched down to kiss the floor, mistaking it for Jerusalem, again. They were handed basic provisions and taken to the mess deck where they were given tea, bread and jam.

Dani, Marcel and Yoni boarded the *Bat Galim*, where they met Buchris, Tarzan and Zimna. Over a meal of shnitzels and French fries they talked about the operation and all that had happened (Dani informed Tarzan that the evacuations could only be done by the Zodiacs from now on). Dani also passed Buchris a package from Rubi. It contained mangoes and rugs – a gift for a contact of his in Eilat.

After that, the agents departed and headed back to the shore. The rising and falling of the water made it impossible to sit down, so Dani stood on the bow, clutching his walkie-talkie and holding onto a rope to keep steady. As they crashed through the waves, a huge surge came their way. Yoni steered in one direction, Dani went the other and was flung into the sea. He lost grip of his Motorola, which disappeared into the murky depths. Knowing he would get charged for the loss of an expensive piece of equipment, Dani went under the water, scrabbling around to try to find it, resurfacing to the sight of torchlights. His colleagues found him and fished him out. (Later on, HQ tried to recoup the cost of the walkie-talkie from Dani's salary, but eventually backed down).

Back on the ship, with the last Zodiacs and Snunit boats back inside the hold, Buchris and Zimna came to talk to the Jews and explain what was going on.

'These people were so frightened and overwhelmed,' recalls Buchris. 'It was like this every time. I saw it myself. To them, it was like being on a different planet.'

They had no knowledge of modern conveniences and had

to be shown how to use everything they would need. The crew taught them how to prepare food in non-traditional ways, and how to use the toilets and showers. They were also shown how to wash their clothes by tying them to ropes and throwing them over the stern so they got dragged through the water. There was also entertainment. They were shown films on a screen in the hold – amazed at something they had never encountered before – and were played recorded music, another medium which was new to them. The crew also broke down barriers by singing and dancing. Film shot on board the ship shows scenes of Ethiopian Jews gathered around, smiling and laughing, as crew members in T-shirts and shorts perform Israeli folk dances for them, clapping, stepping, skipping and turning. In return, the Ethiopians are seen demonstrating their traditional dance, the Eskista, shrugging their shoulders and jutting their chests to the beat of the clapping crowd.

By morning light, the area where the ship had picked up the refugees was busy with smugglers' boats taking contraband to Saudi Arabia on the other side of the Red Sea. The *Bat Galim* by now was already at a safe distance much further at sea, and out of sight. There it would roam around for three days, while the agents carried out a second pick-up from the camps.

Dani and his team made a repeat trip to Gedaref. They collected dozens more Jews, smuggled out of the camp under cover of darkness again, and took them on the long drive back to the coast, stopping from daybreak to nightfall at Nakeb al-Yahud. This time they rendezvoused with the Zodiacs at Marsa Fijab, and the Jews were taken to the ship by the dinghies alone. From now on, all the evacuations would take place from this cove.

Buchris counted the total number of passengers – 264 – and reported the successful conclusion of the first operation to Navy HQ.

Even at this stage, only a handful of Israeli cabinet members knew about Operation Brothers. The Knesset did not know and the operatives did not even tell their own wives and partners.

When the *Bat Galim* arrived back at Sharm el-Sheikh, the Ethiopians disembarked. Top officials from the military and the Mossad (including Hofi) had assembled at the port to greet them. Some of the dignitaries delivered stirring speeches, lauding the servicemen for their actions and welcoming the Ethiopians to the State of Israel. From there, the refugees were flown to Eilat and bussed to absorption centres around the country. Even their presence there had to be hushed up. The Israeli public was not allowed to know and there was a media blackout. If news of the arrival of large groups of black Jews got out, it could jeopardise everything.

By the end of 1981, Israel was in the final stage of its phased withdrawal from Sinai and the Red Sea Naval Command Center was in the process of being evacuated.

The *Bat Galim* was redeployed to the port of Haifa in northern Israel. To get there, it had to sail up the Suez Canal, through which Israel had just been given the right of free passage under the peace treaty with Egypt. Under the rules of the canal, all ships using the 190-kilometre waterway had to be handled by an Egyptian pilot, who would board at one end and disembark at the other. Before the *Bat Galim* left Sharm el-Sheikh, Buchris' wife joined him on board to reinforce the impression that it was a civilian vessel. The Egyptian pilot did not suspect he was steering an Israeli military transport ship, and handed back control at the end of the canal. From there, Buchris continued up the Mediterranean to Haifa. There workers dismantled the ship's temporary facilities. It was not known if it would be called into action again. That would be a decision for the Mossad.

Meanwhile, in parallel to the naval evacuation, covert passage through Khartoum airport was still in operation. Jews were continuing to be transported there under cover of both UNHCR safe passage, and clandestinely by Mossad agents, hidden in safe houses and eventually flown out.

The movement of lots of people, however, even when it was done secretly and with great care, had not gone unnoticed. The local security forces had got wind that something was going on, and they were determined to put a stop to it. This was unwittingly revealed to Dani by Mohammed, the head of the secret police in Gedaref, when Dani went to visit him late one night. While they were talking, Mohammed asked him if he knew any Jews.

'Yes, of course I know Jews,' Dani replied. 'I studied with Jews, some of my friends are Jews.'

'How are they, these Jews?' asked Mohammed.

Dani played laid-back.

'They're like any other person,' he said. 'Some good, some bad, some good-looking, some not good-looking.'

'Do you know about black Jews?' asked Mohammed.

'Black Jews?' answered Dani, feigning ignorance. 'Are you sure?'

'Yes. Black Jews.'

'No,' replied Dani, 'I've never heard about black Jews. I know some of them from north Africa, they're a bit dark.'

'No, not dark – black, totally black, like me,' said Mohammed. 'I learnt from the Ethiopians, that they're coming to the camps here with the other refugees, but they disappear in the night.'

Dani did not flinch, but at that moment, more than any other time, he thought the game was up.

'Yes, they disappear in the night,' continued Mohammed. 'There are some of those Zionist bastards, they come in and they kidnap them and they take them to be cannon-fodder for the Zionist Army. They put them in the front lines so they get killed first.'

'Wow! Are you sure?' asked Dani.

'Of course I'm sure,' answered Mohammed. 'I've got people telling me this. These Zionists come and then they disappear into thin air – but we will catch them,' he said, wagging his finger, 'we will catch them!'

'Well, I wish you luck,' said Dani.

As it was late, Mohammed offered him a room for the night. Dani figured that if he was going to get arrested, it would happen either way, so he accepted. In the morning, Mohammed's wife served him breakfast, then the two men bade each other farewell and Dani left.

With the completion of the first naval evacuation, the team prepared to leave Arous.

Dani found Rubi and took him to one side.

'Remember what you told me?', Dani asked him. 'That you're willing to stay? Okay, I give you the chance – but you'll be here on your own.'

Rubi could not conceal his delight.

'It's fine, I won't be here on my own,' he replied. 'Abu Medina is here. I have a jeep. I don't need electricity, and I can fish for food. Don't worry, I'll manage!'

Before he left, Dani took Rubi to meet Mohammed's brother, Major General Youssef, the head of the Sudanese Navy, at Flamingo Bay. He introduced Rubi as 'James', the *mudir* (manager) of Arous, and they sat down to talk.

'You know, when the Italians were running the village we had an arrangement whereby they would bring me fresh lobsters every Thursday night,' the major general said. 'If you will do this, then maybe there is something I can help you with in return.'

One of the problems they had with their plans for the village was that if they were going to take guests diving, no insurance company would cover the resort unless it had access to a decompression chamber to treat divers suffering from decompression sickness, or the bends. Without it, in the event of an incident, the Mossad would have to pay any medical bills. Dani had discovered that when the Sudanese Navy had an active divers' unit (by that time defunct), they had a chamber at the site. If the village could use it, he thought, the major general could have all the lobsters he wanted.

He started to explain his proposition, but Youssef did not understand English well enough and summoned his deputy, a brigadier general, who had previously been the commander of the unit. The deputy had been trained at Sandhurst military academy in the UK and spoke perfect English. Dani told him they needed the chamber, and could give them lobsters in return. Rubi leant over to Dani and, in Italian, said they should also offer to retrain their Navy commandos. Dani put the suggestion to the deputy, who liked the idea.

'Yes, you can use the decompression chamber, but it's broken,' he said. 'It's leaking and useless. It's a German model, so if you can get a technician from Germany to fix it, then you can have it.'

'Okay,' said Dani, and they shook on it.

'And when you want to come here,' the major general said to Rubi, 'just tell them at the gate you are "Jam-ez from Arous", and they will let you in.'

Later on, the Mossad actually flew over a technician from the manufacturers, who repaired the decompression chamber, and flew him back again, at a cost of about US$10,000. The major general said they could take it back to the resort, but the machine was too heavy to shift. Instead, they agreed to establish direct radio contact from the village to the major general's office, and if there was a diving accident, the village would alert the office, which would send Youssef's personal helicopter to pick up the casualty and fly them to the decompression chamber, a journey which would take only minutes. To test the system, the major general sent his helicopter and pilot to pick up Dani and take him for a tour. For the first time, Dani could see the layout of the village and the surrounding area from above. He took photographs, and passed them onto Mossad HQ.

After the introduction to Youssef, Dani told Rubi he would check in with him from Israel once a day on the code machine at the village. The message sent from Tel Aviv would be from 'Simba to Grillo' (codenames based on characters from the *Tarzan* movies of the 1940s and the children's book *The Adventures of Pinocchio*), and in the event that Rubi was under threat and could not speak freely he would signal by responding with an agreed phrase.

With that, the team departed, leaving Rubi to look after the village.

'And so began the best time of my life!' recalls Rubi.

For him, the place was heaven-sent. He had boats, diving equipment, and companionship in Abu Medina. Abu Medina knew some Italian from the era of the previous owners of Arous, while Rubi knew Arabic, so they were able to converse. They would go fishing and boating together. Abu Medina would dive without a mask to depths of up to ten metres and spear barracuda, and catch lobsters at night in improvised nets made from stockings left by guests in the 1970s. The sea there was teeming with all kinds of colourful species – red snappers, groupers, parrotfish and more.

It was also home to an array of larger sea creatures: squid, octopuses, turtles, dolphins and manta rays, which would swim right up to their boat. There were also sharks – from grey reef to hammerheads – species which Rubi knew from the waters off Neviot. Wild camels also roamed around, and just off Arous, ospreys, herons, pelicans and flamingos would feed and nest among islets and lush green mangrove stands.

Coming from the local Hadandawa tribe, Abu Medina had lived in the area all his life and knew the land and sea there intimately. He showed Rubi the reefs up and down the coast and where shipwrecks lay. One, the *Blue Bell*, had sunk four years earlier just off Marsa Awatir after hitting the reef there. It was carrying vehicles from Saudi Arabia at the time and came to rest, keel up, some 35 metres down. Rubi went to investigate, and dived down to the sponge- and barnacle-encrusted wreck. Scattered on the seabed was its cargo of Toyotas. Some lay upside down, others the right way up, covered with accretions but remarkably intact.

'Now *these* are the cars we need!' he thought.

Diving, fishing and sailing became part of Rubi's daily routine. There was not much else to do. Back at the village the original air conditioning units were broken and there was no electricity anyway (the small generator had stopped working). This meant no fridge and warm beer. At night, there was no light but for a handheld torch, though Rubi did have a Sony Walkman with classical music cassettes, and books, and when the sun went down he would sit in a deckchair on the beach and play his flute. (He was an accomplished flautist. Once when the agents were at Kassala market, a boy was busking, playing a flute, but poorly. Rubi stepped in to help, asked the boy to lend him his instrument and began playing it like a maestro. Passers-by stopped to listen, throwing the boy change. After a couple of tunes, Rubi, with a wink to Dani, started playing Israeli songs and the gathered crowd, not recognising the music, cheerfully clapped along.)

Rubi felt that his stay at Arous was a second chance to enjoy a peaceful life by the sea, in the face of imminent eviction from Sinai.

'Thank you, Allah,' he would say to himself. 'This is where I want to stay!'

The village was not yet operating as a resort and no one came near. But all that changed when, one morning as he was returning from a swim, Rubi spotted military vehicles and armed soldiers gathered on the village beach. He assumed something had happened and that he was about to be arrested.

'Mr Jam-ez! Mr Jam-ez!' called Abu Medina, standing with the soldiers, waving his arms.

Rubi, in Speedos, facemask and snorkel, went to meet them. A man in uniform stepped forward, reached out, and shook his hand.

'I'm Colonel Mahgoub, I'm the *mudir* of the Tourism Corporation, and I have a few people here – Salah Madaneh, the head of our office in Port Sudan, and this is the *muhafiz* [governor] of the whole of the Red Sea State, Mohammed Alamin. We have come to help you get set up.'

Rubi introduced himself as a diving instructor who was looking after the village while it was in the process of being renovated. Mahgoub had brought food and drink, and boxes of bedding, towels and other items for the resort. Rubi thanked them and invited them to stay for breakfast. They took tables in the dining room, and the Mossad agent sat down with the Sudanese soldiers and military chiefs. There they ate, drank and talked together.

'I will get you a carpenter to fix the beds and an electrician to repair the generators,' Mahgoub told Rubi, 'and we'll bring you water in a big tanker. Maybe you need some staff? We have a driver and a cook,' he said.

'Slowly! Slowly!' replied Rubi. 'One thing at a time! Let's do up the village first, then we can start worrying about bringing people.'

Rubi did not want the Army appearing at the village spontaneously. He had got word that another operation was on the horizon, and his mind was on that.

'Where's Mr Daniel?' asked Mahgoub.

'He's gone to Switzerland, but maybe he'll bring some tourists back,' said Rubi, hoping Mahgoub would mistake incoming agents for guests.

'Mr Jam-ez,' the governor said, 'you are like Robinson Crusoe, with comfort!'

When they had finished, the visitors thanked Rubi for his hospitality, returned to their vehicles and left.

The following day, Rubi made good on his promise to retrain the Sudanese Navy divers. He took sets of diving gear and went to the naval base at Flamingo Bay. He announced himself as 'Jam-ez from Arous' and the guard let him in. The major general came to welcome him and introduced him to their sole diver – a Sudanese seaman of retirement age – and four trainees: two Sudanese, and two Zanzibaris on attachment. They went to the edge of the bay, where Rubi wanted first to test how accustomed the trainees were to water. He threw in plates he had brought from the village and told them to dive in and retrieve them. The four men plunged in haphazardly. The Zanzibaris could just about manage, but the Sudanese splashed about chaotically, coughing and gasping. The major general slapped his palm on his forehead.

'Oh my God! They can't swim!' he said in exasperation.

'Okay, you and you are out,' Rubi said to the Sudanese, before carrying on with just the Zanzibaris.

He then produced a weight belt. 'I want you to put it on and tread water, for two minutes. If you feel like you can't cope, just open the buckle,' he said, demonstrating the release mechanism.

The first of the Zanzibaris put on the belt and sank like lead. When he did not resurface, Rubi dived down and pulled him up.

'You want to die?' he asked him, rhetorically.

'I want to see how long I can hold my breath,' the Zanzibari replied.

The major general intervened. 'Thank God we're so afraid of sharks. We're not going to continue.'

*

With the success of the first evacuation, the resort had proved itself as an asset to the Mossad, but without showing signs of genuine activity, sooner or later the Tourism Corporation would wonder about its profitability and start asking questions. Dani knew that Navco needed to show it was a serious business. Mahgoub had been right. If Arous was going to have guests, it was going to need staff. So far it had Abu Medina and a handful of temporary workers, but bringing in full-time employees would heighten the risk of its secret being discovered.

Dani instructed Rubi to get recommendations from Salah Madaneh and start recruiting. Madaneh provided some names and Rubi called them to the village to test them out. There was a waiter, three cooks, a driver and another ghafir. The waiter, Hassan, was previously employed there under the Italian management and knew the ropes. He said he spoke several languages, which was good for guests but dangerous for the Mossad team, in case he understood what the Israelis were saying between themselves in some European tongue. Nevertheless, Hassan and the others were put on a month's trial, then asked to stay on.

Although the village was in reasonable condition, it still needed a considerable amount of work to get it to a standard which would meet guests' expectations. Madaneh sent maintenance workers to fix the electricity and plumbing, and repair broken fixtures and fittings. One day in November, a joiner who had been fixing the beds appeared in the main building, tears running down his face.

'What's wrong?' asked Rubi.

The man had been listening to the radio.

'Moshe Dayan *mat*! [died]', he replied sorrowfully.

Dayan, the general who had led Israel to victory over the Arabs in 1967, had died from a heart attack a month earlier, but the joiner had only just heard the news. This man, an ordinary Sudanese worker, had, it seemed, held Dayan in high esteem.

It was not long afterwards that, while Arous was still being renovated, it received its first, unexpected, guests. Abu Medina had come to find Rubi, and was looking rather perturbed.

'*Fijesh hinak!*' ('Army is there!'), he said, pointing at the hills.

'*Jesh?*' ('Army?'), replied Rubi. 'What do you mean, *jesh?*

'Soldiers! Army! Army!' replied Abu Medina. 'Soldiers! Over there!'

Rubi scoured the hills but could not see anyone.

'Where?' he asked.

'There!' replied Abu Medina. 'Come. Come with jeep.'

They took the vehicle and drove up into the hills. They stopped by a rock and Abu Medina pointed to a bush. Rubi peered closely, and saw some figures in camouflage crouching behind it.

'Okay, you can come out now,' he said in English.

The figures stood up. They were soldiers, but they were not Sudanese. They were white. One of them came forward and introduced himself. He said that they were British and asked Rubi who he was.

'My name is James and I'm the temporary manager of the Arous village,' he replied. 'We're not open yet, but if you want, you can use one of the rooms. Just come and help yourself. No charge.'

Rubi suspected they were British special forces, possibly SAS, on a training exercise or operation.

The soldier thanked him and Rubi and Abu Medina returned to the resort. Rubi left food and drink in one of the chalets which had been fixed with a working shower and toilet. He did not see or hear anyone that night, but the next morning when he checked the room, the food and drink had been consumed. Whoever had been there had left a note, thanking 'James' for his hospitality.

Some proper guests started to come towards the end of 1981 after Salah Madaneh marketed the new European-style resort on the coast to diplomatic circles in Khartoum (there was, literally, nowhere else for them to go on vacation except outside the country) but to begin with there were not many. To supplement the numbers for the sake of appearance, veteran Mossad agents who knew how to sustain a cover story came simply as holidaymakers without any specific mission.

Now that it was receiving clients (real or illusory), the resort needed a general manager, since for a lot of the time Rubi was busy out at sea with the guests. For this, Dani brought in a man by the name of Apke, who ran the kitchens in Mossad HQ and had experience in managing hotels in Germany, where he was born and grew up.

Dani was still in Tel Aviv, planning the next operation, when word came through of a serious incident. While smuggling some 35 Jews from Gedaref to Khartoum in the back of the pickup, Shlomo had been shot at after running a checkpoint. He reported that a guard had opened fire from behind, though without hitting the vehicle. Mossad HQ decided that, combined with the suspicions raised at the Interior Ministry when Dani tried to obtain 74 blank passports, and the sudden appearance of patrol cars at checkpoints which had begun to give chase (the pickups had managed to give them the slip each time by going off-road), it had become too dangerous to smuggle Jews to Khartoum in this way as they had been doing for the past year and a half. The order was given to stop with immediate effect. Jews would continue to be transported with UNHCR passes but the agency now needed to find a new way too. The thinking was to do it as legitimately as possible, the idea being that the less subterfuge involved, the less cause there would be for suspicion. With this in mind, the Mossad turned to one of the major international agencies helping in the resettlement of refugees, the Intergovernmental Committee for Migration, or ICM.

At that time, the ICM did not have an office in Sudan, so a plan was hatched to recruit a trusted and capable individual, who was not a Mossad agent, to represent the ICM in Khartoum. Halevy contacted an influential figure at a foreign Jewish relief agency whom he knew, and asked him for help. This figure provided the Mossad with one of his most experienced and capable staff, a woman by the name of Ruth. In February 1982, Ruth, who was 74 years old at the time, was posted to Sudan, where she lived in and worked out of a room in the Hilton. There she handled all the relationships with the Sudanese authorities and could officially request exit visas and passports for all refugees. Like a number of others on the front line of the operation, Ruth had memories of the Holocaust. For these people in particular, coming to Sudan to help Jews in camps was like closing a circle. Uri had been orphaned by the Holocaust and Apke had survived Dachau. Ruth herself had witnessed displacement and worse horrors first-hand when, as a lieutenant in the US Army, she had been among the first troops to enter Buchenwald concentration camp in Germany after its liberation in April 1945. Ruth was, says Halevy, 'a model, a real unsung hero in every sense of the term.'

Uri (and a British-born agent who filled in for him when he took leave) was named an ICM official, meaning he could now act openly and worked hand-in-hand with Ruth, his ICM 'boss'. The legitimacy provided by the ICM and its Sudanese office, which came under Dani's overall responsibility, allowed the Mossad to cease obtaining passports under false pretences from the Commissioner for Refugees. Uri continued the process of getting entry visas from the embassies and meeting with Committee Men to give them funds to distribute to the Jewish refugees, and to tell them how many Jews to put on the next evacuation list, but a significant element of risk had now been removed.[4]

Back in Haifa, the Navy, at the Mossad's request, recommissioned the *Bat Galim* for the second operation. This time, it was decided to prepare it for many more refugees. The ship secretly underwent a major refit, doubling its capacity. Around 400 bunk beds and additional showers were installed, the mess hall enlarged and the kitchen more substantially equipped. A Mulit rigid hull inflatable boat, sturdier than a Zodiac and capable of mounting a beach, was bought from the UK, flown over and loaded on board. The ship was also fitted with two concealed 20mm guns.[5] It set sail in mid-January, 1982.

The Israelis had in the meantime returned to Arous. They had brought with them a member of staff from the office, Belgian-born Jacques, to pose as a guest.

William had decided one operation was all he could take and had gone back to New Zealand. As a measure of the man of honour that he was, for decades he never spoke about what he had done, not even to his own wife.[6] Dani recruited a replacement, a former journalist at Israel Radio and ex-Mossad agent named Gad. Gad had resigned from the agency (from where he knew Dani, although the two had not directly worked together) just three months earlier. Fluent in Arabic and German, Gad had assets which Dani was looking for, and was keen to join the operation, so he got him accepted back into the Mossad on a short-term contract. Within about a month of their meeting, Gad was on his way to Sudan with Rubi, who had been on sojourn in Israel. They checked in to the Hilton, and after a week set off for the village, in the Land Cruiser used by Shlomo when he had been shot at. On the way they were stopped by police at gunpoint and ordered to go to the station in Gedaref. It transpired that a soldier had recognised their vehicle (it had been specially fitted with a metal frame around its cargo bed for covering with tarpaulin to hide the Jews) as the Toyota which he had opened fire on after it ran the checkpoint two weeks earlier. The soldier was convinced he had hit the car, but there were no signs of bullet-holes, so Gad and Rubi were released.

As far as the local staff were concerned, the new people who came to operate at the village belonged to Navco. There was no reason for them to assume otherwise, nor did it matter. For the staff, the village was a source of income. Nor did they suspect anything when, a short time after their return, Dani told them his team was going away for a couple of days (the pretext given, according to an agent, was that they had an arrangement to meet female Swedish volunteers from a clinic in Kassala), and they all headed off in a truck and two pickups. Their destination was a quarry (there were two or three quarries which the Mossad would use for collecting the Jews, out of sight of the road) outside Tawawa, a large refugee camp five kilometres north of Gedaref.

For the refugees in Tawawa, conditions were dire. Disease was rife, food was scant and children were dying by the day. It was also considered so dangerous that even aid workers dared not venture there beyond late afternoon.[7] For non-Jewish refugees, it was bad; for the fewer Jewish refugees, having to hide their identity on pain of death, it was even worse.

The night of the pick-up, eight-year-old Zude Mulu could not sleep. His mother had told him that, after dark, 'white people from Jerusalem' were going to come and take him to the Promised Land. The family had left their village of Gudulo in Tigray a year earlier, after rumours began to circulate that Jews from Jerusalem had come to Sudan to take the Ethiopian Jews back with them. Zude, his parents and two younger sisters and brother, walked for two months through forests and desert before reaching the camp. They had been told they could be there for up to three years. Desperate to get her children to safety, Zude's mother managed to get him onto the Committee's list. She told two older people on the list to take care of him and to pretend he was their son. Zude had never met them before.

'That night, it was very dark,' Zude recalls. 'We walked out of the camp, very quietly, and across a road. Then I saw some white people, but I didn't know who they were. Suddenly in the distance we saw a car coming towards us. The white people told us to fall to the ground and lie down, which we did. After the car passed, we got up and made our way to a truck.

'I was one of the first people to get on, and a couple of minutes later it was full – men, women and children, packed in like sardines. I was very frightened, everyone was, but not a single person complained. They threw a tarpaulin over us and we began the journey.

'It was very uncomfortable and hot and people started being sick, but we stayed very quiet the whole time, just as they'd told us to.

'I lost track of time, but after many hours we stopped at a place between two mountains. Then they gave us food and cartons of juice to drink. I had never seen such a thing before. When I sipped it, I wondered why it tasted so sweet. Then I thought to myself, "Ah, it must be water from Jerusalem!"

'We got back in the truck and later we arrived at a place where I had no idea where we were. It was dark under the tarpaulin and I could hear a strange noise. It was very loud. None of us had heard anything like it before and we did not know what it was. We were frightened for our lives and started to pray. Then they opened the truck and we all tumbled out.

'The noise was suddenly even louder and I looked around. Then I saw where it was coming from. It was the sea. The Red Sea. I had never seen the sea before, and the noise was the crashing of the waves. I thought this was like the story of Noah in the Bible and that the whole world was going to be under water.

'I was so scared, and as I looked towards the sea, suddenly I saw two figures coming out of the water towards us. I did not believe men could just walk out of the water – for me, this was just not real – so I thought they must be angels.

'Then one of them came to me and hugged me! They cried and we cried. At that moment, I felt more confident, more sure.

'They put us in boats and we went out to sea. I saw a lot more boats like ours on the water and the commanders signalling to one another. All our clothes were completely wet and everyone was in shock.

'I remember going into the hold of the big ship, and they gave us juice and food. We were all dancing together and kissing the floor, because we thought this was Jerusalem!'[8]

Zude Mulu would grow up to become an Orthodox rabbi, known as Sharon Shalom, an educator with a PhD in philosophy and a leading member of the Ethiopian Jewish community in Israel. Two years after Zude arrived, Dani had a son. Later in life when Dani's son got married, Rabbi Shalom performed the wedding ceremony.

After a brief respite at the village, the agents made another trip to Gedaref to pick up more Jews and bring them back to the ship. After the two trips the team was exhausted, but Tarzan, who was on the *Bat Galim*, sent Dani a challenging message.

'In the paratroopers you never stop – we still have a lot of space on the boat,' he said. 'Go another time.'

The agents were at the end of their rope, so Dani put it to a vote. All but one agreed to do it, knowing it could make the difference between life and death for some 100–200 more Jews sitting in the camps. Shlomo said he would give the drivers Benzedrine to keep them awake. The team set off again on a round trip of some 1,800 kilometres, the second time in 24 hours and without having had a break. They collected another big group of Jews from near Gedaref, but the return leg of the journey in the dark, with its long monotonous stretches, had the drivers struggling to stay awake (as one agent would later comment: 'I knew that I was falling asleep when I saw Snow White on top of the engine and all the dwarfs screwing her').

Despite having taken the Benzedrine, Shmulik slept the whole way there and back, effectively leaving them without a spare driver. Dani himself, in the lead vehicle, which was not smuggling any Ethiopian Jews (as per operational rules), could not stay awake and asked his co-driver to take over for twenty minutes. They swapped places and Dani fell asleep, but the co-driver was also suffering from fatigue. A short time later, he lost his concentration and swerved, careering into a barrel on the road. In a stroke of bad luck, at that moment he had crashed into a roadblock. He slammed on the brakes, but the truck behind was too close and went into the back of the vehicle; the third vehicle also braked sharply but ploughed into the one in front. Despite the shock of the jolt, the passengers stayed completely quiet. Suddenly guards shining torches came running towards the concertinaed convoy. The agents got out and Dani told them: 'Okay, if we don't manage to stop these guys, we have to take care of them.' They knew what he meant and were ready. Dani took some biscuits from his vehicle and went towards the nearest soldier to distract him.

'Who are you?' the soldier shouted at him.

'I'm sorry,' said Dani, 'we had a little accident but everything's okay now. We're taking care of it and will be gone in a minute. Here, have some of these,' he said, offering the soldier the packet.

The soldier ignored him and brushed past, walking determinedly up to the convoy. He stopped at the first truck with the Jews hidden inside and asked the men standing by the cab what was going on. As they talked, the soldier reached with his hand towards the tarpaulin.

'He was within 30 centimetres of lifting this up and at that moment we would have to kill four or five soldiers,' recalls Dani. 'But then for some reason he stopped. He just didn't do it.'

The soldier told the group it was okay and that they could carry on, then he walked back to the guards' tent. The vehicles which collided were only slightly damaged and none of the passengers were hurt. The convoy manoeuvred back onto the road and carried on, passing the guards and the upturned barrel. It had been an extraordinarily near miss for everyone.

For the third time in a week, the agents arrived at Marsa Fijab with Jews, where they were picked up by the Zodiacs and taken to the ship. The *Bat Galim* set sail for Israel with 350 evacuees on board, their nightmare ordeal behind them.

The following day, and still at sea, one of the crew members conducted a headcount. It came to only 349, so he counted again. Still 349. There was one person missing. He reported it to Buchris. There was a possibility that one of the Jews had been lost overboard. Buchris needed to be certain before informing headquarters, which would launch a search and rescue mission. He ordered all the evacuees to go to one end of the ship and closed off the area. Then he took a box of sweets and counted out 350. He told each person to come to him, individually, take a sweet and move to the opposite area. The first one stepped forward, took a sweet and moved on. 'One.' Then the second. 'Two.' The process carried on until the last person, who took a sweet and joined the rest of the group. There was one sweet left in the box. Suddenly Buchris had a thought. He instructed everybody to walk past again, one by one, and as they did so he touched the women's backs. Then he found the answer. Concealed in an *enkalwa*, or fabric bag for carrying infants, worn by one of the mothers was a baby. The infant was the 350th passenger. Everyone was accounted for.

Details of the operation and its success were reported to the prime minister, Menachem Begin. He was delighted and commended everybody involved. His feelings were conveyed in a letter which Efraim Halevy sent to Dani:

> My very dear friend
> I will be brief. The escapade of last week was highly praised by the PM at his weekly cabinet meeting. I was told by an independent eyewitness that there were genuine tears in many eyes when the story was told. I was asked to pass to you and team the highest regard and appreciation of PM. I am happy to be the conduit of this item.

The letter ended with: 'Take care brave man. Yours E.'

In the wake of the second operation, Dani took a break from Sudan to volunteer to do his *miluim*, or reserve duty, in the Army. It is a requirement for anyone who has completed their compulsory national service at the age of 21, although Mossad agents can be exempt. He was on manoeuvres in Israel's southern Negev desert when a message came through from Hofi summoning him to the prime minister's office immediately. Dani took the division commander's jeep and drove to Jerusalem. He got there, and still in uniform and dusty, met Hofi outside Begin's room.

Hofi took one look at him.

'You're doing reserve?' he asked him in surprise. 'You were in Sudan!'

'This is my vacation,' Dani replied, jokingly.

The two men were called in. Begin, who was sitting at his desk, got up and greeted them. He looked at Dani and said to Hofi: 'What, your people wear military uniforms now?'

'No, only those who volunteer for national service,' replied Hofi. 'We have a few crazy ones, like this guy!'

The three men sat down and Begin started asking about the Ethiopian Jews, the conditions they were living in and how the operation was going. He asked if the Mossad was doing the maximum possible, how they were providing for the Jews and if there was anything else he could do to help. From the kind of questions he was asking, it was clear his interest in the Ethiopian Jews ran much deeper than a political level.

It had been Hofi's idea that the prime minister should actually meet the people who were doing the work smuggling the Jews to Israel, and for the people who were doing the work to meet the prime minister and get to know what kind of person he was. Later on, Dani was also brought for the same reason to meet Begin's successor, Yitzhak Shamir, who continued the operation begun by his predecessor.

10

AMBUSH ON THE BEACH

With the naval evacuations proving effective, a third operation was planned for just two months' time, in March 1982. This time, though, it would come closer to catastrophe than ever before.

As previously, the team of agents rendezvoused with the young refugee smugglers, the Berare, outside Gedaref and quickly loaded 172 Jews onto the trucks. They drove through the night, stopped for the day, then continued on their way, reaching Marsa Fijab late on the second night. Dani and the commander of the Shayetet unit, Lieutenant Colonel Gadi Kroll, took the decision to bring what amounted to sixteen Zodiacs ashore eight at a time, in order to avoid overcrowding on the beach, as had occurred during the earlier operations. Once the first set of Zodiacs had loaded up with Jews and left, the second set of eight would move in. All was quiet and calm, but with smugglers and Bedouin around, there was always a risk of being seen, so Dani positioned Gad on a hill as lookout with night-vision goggles and a two-way radio.

Down on the beach the first Zodiacs had arrived and the teams were loading the Jews on board when Dani's radio crackled into life. It was Gad.

'Two people are coming,' he said. 'They're soldiers and they have rifles on their shoulders.'

Dani deduced that from the way they were carrying the rifles the soldiers were not coming to fight. He sent Jacques to go and talk to them, see what they wanted and try to get them to go away. After a few minutes Jacques came back.

'It's okay, I gave them some cigarettes and they left,' he said.

There was something unusual about it, though. It was the first time soldiers had come to that particular cove, and tonight in the middle of an operation. Dani thought there must be more to it.

He went over to tell Kroll, who was directing the commandos putting the Jews into the boats. It was not a quick process. One of the lessons learnt from the first operation in the storm was the need to keep passengers safe on the long trip to the *Bat Galim*, which was anchored 25 kilometres offshore. Since then, they had put life-jackets and safety belts on every person (with small-sized safety belts for the babies, manufactured specially for the operation at the Mossad's request), and performed a headcount before they set off, all of which took time.

'Gadi,' said Dani, 'listen, two soldiers came and they went away, but I don't like it, and I think that we should accelerate everything. That means bring the other eight boats now. They can squeeze into the spaces in between. It's going to be crowded but it'll give us the chance to fill them all immediately. The belts and the counting – let's do it once they're already out at sea. We need to get everyone off the beach – that's the Jews and you and your men.'

Kroll did not deliberate.

'Okay, let's do it,' he said, and called in the remaining Zodiacs which were waiting just outside the cove.

The boats came, landed wherever they could and everyone stepped up the pace. Sixteen Zodiacs and 32 commandos were crowded on the narrow beach at once.

Gad came back on the radio.

'Now I see four people coming,' he said, 'and they're holding their guns like they're ready to shoot!' Three of them were soldiers, he said, and a fourth was a tall man in civilian clothing. Dani ordered Gad to leave the lookout and join the team loading the Jews – with none to be left behind. He gave the same order to Marcel, putting him in charge of the evacuation, and told Rubi to take a dinghy which had been brought there earlier from the resort and go and wait with it in the cove until the last Zodiac was ready, then guide them through the coral reefs and out to sea. He instructed Rubi to then wait for a signal from him before going with the dinghy back to the village.

As soon as Zodiacs were full they were pushed back out onto the water and moved off to where Rubi was positioned about 50 metres from the beach, while others were still being loaded to try to get away as quickly as possible.

Dani went back to Kroll and told him about the four armed men approaching.

'I'm going to try to intercept them and buy some time,' Dani said. 'If something happens, don't shoot, unless I'm dead or I give you permission to shoot.'

Kroll was one of the most decorated officers in the history of the Shayetet. He had led deadly commando raids, sunk an Egyptian missile boat with a mine during the 1973 war, and fought many times in hand-to-hand combat. He had also acquired a reputation as an expert marksman.

'I knew him, he's a fighter,' Dani later recalled, 'and for him to take out a company of Sudanese soldiers, even if it's three times more than his, he'd do it in the blink of an eye. But there were still several thousand Jews in the camps, and the main thing was to keep this operation alive.'

Dani took Shlomo and Shmulik – an expert knifeman, with a dagger concealed up his sleeve – and started to walk towards the armed Sudanese. '*Englese! Englese!*' Dani called out. The Sudanese stopped in their tracks, seemingly surprised. They apparently did not expect to find Westerners on the beach. The two groups started shouting to each other, the Sudanese in Arabic, the Israelis in English.

'Don't move or we'll shoot!' one of the Sudanese ordered them.

'We don't understand Arabic,' the Israelis shouted back. '*Englese! Englese!*' they called again, deliberately confusing things to stall the intruders and allow the boats to get away.

Dani leaned over to Shmulik. 'No knives until necessary,' he whispered.

The two groups faced off, yelling at each other, Dani glancing every few seconds to check what was happening with the boats. He could see one Zodiac after the other moving off, until there was just a single boat remaining, full of passengers but stuck on the beach with commandos struggling to get it loose.

Suddenly, one of the soldiers spotted what was going on and started running towards the sea.

'Shmulik – the boat – go!' Dani ordered. Without hesitation, Shmulik darted back towards the shore, dashing to beat the soldier to the stranded vessel. As the soldier ran past, Dani turned and gave chase. Catching up, he barged the soldier with his shoulder, deflecting him from the direction of the trapped boat, but as the soldier got to the shoreline he released a burst of gunfire from the Kalashnikov grasped at his hip.

Dani grabbed him and dragged him to the ground, both of them wrestling in the sand. During the commotion, the commandos managed to release the last Zodiac and get it out to sea. Gad and Shmulik had also made it onto boats and were out of sight.

Israeli medics who were on board the Zodiacs with the commandos checked to see if anyone had been hit by the gunfire. Miraculously, the spray of bullets had missed, and everyone was safe.

As Dani and the soldier grappled, the three other Sudanese reached them, grabbed Dani and hauled him up. Shlomo and Marcel were there a moment later. Then out of the dark a whole platoon of Sudanese soldiers appeared, all with their guns pointing at them. They had the three Israelis surrounded. Neither Dani, Shlomo nor Marcel knew where the other members of the team – Gad, Shmulik, Apke and or Jacques – were or whether they been captured or worse (only Rubi they knew had got out to sea).

Kroll, who was on one of the Zodiacs, messaged the mother ship to report what had happened, and that Dani and others were being held at gunpoint. Kroll wanted to take his troops and rescue them but Rubi persuaded him to wait and let Dani deal with the situation.

A counter-attack by the commandos would certainly be overwhelming but it would also risk triggering something much more serious. Sitting on standby at an airbase in Israel were two F-16 fighter planes, with pilots at the ready in the cockpits. Their job was to protect the *Bat Galim*, which, anchored off the coast of an enemy country, was essentially a sitting duck. If the Shayetet got into trouble, or the ship was attacked by whatever the Sudanese Navy could muster, the F-16s would soar down the Red Sea and obliterate the threat. Should that happen, the consequence would be not only the end of the operation, but an international crisis, or even a Middle East war.

Back on the beach, the tall man in civilian clothing grabbed Dani by the wrist to try to take him away, but Dani pulled himself free. The man shouted at Dani in Arabic, and Dani shouted back.

'Speak English!'

'What are you doing here?' the man demanded to know. 'What are *you* doing here?!' Dani snapped back. 'We're here with the agreement of Major General Youssef!'

The man stopped at the mention of the name.

'You know Liwa Youssef?' he asked.

'Yes. He is a good friend of ours,' replied Dani, angrily. 'I was in his office only yesterday. We are running the resort at Arous and these people your soldier was shooting at were hunting lobsters for Liwa Youssef's dinner! First thing tomorrow, we're going to complain to him about what just happened and you're going to be in a lot of trouble!'

The tall man hesitated.

'You know Liwa Youssef?' he repeated, in a disbelieving tone. 'Okay, I will check.'

He told the soldiers to stand down and ordered two of them to go back to the village with the foreigners and hold them under house arrest there while he investigated. With that, the man and the rest of the platoon left. It was clear the Sudanese had not noticed that the people in the boats were Ethiopian refugees, so there was no reason for the agents to 'take care of' their two guards.

As soon as the troops' vehicles had gone, Dani told Marcel to take the guards in his jeep to the village and said he and Shlomo would follow in the trucks.

At a safe moment, he radioed the *Bat Galim* and spoke to a senior officer, Colonel Dov Bar (on board to take command in the event of something happening to Buchris). Everyone was free and unharmed, he told Bar, and implored him not to report the incident to HQ immediately as protocol demanded. The job was done. The Zodiacs had got away with all the Jews, the F-16s had not been called – and it was time to go back to the village.

The guards left with Marcel, and Dani radioed Rubi to give him the green light to also head back to the resort. Rubi informed Dani that he had picked up Gad and Shmulik and they were safe.

Dani and Shlomo made their way to the trucks. As they got there, two figures emerged from in between the two vehicles. It was Apke and Jacques, who had been hiding there since the soldiers appeared.

'Oh my God!' declared Apke, white as a sheet and trembling. 'I survived the Holocaust but I'm going to get killed on Sudanese soil!'

Shlomo immediately checked his pulse and other vital signs.

'We need to get him out of here as quickly as possible!' he said, fearing Apke was on the verge of a heart attack. (Dani got him on a flight back to Israel via Europe three days later.)

Jacques, who had also gone through Nazi death camps as a boy, was not as shaken up and was himself due to go back to Israel soon anyway.

The four of them got into the trucks and headed off.

Fifteen minutes later when they were back at the village, Dani told Hassan the cook to make the two Sudanese guards a big meal and made sure they had plenty of alcohol. Full up and drowsy, the two men fell asleep, at which point Dani called a team meeting.

'I'm going to Port Sudan to try to solve this problem in a way which will allow us to keep the village and the operation going,' he told his colleagues. Then he warned: 'If I'm not back by tomorrow afternoon, it means they have arrested me or something – so you go. Take the cars but just leave me some communication gear so I can get in touch with Israel, *if* I make it back here.'

It was understood that 'go' meant abandon the village and head north, cross the Egyptian border, and from there escape to Europe.

Dani left the village and drove two hours in the dark, on rugged ground, down to Port Sudan. His plan was not to try to justify their activity on the beach but to complain aggressively in order to turn the situation in their favour.

He went to the officers' quarters in the northern part of the port, and, not knowing where Major General Youssef lived, started knocking on doors. It was well after midnight. At one unit, a door was opened, with a groggy woman standing there.

'I am sorry to disturb you, but I'm looking for Liwa Youssef,' said Dani.

'He's not here,' replied the woman, shutting the door on him.

He had found the major general's house, but to no avail. With Youssef not around, Dani started looking for his deputy instead. At another unit, a second woman opened the door.

'I am sorry to disturb you,' said Dani, 'but I'm looking for the brigadier general.'

'He is my husband,' said the woman in good English. 'Who are you?'

'My name is Daniel, I'm the director of the company that is running Arous, and I need to speak to the brigadier general urgently.'

'Please, come in,' she replied.

The two went into the living room of the house.

'My husband is not in at the moment. He's in the air with his commander. There's an operation going on to catch smugglers,' she told Dani.

It was the first piece of information to suggest why they had been ambushed on the beach. The platoon had been trying to catch smugglers trafficking goods – usually sheep and goats, but also women for slavery – to Saudi Arabia. They had not been on the look-out for the smugglers of Jews. If they had, there would have been a bloodbath. To find 'Westerners on a diving expedition' had clearly taken them by surprise.

'You can wait here until the morning when my husband will be back,' the woman told him.

Dani sat on the couch, lay down and fell asleep. He had been out for some time when he felt himself being shaken.

'What are you doing sleeping on my couch?' asked a voice, jovially. It was Liwa Youssef's deputy, the brigadier general.

Dani sat up and acted angrily.

'Look, I'm sorry I came here in the middle of the night and woke your wife up, but I came to tell you that I'm closing the village and leaving!' he said. 'I'm taking my team, we're going to Khartoum and we're going to complain directly to the brother of the president.'

The deputy's face fell.

'Why? What happened?' he asked.

'What do you mean, "What happened"?' replied Dani. 'You know every Wednesday night we go out to hunt for lobsters for you and the major general. Well, some people came from the sea – no idea who, probably came from yachts to get supplies. I didn't even have time to speak to them when all of a sudden your soldiers came and this guy starts shooting and I have a fight with him and some civilian guy wants to arrest me.'

The deputy looked shocked.

'Luckily we didn't have any guests on a night-dive,' said Dani.

'What? It was you? On the beach?' replied the deputy.

'Yes!' said Dani. 'And your people were trigger-happy. We were caught in the middle! I can't risk such a thing happening to anyone, and besides, if it gets known, tourists will not come!'

'No, no, wait,' said the deputy. 'I will sort it out, I'll check …'

'The only way I'm keeping this village,' Dani interrupted, 'is if we get a formal letter of apology from that *tawil* [tall person], the one who tried to take me.'

'Ah, him,' replied the deputy. 'He's the head of the secret police in Port Sudan. I can't tell him what to do.'

'That's your problem,' said Dani. 'I need a letter of apology.'

'Okay, okay. Let me talk to the major general. We'll get you some apology from the Army. I can't guarantee you anything from the secret police.'

'Yes, but I need your assurance that this guy's not going to bother us like that again,' said Dani.

'That I can guarantee you. The village will be off-limits for anyone except for us,' the deputy replied. 'Come tomorrow and we'll have a meeting.'

Dani realised it was already late morning and he had told the team to evacuate the village if he did not return within an hour or so from now. He left quickly and drove at high speed back to Arous, the four-by-four rattling and racing its way over miles of rough ground and sand.

He got there an hour after the deadline, but the team had decided to give him a bit of extra time before pulling out. Any longer, though, and they would have been gone.

He went inside where he was greeted with serious news. The two soldiers were gone but an order had come from Mossad HQ: 'Evacuate the village'. The senior officer on the *Bat Galim*, Dov Bar, had filed a report on the ambush at Marsa Fijab (though he was reprimanded for not reporting it in real time). It was a crisis. The order had come from Dani's superiors and was expected to be obeyed, but to do so would also mean extinguishing the only hope for thousands of Jews languishing in the camps. Dani had an issue with discipline when he felt orders were misplaced.

He took the communication device, went to his chalet and sent a short, coded response.

'Met officers in charge. Think incident behind us. Everything okay.'

An encoded radio message came back.

'Still, we want you to evacuate, and we want you all to leave Sudan.'

Dani replied, curtly.

'No reason to evacuate. If do, cannot come back.'

The response was not what Dani was expecting.

'You will obey as instructed,' came the answer, directly from Hofi himself.

Challenging an order from a senior divisional figure was one thing, but disobeying the chief was unthinkable. The only alternatives were to resign or be fired.

Dani decided to put it to a vote and assembled all his team. He was prepared to go to Israel and fight the order, but if they stayed in the meantime it would render them renegades. The consequences of that would put them all in the firing line. On the other hand, to leave would mean everything ending, but without the repercussions.

'All those in favour of staying?' he asked.

Without hesitation, all hands went up, bar one. The dissenter's opinion was that the operation carried too many risks, but this person was overruled.

'Who cares?' said one of the team. 'Most of us are on contracts. We get fired, so we just go back to ordinary jobs!'

'Okay,' said Dani. 'Give me 24 hours and I'll send you a message from back home, telling you to leave or stay.'

First, though, he had an appointment to attend.

At daybreak the next morning, Dani and Rubi went back to Port Sudan, armed with a bottle of cognac and fresh fish prepared by chief cook Moussa. They walked into Liwa Youssef's office and waited. The major general arrived half an hour later, tired.

'Ah, Mr Daniel, Mr Jam-ez!' he said, greeting them with an outstretched hand.

Dani was too riled for pleasantries.

'Your people are trigger-happy!' he said, jabbing with his finger.

'What do you mean?' asked Youssef. He had not yet heard about what had gone on.

'Let's eat and drink first, hey?' suggested Rubi.

The three sat down and Youssef's secretary brought in plates, cutlery and glasses. The major general opened the aluminium foil containing the fish and inhaled the aroma.

'Don't worry, Daniel, our friend will sort it all out,' said Rubi, pouring Youssef an ample measure of cognac.

They told him what had gone on at the beach and he was both angry and contrite.

'Mr Daniel, Mr Jam-ez, I am sorry about what happened,' he said. 'What do you want me to do for you?'

'Well,' said Dani, 'if you can give us a permit saying we are from Arous village and are on official business under the auspices of your office, then we could reconsider closing down.'

Youssef agreed, wrote it out and got his secretary to type it up. It meant that if the team got stopped at roadblocks in future, they could show the pass proving they were bona fide and not have to worry about being questioned.

The two agents thanked the major general and left.

On the way out, Rubi turned to Dani and, in Hebrew, said: '*Yesh lanu ta'odat kashrut!*' ('We've got our kosher certificate!')

Dani took a flight from Port Sudan and Rubi returned to the village.

When Dani's plane landed at Zurich airport, he contacted the senior figure in his division who had issued the evacuation order.

'I'm on my way,' he said. 'Please, hold your instructions until you hear what I've got to say. My team are on their own and I take responsibility for telling them to stay there. Let me just talk to you first and then you decide.'

He got the official's agreement to suspend the order until he could get to the office.

Dani took a connecting flight and landed in Tel Aviv. There a car was waiting for him and it took him to the Hadar Dafna building, a tower block on King Saul Boulevard which was the Mossad's headquarters. Dani took the lift up to the eleventh floor. As he stepped out, Hofi's chief aide, with whom Dani was friends, saw him and, with a smile, drew his finger across his throat.

The official who issued the evacuation order was also there, and together they went to Hofi's office. After the two previous operations, when Dani and the senior official reported to Hofi, he would greet them warmly, with a pat on the back and expressions of gratitude. This time he stayed seated behind his desk, without as much as a 'hello'.

'You wait outside, all of you, except for Dani,' he said, sending away the official and his chief of staff. Then he turned to Dani. 'Okay, you've got five minutes to tell me your story.'

'Even before I start – here,' said Dani, reaching into his pocket and bringing out the keys to his house and his motorbike. He put them on the table.

'I can be replaced straight away. My deputy Marcel can take over,' he said. 'If you decide I shouldn't go back, then fine.' Then he asked: 'May I use your whiteboard and marker pen?'

Hofi gestured for him to go ahead.

Dani drew him a diagram of Marsa Fijab, the coastline and the sea, and explained minute-by-minute how the events of the night unfolded, how he and Kroll speeded up the evacuation process, how he told Dov Bar to delay reporting the incident, and how he got the permit in Port Sudan. He took it out of his pocket and showed it to Hofi.

'Haka, you can decide what you want, but it will be a *crime* to abandon the village, because to construct a new cover, it will take a year, and you'd have to build a new team from scratch. So for a year, there'd be no evacuations, and all the while more Jews coming into the camps. There are still about 3,500 there right now.'

Hofi listened without interrupting. After Dani had finished, the chief called the other two men back in.

'Okay,' he said. 'I've decided Dani will be reprimanded for disobedience, and at the same time, I'm giving him a citation for doing the right thing. Both will go into his file. He will go back and continue in charge of the operation.'

In other words, Hofi determined that Dani had disobeyed an order, but that he had been right in doing so. As a result of that decision by the head of the Mossad, the operation was saved and with it a lifeline for many thousands of stricken Ethiopian Jews.

Hofi then turned to Dani and said: 'You have two daughters – go and see them, then go back to your team in Sudan.' The fact that the chief of the Mossad displayed a measure of humanity in that moment touched Dani deeply – and for him defined Hofi as a great commander.

With a resurgence of will to carry on, Dani thanked Hofi and left the office. He then sent a message back to the village: 'You are kosher, you can stay.'

It came as a relief to the team, but in the village they were faced with another problem. Now that Apke had been sent home, they had to find a new general manager.

11

'ADVENTURE, À LA CARTE'

A few months earlier, on his brief return to Israel, Rubi had told Dani about a woman he knew who worked for El Al and ran a tourist operation in Eilat.

'She's the one I sent the mangoes and rugs for with Buchris,' he told him. 'Her name is Yola. She's originally German, speaks languages – and she's fearless.'

Rubi had met Yola when he worked as an El Al air marshal after he retired from the Shayetet. Yola co-owned a yacht, the *Yamanji*, in Eilat, where she would take tourists on trips down the Gulf of Aqaba in between working as a purser on flights. They hung out together in the port city, where Rubi taught her to dive. Every so often, Rubi would disappear, without telling her why. Then, one day he came back after one of his absences.

'There's someone I want you to meet,' he told her, without explaining.

It was late July 1982 when Dani, who was in Israel at the time, flew to Eilat and met Yola. They talked, with Dani displaying particular interest in the fact that her mother-tongue was German, she knew how to dive, and that she ran a small tourist business there. She was blonde, less typical of Israelis, which would be an advantage for undercover work. It also occurred to

Dani that having a female in charge of the day-to-day running of the place would help lower any suspicions.

He asked her if she wanted to come and work with him and Rubi on 'something for the government'.

Yola had an inkling it was to do with one of the intelligence agencies, but did not say so. A passionate Zionist, the prospect of working in the service of the state excited her. She was also motivated by the tragedy which had befallen her own relatives in Germany when the State of Israel did not exist. Dozens of members of her extended family perished in the Holocaust. Her mother survived by hiding for years in a cellar; her father escaped to Russia. Three of her grandparents were murdered. Every time she flew to Germany with El Al, it made her think of what had been done to them there.

Besides this, Yola was adventurous by nature, and smart. She also loved detective novels, reading Agatha Christie in English as a child. Without hesitation, she accepted Dani's proposition.

There was some consternation back at Mossad HQ about recruiting a woman to work, undercover, in such a dangerous operation, but Dani got Halevy's and Hofi's consent.

Yola was called to a meeting in a cafe in Tel Aviv with Halevy, who wanted to test her suitability. She still had not been told any more about who it was for or what it was about. The verdict of the meeting was that she passed 'with flying colours', so she would later be told. Yola was then put through a series of tests with other candidates – a psychological examination at Mossad HQ and trials in the field designed to assess resourcefulness and aptitude for lateral thinking, such as Rubi himself had undergone when he had to evade agents on his trail at the airbase at Tel Nof. She made it through and was then put on a course on surveillance, counter-surveillance and secret communication techniques. By the end, several candidates had quit or been rejected. Having impressed her instructors, Yola was accepted – the single criticism of her being that she showed 'too much *chutzpah*' (a Yiddish word, often defined as 'brazenness').

Dani told her what it was all for. He told her about the diving resort, how they were using it as a front for smuggling Jews out of Sudan, and how the agents took on roles there. They wanted her to be the manageress, following on from Apke – making sure the village ran smoothly while helping out with clandestine operations. He offered her the job and she happily accepted. She was released from El Al under a special arrangement between the company and the Mossad. None of her colleagues at the airline knew.

Yola, in fact, was to be the first of three Israeli manageresses, who would rotate every two months.

Like the other members of Dani's team, Yola had to adopt an alternative identity. She was given the name and passport of a real person, a non-Jewish woman who had moved to Israel from a European country. The woman had changed her name and had volunteered her passport to be used by the Mossad. Yola was flown to the woman's country of origin under instructions to learn all about her home town, as if she had grown up there herself.

As much as she liked the thrill, she was under no illusions about the dangers. At one briefing she was told that if something happened, such as the village getting exposed, and she was alone, she would have to run for her life. She was told that in such a situation she should take a homing device, jump into a Zodiac and head out to sea, where she would be rescued.

It was in September 1982 that Yola made her first trip to Sudan. She flew from Israel to a European city, using her genuine documentation, and met up with a Mossad agent, who handed over her false passport, driving licence and other papers. Normally, new operatives would fly on to their destination with a second agent, but at that time there was none available, so she travelled to Khartoum alone. The plane was full of Sudanese, and the white, blonde woman by herself was a curiosity for the other passengers. She had grown up on stories of exotic travel and discovery, so arriving in Africa filled her with excitement. She spent the first night in the Hilton, where she met Dani on his way back to Europe, then the next day flew to Port Sudan. There she was picked up at the Red Sea Hotel by her old friend, Rubi. It was already evening by the time they got back to Arous.

'I was really amazed by the place,' recalls Yola. 'It was so beautiful, so serene – completely untypical of what you see in Sudan. And then life really started there.'

At that point, Arous was still some way off being ready as a fully functioning resort. The rooms were in disarray and nothing was organised. It also lacked equipment. The only thing to eat was fish freshly caught from the sea, but there was nowhere to store the catch. Sorting out the kitchen was a priority, starting with a new fridge and deep freezer, trucked in from Port Sudan. If there was to be a proper service for guests, they would need breakfast, lunch and dinner, so Yola devised a menu with Moussa, inventive enough so that no meal would be served twice the same week. Ingredients were bought in Port Sudan, and lamb, veal, fresh vegetables and salad were added to the large variety of seafood on offer, while cheese and other delicacies not known in Sudan were also available, picked up in European airports on the way in.

'Yola made Arous,' one agent would later comment. 'She was like "you do this, you do that, you go and buy this, you go and buy that".' As the village took shape, local people would stop by to ask Yola for help with problems or for medical advice. Ironically, they would call her 'Golda' after Israel's former prime minister Golda Meir – known throughout the Middle East as a strong and capable woman – and would bring her gifts of animals, including dogs, birds and even a fawn.

Electricity was working after the generator got fixed, but it depended on fuel to run. Yola would make sure there were always enough barrels, and when they ran low either she or one of the workers would go to a depot in Port Sudan and get some more. Stocking up on fuel 'for the village' was also a convenient cover for making sure the trucks and cars had enough reserves ready for going out on operations. There were no fuel stations between Gedaref and Port Sudan and the team had to have enough for the long drive there and back. Yola would start collecting barrels of fuel weeks in advance, so as not to arouse suspicion as to why they needed so many at once. There was also now regular provision of drinking water. Every few days, one of the staff would drive the one working tanker to the Khor Arbaat basin in the Red Sea Hills, and fill up with potable water (the tanker took a battering, overturning at least twice and losing its windscreen, but it kept going). The team had actually found a desalination system, still in its crates from the era of the Italians, but its parts had decayed and it was inoperable. On close inspection, they discovered, bizarrely, Hebrew lettering on the equipment, meaning the apparatus had been made in Israel. According to Abu Medina, it was gifted to Sudan by Kuwait. Whoever had tried to conceal its provenance had not done a very good job.

In between operations, there were only two members of the team permanently at the village (later on, at busy times extra Mossad agents who were not specifically part of the mission would be drafted in to help out). When Yola arrived, it was just she and Rubi for four months. In the run-up to an operation, Dani's team would start trickling in, one after the other. London-born Halevy, the head of the division, himself went twice, posing as Navco's bookkeeper. After an operation, the agents would depart, with just the resort's manageress and a diving instructor staying on.

After getting the kitchen running, Yola started on the bedrooms, clearing them out and cleaning them up. The rooms on the north side of the main building and a few on the south were reserved for guests. The others were set aside for Mossad agents and for storing diving gear and secret equipment, including the two modified air cylinders. The store room was out of bounds except for the management.

By the winter of 1982, refurbishments were finished and the village was properly ready for business (it ended up costing nearer $100,000 than the estimated $1.1 million that Noam had calculated).[1] So far it had been catering for small numbers of local guests, but to keep the Tourism Corporation happy, the resort had to begin attracting foreign tourists and diving enthusiasts. It was time to start publicising, in a low-key way, the holiday village run by secret agents.

One of the travel agencies which had sent divers to resorts in the Sinai was Irene Reisen, a small, Israeli-owned company in Zurich, specialising in diving holidays. Rubi knew the director, 'ZL', and contacted him. He told ZL he had relocated and was 'doing something for Israel' but without mentioning the Mossad.

'Only I'm not Rubi,' he told him, 'I'm now called James.' He told him about Arous, and asked him to sell it as a sub-lime holiday experience for scuba divers and adventure-seeking travellers.

ZL contacted Michael Neumann, a local biology student and diver, who he would sometimes pay to scout out new des-tinations, and asked him to go and check out Arous.

The idea appealed to Neumann, so, in November 1982, he and a friend – a sales manager at Euro Divers, a Zurich-based company specialising in diving holidays in the Maldives – went down to Port Sudan. From there they got a lift on the back of a truck and travelled up to Arous (Neumann had to first obtain a new passport, because his current one had Israeli stamps, which would have barred him from Sudan). Once there, Neumann says, he sensed there was more to the place than met the eye.

'There was this village with a central building and all these bungalows and nothing around it at all, on this bay,' he recalls. 'There were two people working there – a woman and a guy. They said they were European but their accents made me not so sure.

'There was this big open-plan restaurant and we would have our meals there. The man and the woman would be sitting in one corner and we would be assigned a table in a completely different corner and we were the only four people there. I thought that was a little unusual, for the staff of a diving resort to do that, especially with people who had come to check out the place in order to then bring tourists.

'They kept themselves to themselves, but then of course we were diving together every day and after a while we started sit-ting together, and went out in the Zodiac; and then things were a little strange because the guy would take off at dusk in the Zodiac and he would come back at night completely shattered.'

Neumann had taken publicity shots at Arous and they were used in a glossy advertisement which the Mossad produced by the thousands, distributing them in travel agents and dive stores across Europe.

'Arous. A wonderful world apart,' read the headline set against an azure sky above a turquoise sea. Underneath, an idyllic scene of whitewashed chalets on a sun-drenched beach. The poster was illustrated with exotic scenes, including a blonde, tanned bikini-clad woman, diving cylinder on her back, a pair of blue-cheek butterfly fish, a scuttling ghost crab and a Sudanese man and woman smiling warmly (it was Abu Medina and Noora, the head chambermaid). It also showed, from behind, the figure of a man in blue trunks and a dark top walking across the sand. The man was Rubi, who intentionally got himself into shot as a stunt for his amusement.

The advertisement alluringly promised 'adventure à la carte'.

'Rarely has nature been so generous or so varied,' it said. 'Exotic fish of many kinds swim by, their brilliant hues enhanced by the exceptional clarity of the water. Here, too, are turtles, mantas, bottle-nosed dolphins, graceful sailfish and, in the depths, various species of sharks.

'Cormorants, cranes, flamingos, ospreys and pelicans wing their way through the unpolluted air. At night, after the landscape colours have paled, there are breathtaking views of the heavens, aflame with millions of stars.

'At the end of an active day, relax in the friendly atmosphere of the games room. Have a refreshing drink, a game of darts and then an excellent meal in the Arous restaurant, where fresh fish is served daily.'

The resort was, it said, 'unique in all the world' – a claim which in this case was without doubt true.

The advertisement provided information on how to get there, including flights from nine countries in Europe, as well as from Jeddah and Khartoum. It advised that visas were required for overseas visitors, which, it said, could be arranged by 'the Sudan Tourism Corporation, or Navco Aviation Co'. It gave the address of Navco as Rue des Alpes, Geneva.

Dani and Salah Madaneh, the head of the Port Sudan tourist office, drew up a price list, based on the tariffs from the time of the Italians. Rates began at US$65 per night for a single occupancy, half-board, to $120 per night for a double room, full-board. There was no charge for children under three years old. There were also prices for various water sports including windsurfing, water-skiing and boat trips (the sole windsurfing board came from a surf shop in Tel Aviv and had been smuggled into Sudan). Boat trips, the price list said, included the use of 'shuftascopes' – or, to use the proper name, hydroscopes – a glass-bottomed instrument for peering into the water. The word was a portmanteau invented by Abu Medina, based on the Arabic word *shuft* ('look').

It offered introductory diving lessons with diving equipment for hire, and day trips to Arbaat and Suakin, an ancient port famed for its Ottoman-era coral buildings, 65 kilometres south of Port Sudan. Navco marketed the resort, putting advertisements in *Tauchen* ('Diver') magazine in Switzerland and in *Sudanow*, a local monthly English-language magazine read by expatriates.

The uniqueness of the holiday village caught the attention of divers and independent travellers looking for something different. The first foreign bookings were made, and groups began to arrive, flying into Khartoum, then taking a connecting flight to Port Sudan. There they would be picked up by Ali the driver and taken on the long, bumpy ride to Arous.

Within weeks, the resort was almost sold out. A letter sent by the liaison office of the Sudanese Tourism Corporation to a planned large delegation of military attachés in Khartoum in December 1982 urges final confirmation as 'the village is nearly booked by tourists from Europe'. It shows the following provisional tally of attachés and their families with reservations for 27–31 December: France – up to eleven guests, six rooms; Britain – up to nine guests, four rooms; West Germany – at least four guests, one room; USSR – four guests, two rooms; Sudan – two guests, one room; US – two guests, one room; Ethiopia – one guest, one room; and an unidentified 'Colonel Tucker' – four guests, two rooms.

One of the most regular visitors to the resort was a French military attaché by the name of Christian de Saint-Julien. A veteran of the Algerian War, Saint-Julien would come with his wife and child for holidays. He was well-liked by the Israelis, but never knew who they really were. He would sit and talk with them about things going on outside, with the agents playing naive. They would ask him questions that would sometimes yield intelligence, including, according to one of the operatives, 'military secrets', without elaborating. They made sure he was looked after and always came back.

Diplomats from the highest level came to stay at Arous. They included the US Ambassador to Sudan, Constantine William Kontos and his wife, Joan, and the US Ambassador to Egypt, Alfred Leroy Atherton Jr (a Middle East expert who had helped to negotiate the peace treaty between Israel and Egypt) and his wife, Betty. The Egyptian Ambassador, Ahmed Ezzat

Abdullatif, was also a guest, and would while away the hours chatting and playing backgammon with the diving instructors, unaware that they were Mossad. Abdullatif was not the first Egyptian to stay there. Once, before it had officially opened, a unit of Egyptian soldiers on a training exercise in the area were put up in the village for a couple of days, at the hospitality of Rubi and Gad, where they played football together and talked over cups of tea.

Once, on the last day of their holiday, three European ambassadors went fishing. The sun was beating down and it was unusually hot. Their flight to Khartoum was due to leave at 4pm that afternoon, but at midday the Tourism Corporation radioed the resort to say they had been informed that the Saudi pilot had decided to leave early. The ambassadors were out at sea with no means of communication. Flights from Port Sudan had never before left on time, let alone early, and sometimes did not even go at all, so to miss the flight would have left them stranded. A manageress jumped into one of the cars and drove at high-speed to the airport (in reality, it barely qualified as such, being little more than an airstrip with some benches). She ran onto the plane and grabbed the pilot.

'Listen, you have three ambassadors in Arous now,' she told him. 'If you leave without them, I'll make sure there'll be a diplomatic incident between their countries and Saudi Arabia, and I'll see to it that they know it's all your fault!'

The pilot was flustered but agreed to wait until four. Nobody got off the plane, and it stayed sitting there for hours, along with goats and sheep which were customarily transported in the cabin. The heat was stifling and the air conditioning switched off. The ambassadors arrived, on time, oblivious to the hold-up.

Apart from the diplomats, most of the guests were ordinary

tourists or Westerners working in Sudan, or, occasionally well-heeled Sudanese nationals. A handwritten register from the village shows visitors from Britain, Switzerland, Germany, the US, Spain, Sweden and France, with diverse jobs, including engineers, teachers and a 'dairyman'. Others came from locally based operations such USAID (the United States Agency for International Development), Mobil Oil and the British Red Cross. Among guests recorded as having stayed there were an Iraqi manager of the National Bank of Sudan and the 'Sudanese director of the president – office of the Council of Ministers' – both of whose countries were technically at war with Israel. Some of the handwritten entries are annotated with observations, including: 'lovely family', 'chatterbox', 'miser', and, somewhat intriguingly, 'CATASTROPHE!!!'.

American Emily Copeland was working as a local hire for the UNHCR when she went to stay at Arous. She had been near the border with Eritrea carrying out surveys of refugees suffering from malnutrition, when someone suggested a trip to the village.

'At the time, that was really the only place international staff could go that would be a vacation break within the country,' she says. 'So, a bunch of us went up to this dive resort for a few days of R&R.

'After you've been in the camps – and I'd been doing this for six months – it was the first place of its kind I had seen. The only other places where you could go and relax were like the Sudan Club [a British colonial-era institution in Khartoum], but you had to have an invite to get in.

'Arous was really beautiful. They had these lovely little vacation cabins and you'd go out on boats and go diving or snorkelling. The underwater scenery was just breathtaking.

'I remember the European staff all looked young and really healthy and fit, and at dinner time, people would say: "Why the heck [build a resort] here?" Of course, the answer was it was totally gorgeous and unspoilt, and people were saying: "Wow, I hope they can make a go of it."

'The interesting thing was,' she continued, 'nobody knew they were Israeli. If it was a front, it was a pretty good one, because they really provided a service. They seemed very legitimate.'

The holiday village was also a welcome place for overseas staff of companies mining for gold in the Red Sea Hills.

'It was our chance to escape every now and again,' recalls Briton Phil Newall, who worked for Robertson Research consultancy, which ran an operation in the Gebeit mine, about 90 kilometres north-west of Arous. Newall remembers Arous as a 'stunning place, with very impressive diving gear, and a bunch of well-toned guys'.

He and three colleagues visited at a time when there were no guests. 'It was very exciting but it just struck you, as soon as you went in this place, it was weird. It was all very tidy – everything looked really new and shiny. It was bizarre because there were so many people there to help you, but no one actually staying there.

'It was like "Yeah, come in, what do you want to do? Snorkelling? Sub-aqua?" Whatever we asked for they said "Fine. You can use this or that", and we just paid a few dollars.

'The thought in my mind at all times was: "How has this company managed to put all this infrastructure in place and there's nobody here at all? Who's paying for this?" But they were very friendly – it's as if they were just happy to have us there.'

Some guests were not who they seemed to be. On one occasion, three American visitors arrived and asked to stay for two weeks. The Mossad staff immediately suspected they were spies. 'I think if they came with a sign on their forehead saying "CIA", they couldn't have been more obvious,' one agent recalls. 'Even though they were all divers, there was something about their behaviour.' It is possible the CIA officers were sent to check out the resort which had sprung back to life on a barren stretch of coast. This created the strange situation of undercover US officers and Israeli agents trying to outfox each other with neither knowing for sure who the other was. If the Americans did put two and two together, they never let on.

One CIA officer who definitely did go there was one of the predecessors to Milton Bearden, the CIA station chief in Khartoum. Bearden himself stayed away, but his predecessor was part of the Mossad's emergency contact plan, so the Israelis knew him and he knew them. 'We mingled with the guests, but we pretended of course not to know him,' another of the undercover staff recalls. 'Of course, he knew what was going on, but he never gave a sign and we never gave a sign.'

However, there were at least two occasions when guests did uncover the truth – incidents which threatened to put the whole operation at stake. Both times, the guests were Jewish – which paradoxically, being more attuned to the idiosyncrasies of Israelis, carried more risk than non-Jewish guests.

The first time happened when an agent was with a group of guests on a dive. One of them, a Swiss man, noticed that the agent made a hand signal for 'Okay', used in the military instead of the more common 'thumbs up'. He asked the agent a question in Hebrew, and the agent inadvertently replied with the Hebrew word 'ken' – 'yes'. Alarmed at his slip-up, the agent tried to cover up.

'What did you say?' he asked.

'Look, I understand you're Israelis,' the man replied. 'But don't worry, I'm not going to say anything.'

The agent pretended to be puzzled, as if he did not know what the guest was getting at in the hope the man would doubt himself. But his verbal blunder rang like an alarm bell in his head and he hurriedly went to find Dani.

'I'm burned!' he told him, explaining what had happened.

'Right,' said Dani, thinking quickly. 'I'll sort it out.'

The guest was back in his room when there was a knock at the door. He opened up to find Dani there, looking serious.

'You were on a dive with one of the instructors,' Dani said, making a statement rather than asking.

'Yes,' replied the man.

'I understand you have questions,' Dani put it to him.

The man responded keenly. 'I know who you are,' he said. 'But don't worry, I won't say anything.'

'That's right,' said Dani, 'because I see you have requested a night-dive. Well I'm going to tell the diving instructor to take you to a special reef where there are sharks who *love* kosher meat.'

'No ... no ... I didn't ...', stuttered the man.

'Be careful what you say and who you say it to, because we have ears everywhere,' Dani warned him, before leaving the room.

The man did not mention it again for the rest of his stay and the Israelis heard nothing more afterwards.

On another occasion, they were compromised by a guest who happened to be an activist from the Canadian Association for Ethiopian Jews (CAEJ), a campaign group which had pub-licly assailed Israel for, from its perspective, letting the Jewish refugees rot in the camps. The CAEJ, like its American coun-terpart the AAEJ, did not know about the Mossad's secret operations, which the Mossad considered their public agitations were putting at risk.

The activist, 'Alex', had been working at a clinic in Wad el-Heluw, a camp north-east of Gedaref, close to the Ethiopian border. He was an amateur diver and a colleague suggested they both go on an expedition to Arous.

Alex says he had heard unconfirmed reports that Israelis were operating secretly in the camps in Eastern Sudan, and often wondered whether they were among the white aid workers he came across in the field.

He says he checked into Arous for a long weekend and his suspicions drew him to conclude that the white staff were undercover Israelis.

'From that point on, I basically tried to – without revealing their identity or anything – tell them about the situation in the camps, how despondent the refugees had become and how food and water were a major problem, in the hope that they would do the social thing and ask a few questions about it, but in fact they did exactly the opposite. As soon as I said something they'd switch the conversation to something else. I thought maybe they'd come and approach me more privately, but that wasn't happening.'

One of the agents confirms they realised this guest had discovered what was going on and were trying to avoid him.

'It was obvious that he knew,' the agent says. 'He came to the village and everything fell into place ... for him it was a "Eureka!" moment.'

Frustrated, Alex confronted the agent, who was acting as an instructor on a dive trip.

'I said to him: "Tell me what the fuck are you guys doing here?" He looked at me, obviously surprised by my question and language. So I added in Hebrew: "*Tagidli ma atem osim poh?*" ("Tell me what you're doing here.") His knees buckled and he basically fell down onto the edge of the boat.'

The agent corroborated Alex's account of the exchange.

'I had very few options about what to do. One was to deny and then to take the risk that he won't buy it and he will go to his friends. So I chose – in my opinion the right choice,' he says, without elaborating.

The Mossad pressed Alex not to go public about what happened and it did not come out.

Circumstantial evidence that Israelis were running the resort could perhaps be explained away, but actually being recognised was more difficult. This was a particular risk in the case of Rubi, who had dived with thousands of people during the seven years he worked at places up and down the coast of Sinai. On more than one occasion, ZL would send to Arous tourists whom he had also previously sent to resorts where Rubi was an instructor. One group arrived and said 'hi' to Rubi straight away, remembering having met him before.

'Guys, I know you know me, but here I'm not Rubi, I'm James,' he told them, without explaining. 'Just call me James from now on, and I'll make sure you have a good time.'

On another occasion, a guest from Sweden told Rubi he remembered him from when he taught his brother how to dive in Neviot in 1976.

'No, you're mistaken,' Rubi told him.

All Rubi could do was flatly deny it and move the conversation on.

12

DELIVERANCE FROM ABOVE

The Ethiopian Jews were never smuggled out through the village itself. The closest they came was on the night of the first naval operation, when the agents were forced to move the evacuation point from Marsa Awatir to Marsa Arous, but that was before the resort was open to guests. After that, they had carried out five more rounds of evacuations from Marsa Fijab, about four kilometres north of the resort, up until the ambush on the beach. That incident had caused the Mossad to call a halt to maritime operations and to rethink tactics. Refugees were continuing to be secretly brought out through Khartoum airport under the auspices of the ICM, but on its own this was insufficient so the Mossad needed to find another way. With naval action frozen, only one option remained: airlift.

At a meeting with Dani and Halevy in early 1982, Hofi informed them that he had spoken to Major General David Ivry, the head of the Israeli Air Force, and that it was Ivry's opinion that the IAF could bring more Jews out, and more speedily, than the Navy.[1] It would be difficult and dangerous but, in principle, possible if C-130 Hercules transport aircraft were deployed. Hercules had flown more than twice the distance from Israel to Port Sudan when they were used to rescue the Jewish hostages in Entebbe, Uganda, some six years earlier. As with that operation, if they were used in Sudan they would be landing in the dark, in hostile territory, collecting civilians and swiftly taking off again. At Entebbe, though, the Air Force knew they would be landing on a proper asphalt airstrip at an international airport; in Sudan, they had nowhere to land but desert.

There were many considerations to take into account – foremost, the need for the ground to withstand up to about 70 tonnes of aircraft weight. If a C-130 got stuck, the consequences would be disastrous. The Air Force had no satellite maps of Eastern Sudan and those they could obtain from their US ally were usually censored. The commander of C-130 Squadron 131, Lieutenant Colonel Asaf Agmon, who had co-piloted the first flight of Ethiopian Jews from Addis Ababa in 1977, hit on an idea. On a routine mission to an airbase north of Washington, DC, Agmon approached the operation branch commander. He told him he collected old aerial maps for a hobby and asked the commander if he could let him have any unclassified maps of the Middle East or North Africa. The commander obliged and gave him a set. Two of the maps were of Sudan, one of which showed a symbol of a runway, about 50 kilometres from the coast and less than an hour's drive from Nakeb al-Yahud, the valley where Dani's team would hide with the Jews during daylight hours on their way to the cove. It was not possible to tell if the site still existed, or whether there were military installations in the area, so the Air Force sent a Hercules fitted with a FLIR thermal imaging system on a secret night flight to take photographs.[2] The results showed it was still there and possibly made of concrete. The site was identified as Carthago, a landing strip built by the British during the Second World War for bombing raids against Mussolini's forces in Fascist-occupied Ethiopia. The Air Force informed Mossad HQ, which passed the information to Dani with instructions to go and check it out. If the Air Force's suspicions were confirmed, it would provide somewhere proper for them to land, avoiding the need to penetrate deep into Sudan, which would have increased the risk exponentially.

Dani and Louis drove down to the site, situated on the western flank of the Red Sea Hills, in the desert east of the small town of Sinkat. They found the landing strip (made from gravel, not concrete, but which also suited big planes) and a fairly recent-looking windsock, indicating it was still functioning. Asking around, they learned that Nimeiri himself flew in there from time to time, bringing wealthy friends from the Gulf to his nearby lodge for hunting trips in the hills. What the Air Force was planning to use was none other than the president's runway.

The two men returned to the village and Dani headed back to Israel to brief headquarters and the Air Force.

Even though it was a real airstrip, Air Force planners wanted to check it first-hand. In an operation codenamed Bat Shir (Daughter of Song), they sent three CH-53 transport helicopters carrying a team of runway engineers to test the ground, specialists to intercept Sudanese communications while they were there, and the reconnaissance unit from the Paratroopers Brigade to defend against attack.[3] Dani flew with them. They took off from Tel Nof, stopping at Ofir Air Force base near Sharm el-Sheikh (marking one of Israel's last operations from there) for an initial refuelling. One of the helicopters had developed engine trouble so was grounded, and a decision was made to continue with just the other two. It was still light when they took off again, flying low to avoid detection, at times just fifteen metres above the clear blue water, the sea like a gigantic aquarium with schools of tropical fish shoaling below. The flight time was about eight hours, which meant they had to refuel in mid-air (twice in each direction) – one of the most dangerous and complex manoeuvres, even for highly experienced pilots. After it had gone dark, Hercules roared in overhead, slowing down to almost minimum possible air speed, while the helicopters accelerated to their maximum so that a hose from the aircraft could be guided into place to deliver the fuel.

The helicopters landed near Carthago, which had been cleared and marked with small battery-powered lights by Marcel and Jacques (who had gone back to Israel shortly after the ambush on the beach, but had since returned to Sudan in the guise of a Navco employee) on the ground. Dani and the crew walked to the site, where the engineers tested its firmness with penetrometers while the reconnaissance unit guarded the perimeter. The engineers certified that it could support the weight of a Hercules. Dani stayed and the helicopters and troops flew back to Israel, with the results reported to commanders.

IDF chiefs authorised the plan for an airlift and it was approved by Begin.

A top Mossad official directly involved in the decision to move to airlifts said in many ways it carried a greater risk than seaborne evacuations.

'When we brought in the ship [*Bat Galim*], it was less of a problem because it's anchored outside, but when we had the aircraft coming in, we had no way of giving early warning if the Sudanese were around, except for […] having a small group of armed people who came on the aircraft, who protected the perimeter when the operation was actually being carried out – but if the Sudanese had come in force, there's nothing we could do.'[4]

Unlike the naval evacuations, where the *Bat Galim* would wait at sea for the agents to arrive at the cove, with the air operation the timing was determined by the Air Force. The Mossad team knew what time the Hercules would set off from Israel, and had to make sure they were in position, at Carthago, with the Ethiopian Jews, by the time it landed. Every second of the plane being on the ground was a chance of being spotted and attacked. The Air Force calculated that from touchdown to take-off, the loading of the Jews could be completed within fifteen minutes.

The first C-130 took off after nightfall from Air Force Base 27 at Ben Gurion airport on 13 May 1982. It was piloted by Lieutenant Colonel Natan Dvir, who had flown one of the Hercules aircraft in the raid on Entebbe six years earlier. Dvir flew the entire four-hour flight to Sudan with the lights off – low over the Red Sea, then up and over the rugged chain of the hills, descending close to the slopes which led down to Carthago. Also on board were two co-pilots, two flight engineers, three navigators and about twenty commandos whose job it was to secure the area.

Some 30 hours earlier, Dani and his men had left the village in convoy. There was a new addition to the team – an agent named Gil, a Moroccan-born Israeli with a cool mind under pressure and a wizard with anything mechanical or electrical. He was also masterful at adopting personas and as part of his cover passed himself off convincingly as French.

The Israelis got to the quarry outside Gedaref and quietly collected 172 Jews. Through night, day, and night again, passing some dozen checkpoints, they brought them to the area of the landing strip. After offloading the passengers, one of the pickups was repositioned nearer the runway, pointing towards it with its headlights left on (its cabin empty) in order to provide illumination for the aircraft when it came in to land in the dark. The only other light came from four of the small battery-powered torches – two marking the beginning of the landing strip and two marking the end, 1,200 metres apart (the minimum length for a Hercules to land) – which agents had earlier set up.

The team explained to the Jews, most of whom had barely travelled before, and then by nothing more than donkey, about what to expect – the plane, the noise, the dust – to try to prevent them from panicking. Minutes later, they watched, terrified, as the Hercules came out of the sky, and thundered onto the runway – 'a very, very difficult landing', Dvir recalls, 'but as planned'. It slowed to a near-halt and taxied around to face the way it had come.

The rear of the plane opened and the soldiers dashed out, holding green stick lights and spreading out in the shape of a funnel to channel the Jews into the plane and away from the engines. Dani's men led the evacuees into the aircraft and sat them down on the floor. One of the Ethiopians would later recall the experience as being like that of 'Jonah the prophet going into the belly of the whale'. With everyone accounted for, the soldiers returned to the plane and passed out some crates to the agents. Dani had also fetched objects from his truck and handed them to the commandos.

'And here, my friends, these are for you!'

It was a cluster of swords, bought from a swordsmith in the market in Kassala as souvenirs for the soldiers and crew. (Gifting swords in this way became a routine with future airlifts in this operation. Rubi and Dani would buy several of the hand-crafted weapons at a time, telling the delighted merchant they were selling them on in Europe.)

The two teams wished each other luck, then the loading ramp and door closed and the engines revved. On schedule, the aircraft accelerated and took off again, soaring back out towards the Sudanese coast.

The team loaded the crates into their vehicles, left the area and drove 175 kilometres northwards to Arous. When they got there they unpacked the cargo. Inside were about three dozen air conditioning units for the resort. The appliances were manufactured in Israel by Amcor, an established brand, but the nameplates had been removed and replaced with those of Luxair, a fake name invented by the Mossad.

The first aerial operation was a success, and it was decided to repeat the procedure while still within the phase of the new moon. Just six days later, a second airlift (which evacuated 184 Jews) piloted this time by Agmon, was carried out at Carthago in the same way, without any incident, and a plan was approved for a third. The team was already on its way to Gedaref when a coded radio message came through from Mossad HQ. It was a one-word order: abort. There was no other information and the team did not know why. While some orders could be disputed, 'abort' was categorical, so Dani and the team called off the operation and returned to Arous (the refugees they would have picked up were none the wiser – a benefit of Dani's policy of not telling them until the last moment that they were leaving – and were taken out in a subsequent operation). The agents learnt that personnel in a listening unit belonging to Israeli Army intelligence had intercepted a message between the secret police in Port Sudan and their headquarters in Khartoum. It said two big planes had been seen coming into Carthago and that security forces were going to carry out an ambush there. There was no mention of Jews and they probably thought it was a sophisticated smuggling operation. According to an unconfirmed report, a Bedouin had seen the planes and told the authorities. The report says investigators came to check Carthago and found discarded cans of Lipton Ice Tea, proof of human activity. Had they tried to trace their source, they would have found an ample stock at the diving village in Arous, but as Lipton tea was sold in most of the other hotels as well, nobody came to ask.

As a result, the military and the Mossad froze the airlifts after just two rounds. Thousands of Jews were still in the camps, and while Carthago had opened the way to evacuating nearly 200 at a time (the official capacity of a C-130 was actually 91 people), the sole remaining exit, via the ICM out of Khartoum, could manage far fewer.

However, with the typical unpredictability of the Middle East, it was an event on a street thousands of miles away which was about to derail operations on the coast. On 3 June 1982 Palestinian gunmen shot Israeli ambassador to Great Britain Shlomo Argov as he left a hotel in London. The attempted assassination triggered Israel's invasion of Lebanon three days later, aimed at driving out Palestine Liberation Organisation (PLO) guerrillas, who for years had been using it as a base from which to attack the Jewish state. For the fifth time in its short history, Israel was at war.

The team learnt about it on a TV in Arous when they saw pictures on a Saudi channel of Israeli tanks rumbling up the coast towards the Lebanese city of Tyre. Two things were immediately clear: first, a major conflict was unfolding, and second, it meant that for now the military was not going to divert resources to Sudan. The IAF was preoccupied with attacking targets day and night (just days after the start, nearly 100 Israeli fighter planes were deployed in one of the biggest aerial battles since the Second World War), and for the Air Force, Operation Brothers was suspended.[5]

Dani decided to keep Rubi and Gad at the village and instructed the rest of the team to return to Israel. He was the first to go, grabbing the resort's driver, Ali, and taking the wheel himself to drive high-speed to the airfield in Port Sudan. A plane was already taxiing to take off, so Dani got the director of the airfield, whom he knew well, to flag it down and let him on, even without a ticket. He got to Khartoum, then flew indirectly back to Israel, and headed to his cottage in the middle of an avocado orchard, north-east of Tel Aviv. He was there only as long as it took him to collect his gear, before heading up north on his motorbike to Kibbutz HaGoshrim, situated on the edge of the border with Lebanon (the bike had been bought a few years earlier from a UN officer on the Lebanese side of the border and still bore its UN licence plates). Out of the kibbutz restaurant window, a man watched as Dani pulled up in the car park. The man left the building and walked outside, approaching Dani as he dismounted.

'Dani?' the man asked, with a tone of familiarity.

Dani turned around and, seeing the man, smiled broadly.

'Yossi!' he said. 'Hey, good to see you!', reaching out and shaking his hand.

The man was Yossi Ben-Arieh, also from the Mossad but at that time doing reserve duty as a spokesperson in the Army. (He would later work as Mossad's liaison with Sudanese Vice President Omar el-Tayeb in Khartoum during the secret Operation Moses airlift.)

'What are you doing here?' asked Ben-Arieh. 'I heard you were in Sudan!'

'Yes, but I've come back because of the war,' Dani replied. 'I'm on my way to join my unit right now. But listen – this bike, it's unique – the only one in Israel – Kawasaki, you can't get them because of the [Arab] boycott. If I don't come back, take it – it's yours!'

Dani crossed the border and with transportation organised by his Mossad colleague at the kibbutz, headed 50 kilometres west to join the reserve Paratroopers Brigade in Tyre.

Within a day he was fighting in a battle against the Syrians. Dani spent a month in the war before being released. He returned to Israel and, not having not told his family he was there, turned up as a surprise to see his daughters. It was a rare opportunity where he could just be a father again. After the intensity of war, and the pressure of the mission in Sudan, he took advantage of a brief period 'off' to decompress and get out of the Middle East altogether, taking his girls on an impromptu two-week holiday to the South of France.

By late summer, the main fighting in Lebanon was over – a ceasefire between Israel and Syria was holding and the PLO had agreed to pull its thousands of fighters out of the country. In light of the developments, the Mossad, with the Navy's approval, decided to resume Operation Brothers, and evacuations by sea.

Dani and the others returned to Sudan, and in November, the *Bat Galim*, with Buchris in command, was called back into service. It sailed from Haifa incognito back down the Suez Canal, then up the Gulf of Aqaba to Eilat to refuel. The port was 100 nautical miles north of its previous base at Sharm el-Sheikh, which added a day's sailing time. It took the *Bat Galim* three days to get to its destination, where it anchored several kilometres out at sea north of Port Sudan.

Dani's team (which now included a new member, Micki, whose dual experience as a doctor and as an officer in an elite reconnaissance unit demonstrated an ability for level-headedness in complicated situations) went to collect evacuees. There were 135 Jews to be transported, but the truck suffered a mechanical failure when they got on board in the quarry. It was a stormy night with rain lashing down and the agents could not get the truck moving. Gil took a few tools, lay on his back beneath the vehicle and started banging and clanking away, submerged up to his face in mud. However, after a valiant attempt he resurfaced, conceding defeat. The crippled truck meant they had a crisis. They were going to have to leave it there – clear evidence for security forces to find – but it also meant they would not be able to take all the Jews. Dani had no choice but to send 100 back to the camp, triggering scenes of pandemonium as the team had to stop everyone desperately trying to clamber onto the single working truck. He ordered the younger leaders, the Berare, to quickly escort the stranded Jews back to where they had just come from, resulting in families getting split up between those who went and those who had to stay behind.

Then he turned to Pomeranz.

'Shlomo,' he said urgently, 'you're going to have to go to Khartoum immediately! Get to Ramian and tell him about the truck, tell him exactly where it is so he can send his son to pick it up. And then – you leave the country!'

Shlomo gave a nod of understanding.

'Go to the road and thumb a lift, but whatever happens, get there as fast as you can!' said Dani.

As Shlomo set off on foot, the vehicle with its traumatised passengers started up and headed out of the quarry, leaving the stricken truck where it was.

The following day, Shlomo was already waiting at the Blue Nile Automobil premises on Gamhouria Street in Khartoum when Ramian arrived to open up. He knew Shlomo through Dani – they were two of his best customers. Shlomo told him the truck had broken down and that he needed to send his son urgently to tow it back. 'One other thing,' he said. 'If the police come asking questions, please don't say anything about us, or our business will be ended.'

Ramian told his son, who went with a tow-truck to the quarry on the edge of Gedaref, but when he got there, the truck was gone. The police had got there first and taken it to their compound. During the turmoil of the previous night, refugees had dropped clothing and other belongings at the scene – clues perhaps to the mysterious disappearances of Jews from the camp. The police traced the vehicle to Ramian's rental company and went to pay him a visit. They wanted to know who had been driving the truck. Ramian gave them a false story, telling them it had been one of his employees, who had just left and gone back home to south Sudan. Whatever he told them, he did not say anything about Shlomo or Dani, and they left it at that. Shlomo, who was coming to the end of his assigned period with the operation anyway, left Sudan and returned to his job at Hadassah hospital.

Over the next 24 hours, travelling only in darkness, the team transported their remaining 35 Jewish passengers to the beach. With the waves crashing onto the sand, the Zodiacs came in and loaded up with the Jews, but they could not sail back to the *Bat Galim* because of the treacherous conditions. The Shayetet commander radioed Buchris to say the ship would have to come to them. For the *Bat Galim* it was a hazardous manoeuvre because at 500 tonnes there was a risk it would run aground. It depended on how deep the cove was. The frogmen from the missile boats had previously mapped the area – but what had been written down as the depth was illegible. Buchris had to take a chance. He crossed the outer reef, sailing precariously close to the shore while being buffeted by gale-force winds, and ordered the crew to drop anchor. At 150 metres long, the chain unwound, and kept going, descending into the abyss without reaching the seabed. Fearing the anchor would get caught on corals, Buchris instructed the Zodiacs to sail out to his position. From there, he would use the ship to shield them from the wind until they got further out to sea. So the Zodiacs, with their petrified and drenched passengers, made their storm-tossed way to the *Bat Galim*. The crew tried to weigh anchor but it would not retract. Something was wrong with the pulley. By now it was 5am and the light was coming up. The smugglers' boats were already on the water and the Zodiacs and the *Bat Galim* were exposed.

There was no choice. The *Bat Galim* had to leave, and with the Zodiacs sheltering alongside the towering ship, it headed back out to sea, its anchor trailing as it went. If it snagged, the ship would be marooned – an Israeli vessel, troops on board, smuggling black people, in Sudanese waters – a nightmare scenario. It continued to make its way cautiously, further and further from the coast. At a safe distance, the crew started winching the Zodiacs up with a crane, one by one, a process which took five hours. After the last boat was in the hold, they connected the end of the crane to the anchor chain and managed to lift it up. With less of a burden of weight to hoist, the pulley started working again. The anchor was finally retracted and the *Bat Galim* sailed on, making its way back to Eilat.

Between November 1982 and April 1983, the ship made four more trips as part of Operation Brothers.[6] However, the number of Jews it transported was far fewer compared to the first evacuations a year earlier. With security forces now aware that refugees, specifically Jewish ones, were disappearing from the camps, it was now much more difficult for the Berare to smuggle them out. Non-Jewish refugees informed on the Jews, whom they could identify from certain practices. One of the clearest signs was at sunset on Friday, when Jewish families would extinguish their campfires so as not to transgress the Sabbath, when fire was forbidden, according to their beliefs. Once when Dani slipped into a camp undercover to personally warn the Kessim that this practice was endangering their lives, they respectfully thanked him but said that it was precisely because they observed the laws of the Sabbath that Ethiopian Jewry had survived for so long, under the protection of God.

By the end of its last mission, the *Bat Galim* had carried out eight operations in all, ferrying a total of 1,082 Jews to safety and a new future in Israel.

By early 1983, there had been no airlifts since the outbreak of the Lebanon war nearly a year earlier and Dani was anxious to get them under way again. Resuming operations from Carthago was out of the question, so he suggested using the desert itself, an idea backed by Agmon. Air Force planners were resistant though, arguing that a C-130 needed a proper runway, or approved ground where it could land.

Dani heard that there was a new appointee in the Operations Department at Air Force HQ, Major Ika Brant, and he paid him a visit. Dani told Brant there was an unspecified operation in Sudan which needed the help of the Air Force, but had been told it was not possible. Brant was fresh to the job and eager.

'There's nothing we can't do,' he told him. 'We can do everything.'

'But there's no runway,' replied Dani. 'It's just desert.'

'Don't worry,' said Brant. 'We'll manage.'

'Near Gedaref? That's 500 kilometres inland.'

'No problem! We can do that,' replied Brant confidently, although at that moment he did not know if or how it could actually be done.

Brant brought the issue to the head of Operations, Colonel Aviem Sela, who examined it. Normally, finding and preparing untested landing sites in hostile territory, such as in the Lebanon war, was a specialised job carried out by a particular unit of the Air Force, but it was not feasible to send them to Sudan. Dani's team, on the other hand, knew the terrain. Sela decided they could be entrusted to do it instead and gave the plan the green light.

Sending huge planes deep inside an enemy country in the Arab world required finding a place to land out of sight. It had to be far enough away from military bases, human settlement and roads, and to be on relatively flat ground. It also had to be within the fuel range of the aircraft. The planners studied maps and identified an area about 100 kilometres from the pick-up point outside Gedaref. Dani and his men regrouped in Israel and began a period of intense training with C-130 squadrons. It was top secret. Within the two squadrons (103 and 131) themselves, only the crews picked for the operations knew about it, and even then some of them did not know it was for airlifting Ethiopian Jews. They practised at night-time in the Negev, conducting the exercises as close to the real thing as possible. The Mossad agents scoured the desert for areas of at least 1,200 metres of clear, hard ground, checking them for firmness. Where it was considered okay, they set up two parallel rows of battery-powered lights and called in the Hercules. The plane – lights off – flew in, and the pilot, using night-vision goggles, picked up the airstrip and made a landing in the near pitch-black. The drill was repeated over and over again, night after night.

The air crews planned as much as they could for things going wrong. At all cost, they had to avoid getting stranded. In case of a puncture, the planes were equipped with a spare tyre and a disc-cutter – if the tyre could not be replaced, they were prepared to cut off the struts and take off on one set of wheels – something that had not been attempted before. They practised what to do if the plane was crippled – one scenario involved blowing it up with explosives and getting picked up by another aircraft. Another was deserting a stricken craft and having to walk to the Egyptian border, all the while evading capture by Sudanese troops – simulated by an Israeli Army unit which was sent in pursuit of the crew as part of the exercise.

At the end of spring, the team returned to Sudan. They went into the desert and, working within the coordinates provided by the Air Force, set about identifying areas of the right length and width which could serve as a landing strip. It was a slow process, having to penetrate every part of the ground to check its density, and with the additional danger that it had to be done in daylight, since any miscalculation risked putting the plane in jeopardy. When they notified HQ that they had marked out a place, the Air Force sent a pilot to check it. Originally from Argentina, the pilot had the appearance and language of a South American, giving the Sudanese no cause to suspect he was

Israeli. He flew in on a commercial flight, with a false passport and a cover story as a representative of Navco. The pilot okayed the landing site, stayed in Khartoum for some days under the protection of the Mossad, then returned to Israel.

Although the location was remote, Dani's team had spotted a tank brigade base about 25 kilometres from there. They had it under surveillance and knew its routines, as well as how many of the tanks were operational or out of action. They calculated that in the event of a tank being sent from the base, it would take it about two hours to reach the area, by which time, barring any mechanical failure, the planes would be long gone. They had also gathered information about the Sudanese Air Force, such as what type of planes it had and how many, and passed it to the intelligence division of the Israeli Air Force.

There was one more thing. There were two big radar dishes at Flamingo Bay, and although agents had reported that they did not appear to be working, HQ was not comfortable about this and wanted verification. The only way was for someone to get into the facility for a close-up look. Yola decided it would be more disarming if it was a woman – plus the fact that she had been warned by a senior figure in the division not to drive alone in the desert as a female gave her the determination to prove him wrong. Without letting anyone know, she set off by herself and drove to the base. She pulled up at the north gate, where a soldier came to see what she wanted. He did not speak English, so called his commander, who did. Yola explained she was 'just a simple woman who had lost her way trying to get to Port Sudan'. The commander appeared to take kindly to her and offered to help. He climbed into the car to show her where to go, telling her to drive through the camp from north to south. As they passed by the radars, Yola saw they were rusted and not functioning. They got to the south gate, where the commander pointed her in the direction of Port Sudan and got out of the car. Yola thanked him, drove out of the base then turned round, went back to the village and passed the information to HQ.

13

PANIC IN THE DESERT

On 10 June 1983 – thirteen months after the near-miss at Carthago – airlifts were started up again. A C-130 took off from Air Base 27, shadowed by a command-and-control Boeing 707 which would stay airborne for the operation. After a four-hour flight south, the C-130 crossed over the coast of Sudan, only this time it was going to be far more difficult than before. Whereas Carthago was mapped and identifiable, here the pilot had to find a pin-prick of a makeshift landing spot in the dark, with only the manual skill of flight navigators to get him there. The on-board Doppler navigation system was prone to drifting and as good as useless, while the only maps and satellite photos they had were old and outdated.

That morning, Dani and his team had left the village under a pretext and headed off into the desert to locate and prepare the landing site in the area approved by the Argentinean pilot. They had to make sure that they could find the same spot again at night-time without delay. To do so, they made a marker out of the bones of dead animals and some stones, and measured the exact distance from there back to the main road using the vehicle's odometer and a compass to read its positioning.

However, on the night of the first desert airlift, all did not go according to plan, and the consequence was mayhem.

Dani's team got to the collection point at the quarry near one of the camps but the Jews arrived late. The Berare explained that they had been too afraid to leave because of heightened police presence in the area. The C-130 was already on its way and the delay cost the agents valuable time. They quickly set off with 166 passengers and headed to the landing strip. Dani was in the lead vehicle and turned off the Gedaref-Kassala road at what he believed was the right place. The convoy drove in the right direction and for the exact distance but when it stopped there was no pile of bones. The plane was minutes away, but the trucks with the Jews were in the wrong place. Dani instructed his men to wait and sped back to the road by himself. He radioed the Hercules pilot and command-and-control to inform them he was running late.

'What? Why?' came the harried response from a general on board.

Dani did not want to try to explain.

'I can't hear … I can't hear …' he answered, pretending he was losing reception, and switched the communication off, leaving only the channel to the pilot open. Hitting the road, Dani raced up and down until he found where he should have turned off, just 100 metres away. He sped back to where he had left the group, while speaking to the pilot.

'When are you landing?' he asked urgently.

'Five minutes,' came the reply.

It was not going to be long enough to get back, move everyone to the right place and set up the battery-powered lights for the pilot to see where to land.

'I don't … if it's five minutes …' continued Dani, 'five minutes does not give me enough time! The lights… there are no lights!'

'Right – go to the beginning of the strip, stop your vehicle and point your headlights towards the runway. I'll land over you,' replied the pilot.

Dani raced to the strip, skidded to a halt and flicked on his lights. He did not have the chance to get out of the cabin and to a safe place. Within seconds the Hercules blasted overhead, just a couple of dozen metres above him, the turbulence from the propellers shaking the vehicle like a hurricane.

Dani jumped out and ran to get the group and lead them to the plane. However, because of the mishap the team had not had time to explain to the evacuees what was about to happen. The Jews had climbed down from the vehicles and had been standing in a huddle in the eerie silence of the desert, when the gigantic aircraft had descended out of the night sky with a deafening noise, landing in blinding clouds of dust. In the words of one of the agents, 'to the refugees, it was as if the Devil himself was coming'. With its engines still roaring, the aircraft opened up its rear cargo door and let down its ramp, as commandos appeared and fanned out with the green stick lights. They had just minutes to spare, but the refugees were so terrified of the 'monster with green teeth', as another agent put it, that they turned and ran, scattering into the darkness. There was a frantic scramble to get them back, involving everyone down to and including the captain and co-pilot. As they found them, hiding behind rocks and in bushes, they took them to the plane and put them inside. 'They were so light in weight,' recalls one of the agents, 'that they were being blown away by the wind of the engines and had to hold on to each other.' It took 45 minutes in all, until they were sure they had retrieved everyone. The cargo door and ramp closed and the plane took off, disappearing back into the night sky. As the roar faded, quiet and stillness returned to the desert. Dani and his team brushed away the aeroplane's tracks with branches. They were about to leave when all of a sudden they noticed an elderly woman standing there.

'*Lijoch!*' she said. '*Lijoch! Lijoch! Lijoch!*'

She was an Ethiopian Jew and she had not got on the plane. Tarzan, who had been brought in on the flight to join the team on the ground under the guise of a tourist at the village, understood Amharic.

'She is saying "the kids",' he said. 'She must be the grandmother of some of the children!'

The woman was alone – everyone she knew had gone.

The agents were in a quandary. They could not take her back to the refugee camp because if she told people there what had happened, word might get out and expose the whole operation to the secret police. Nor could they take her back to Arous – they could not hide her in the village, and in any event there were to be no more operations from the coast. The only option left was to take her to Khartoum and smuggle her out on a passport obtained through the ICM. There was a risk that they would be seen – and white men driving a black woman would immediately suggest she was being trafficked for slavery. They put her into one of the cars, concealed her behind a canvas curtain, and headed off on an impromptu trip 500 kilometres to the Hilton. It was daylight by the time they got there and pulled up in the car park. Dani fetched Uri and told him to take care of the woman, but they had to first get her into his car without being noticed. Uri got his vehicle and parked it next to theirs, and when the coast was clear they manoeuvred her out of one car and straight into the other, gently pushing her down to lie on the back seat.

'Straight away she sat back up – sitting there bolt upright, looking like Queen Victoria!' recalls Tarzan. They tried again to get her to lie down, but she sat straight back up, with a look of indignation on her face. On the third attempt she complied. With the woman out of sight, Uri took her in his car to a safe house and organised a passport and exit papers for her. Within days she was flown out to Europe and on to Israel.

One of the Khartoum agents told the Committee what had happened and asked them to look out for anyone else who might have been left behind that night and made it back to the camp. Two weeks later, word came back that there was indeed another woman who had hidden in the desert. Unlike the older woman, she had not come forward, but had some-how managed to return by herself to Gedaref. It turned out she was the daughter of the elderly woman – meaning that her children had gone off into the unknown on the plane without their mother or grandmother. The agents told their colleagues in Khartoum to make sure the mother was put on the next flight. Stories of separation like this one abound. While the case of the two women was the only known instance of refu-gees left alone in the desert, the splitting up of families – be it between those who went to Sudan and those who stayed behind, or children being smuggled out of the camps ahead of their parents in order to save their lives – was one of the many traumas the Ethiopian Jews had to go through on their long and difficult odyssey.

For Dani's team, the transition to desert airstrips was a big advantage. The landing points were much nearer the camps, meaning instead of a gruelling day and night's drive, the trip from the pick-up point to the landing strip would take them less than two hours. It also spared them having to run the gauntlet of a dozen roadblocks between Gedaref and the coast – now they would only need to pass one. However, it meant having to find and prepare a different landing strip before every airlift. They never used the same site twice, because while the team brushed over the planes' tracks after each evacuation, sooner or later it would become clear there had been activity if the ground kept getting disturbed. On one occasion when the team was probing with a penetrometer (brought in aboard the Hercules on the first Carthago operation, and kept hidden in pieces) they were spotted by a Bedouin on a camel. He started shouting that it was his land and demanded to know what they were doing. Dani congratulated him and told him he was going to become very rich, because they worked for an oil company which had found a reservoir under the ground. The Bedouin was elated and left them to it.

In between operations, agents went back home and carried on with 'normal' life. None spoke about their activities. Their friends and family had no idea what they had been doing. The absences and the demands on Dani when he was home took a toll on his family and ultimately led to the breakdown of his marriage. From then on, every moment he had free he spent with his young daughters.

Rubi, meanwhile, got married – nearly all the team from Arous, as well as top Mossad figures from headquarters, came to his wedding at the Sharon Hotel in Herzliya. A senior official broke the news to Rubi's new wife that her husband would not be able to go on honeymoon straight away because he was needed for a mission. (Rubi's parents threw a wedding party at the kibbutz the next day, but Rubi had already left – prompting his wife's aunt to comment that she 'always knew he was a *tachshit*' (Yiddish for someone who behaves in a shameful way).)

Yola's parents never knew where she kept disappearing to. Once, after an absence of two months, which she explained away as a 'government job in Africa', her father said: 'It's okay, I know, you went with [then defence minister] Ariel Sharon to Zaire'. Marcel was rotated to headquarters to continue with Operation Brothers from there after his intensive and exhausting service, and was replaced in the field as Dani's deputy by 'Yuval', a former fighter pilot. Yuval's first operation in Sudan was, as it turned out, the *Bat Galim*'s last. Like the others, in the interim periods in Israel, he blended back into ordinary life, including enrolling in computer programming and systems analysis classes at the Israeli Institute of Technology in Tel Aviv. He would sit in front of another student, who noticed when he would come and go, and return with a tan. They were paired up on projects but she ended up doing most of the work because of his absences. This pattern had gone on for months when curiosity got the better of her.

'I sharpened a pencil to a very fine point and put it against his carotid artery,' the woman recalls. 'I told him: "I have no idea what you're doing, but whatever it is, I want to do that too!"' The woman, 'Chana', was an officer in the Navy and academically brilliant. She had a Master's degree in biochemistry and had served in the medical corps in the Army. She also happened to have grown up in Australia and was fluent in five languages. She was, on paper, an ideal candidate for the Sudan job. Yuval took her credentials and gave them to the recruitment office at the Mossad. Then she was called for an interview. Chana did not know it was the Mossad, or what the interview was for, but she was enthusiastic.

It was the start of a process that took ten months. Chana was put through a series of tests along with other potential recruits, and was one of a final ten who made it through to an intensive three-month training course. Even by this stage, the purpose was not revealed. Only two of the ten candidates managed to complete the course. One of them was Chana. It was then that they told her what she had been recruited for, and that she would be serving undercover as a manager at Arous.

'I thought it was wonderful,' Chana recalls. 'I felt that this was the missing link that I'd been looking for in my life. I didn't want to be a scientist, and I knew a career in the Navy wasn't for me, whereas this fit me like a glove. To be given the chance to be a little part of a big puzzle that was the operation to bring home the Ethiopian Jews – it made me very proud.'

Chana was sent to Club Med-style resorts in Israel to learn about how they were run, given a false identity and passport and despatched to Sudan in late 1983. By then the resort was in full swing and she walked into a well-oiled operation.

Chana took to it like a duck to water – except in her case she was actually afraid of water, and didn't even know how to swim. This led to tensions between her and a diving instructor, 'Itai', who had remained at the village since the last operation. The Mossad would not allow anyone to dive alone in case they got into trouble, which meant that when it was just the two of them at the resort, he was hindered.

'Why did they send this stupid woman with me?' Itai would say in frustration.

After Chana had been there for a few weeks, he asked her to help him test some of the equipment, which required going out in a Zodiac. Although she was frightened, Chana agreed and they sailed out to sea. Once they were a significant distance from the shore, Itai stopped the boat.

'Okay,' he said, 'now either you're diving or you're diving!' He started telling her what to do.

'I thought it was my last day on Earth!' Chana recalls.

He put a diving cylinder and mask on her – and threw her overboard. Chana knew she would drown if she didn't take control and do as he had said. She couldn't swim, but she discovered that she didn't need to in order to flip around and go up and down using the natural buoyancy of the sea.

'After that first time, you couldn't get me out of the water!' she says. From that moment Chana was hooked on diving. She would go on expeditions to shipwrecks with guests and even drew what may well be the first diving map of the coast and reefs in the area, which she hung on the dining room wall.

As the village became more established, it employed about a dozen members of staff, including chambermaids and mechanics, and more ghafirs, cooks (one poached from the Hilton by the offer of more money) and drivers. The agents knew that one of the drivers was passing information about the resort to the Sudanese secret police (they would refer to him as 'The Snitch'), although he didn't know anything about them being Israelis or what they were actually doing. It began after the former chief of the secret police in Port Sudan approached Dani in the early days when he was setting up the village and offered to furnish it with guests in return for payment. Dani had pretended to procrastinate, so the man invited him to dinner at his house to 'talk it over'. When Dani, together with Gad, turned up, they found he had laid on Eritrean sex workers and copious amounts of hashish. Sensing a trap, Dani told him never to contact him again and the pair left. From then on, 'plants' and fake guests were sent to the village to try to find out who these 'Europeans' were. Colonel Mahgoub of the Ministry of Tourism tipped Dani off, warning him that the secret police were using informants to poke around at the resort. As a result, whenever Sudanese came to stay, the Israelis were prepared, though they could never be sure everything was OK.

They discovered that one of the informants was an electrician they used called Sandro, an Eritrean or Ethiopian. Rubi took him aside and told him they knew what he was up to – but if he wanted a 'ticket out', he just needed to tell his paymasters that everything was fine. 'Later on, he found himself in Canada, somehow,' Rubi says.

The village was not without its hitches but was run by people who knew how to find solutions to problems. As water became harder to come by because of severe drought, one of the diving instructors, who happened to also be a senior figure at Israel's Mekorot national water company, got a desalination plant brought in on one of the trips by the *Bat Galim*. They assembled it on the beach and for the first time got purified water piped to the resort. In fact, they began to produce water well beyond their needs and ended up selling surplus to local bedouins. (The system was put out of action for a time when a worker took a pick-axe to the inlet pipe, hitting it up and down, to try to find the source of a blockage.)

Although Arous did not make a profit it did become financially self-sufficient. Mossad agents opened an account at El-Nilein Bank in Port Sudan and used some of the money they made at the village to hire more vehicles to transport the Jews at night. Its busiest periods were Christmas, New Year and Easter. At these times, the Israelis would put on shows for the guests, where they would wear fancy dress and sing and dance. The resort even had a Christmas tree, made by Yola out of planks of wood and dressed in green tinsel and decorations which she bought en route through Europe.

Alcohol was also in plentiful supply at Arous, and remained so even after it was banned across the country when Islamic law was imposed in September 1983. That month, in a public spectacle, thousands of gallons of wine and beer were poured into the Nile, watched by President Nimeiri in person. Despite that, members of the team would stock up on alcoholic drinks at duty free stores in airports on their way back from trips to Israel.

One night, one of the workers came to see Yola to tell her there was a man, known to be a leader of the local smugglers, asking to see her privately. The man often drank coffee at the resort and was given freshly baked loaves of bread by Yola. On hearing he was there, she went to meet him in a dark corner of the village.

'You know I have good relations in Port Sudan,' said the smuggler. 'Tomorrow they're going to raid your place. I don't know what they're looking for but you're my friend and I want you to know.'

She thanked him and the agents set about making sure none of the secret equipment was discoverable and all the alcohol was out of sight (they tied the bottles in a sack, took it out to the reef and submerged it in the water, suspended from a buoy). The following morning, at 6am, Yola was woken by banging on her chalet door.

'*Mudira!*' ('Manageress!'), came a voice. 'We've come to do a search!'

Yola opened up to find soldiers with Kalashnikovs and a commander.

'Please, go ahead,' she said.

The commander gave the order and the soldiers fanned out, looking through the rooms and buildings (there were no guests resident at the time). Not finding anything suspicious, they thanked Yola for her trouble and left.

While the village had ample supplies of food and water, it still depended on the strained Sudanese market for its fuel, and in mid-1984 the country was suffering a shortage. The resort's driver, Ali, went to collect fifteen barrels from the Agip oil refinery in Port Sudan but was turned away. They told him that no one was getting fuel, no matter how much they were willing to pay. The village had only enough for two weeks, and without more supplies, it would have to shut down – meaning an end to operations. Chana took the truck with Ali and the fifteen empty barrels and went back to the Agip plant. Ali stayed with the vehicle as Chana went inside to see the manager. She was shown to a waiting room outside his office, where she took a seat next to a smartly dressed Arab man.

'Hello,' said the man, in polished English. 'Who are you?'

'I'm the *mudira* of Arous,' replied Chana. 'And who are you?'

'I'm the commander of the PLO base near here,' he answered.

The PLO had set up in Sudan after pulling out of Lebanon in the wake of Israel's invasion. It was a shock encounter, but Chana held her nerve.

'Well, it's very nice to meet you,' she responded, feigning a smile. 'Why are you here?'

'We don't have enough fuel,' the commander said. 'We need two barrels a week so we can train at night.'

They continued to talk until the commander was called into the manager's office. He re-emerged a short time later, a smile on his face.

'So, did you get your two barrels?' asked Chana.

'Well I got one!' the commander exclaimed.

It was bad news. If he only managed to get one barrel, Chana thought, there was no chance she would get fifteen.

She was called in next, and had not even sat down when the manager declared: 'God, how I hate these Palestinians!'

She did not react, but, noticing a photograph on his desk of the manager and his wife and children, she remarked: 'Oh, what a lovely family! I'm the *mudira* of Arous. I'd love to have you all over. Have you ever been?'

'No,' replied the manager.

'Well,' continued Chana, 'please come at our expense. The only thing is, we don't have enough fuel so we keep having to ration the power, so, you know, the lights, the air conditioning, the kitchen …'

Chana got her fifteen barrels, and the Agip manager and his family became frequent guests at Arous. They were given VIP treatment, and the village never had problems getting fuel again. As it turned out, 1984 was the busiest year for the resort. It was only the exorbitant cost of the fuel which prevented it from doing well financially.

By this point, Dani's services had been called upon in another part of the Mossad, and he accepted. After almost five years of constant action, tension and detrimental impact on his home life, Dani had felt that the time had been right to assume a new role, one which would enable him to see his daughters more. He had carried the weight of responsibility day and night not only for his team but for the thousands of Ethiopian Jews passing through the system which he created, and both required the kind of innovative thinking where, by his own acknowledgement, he was running dry. Operation Brothers was his legacy and he bowed out. Although Dani went on to serve in other capacities in the intelligence agency, he remained in contact (even after his retirement from active service) with many of the Ethiopian Jews who made it to Israel as a result of his leadership and continues to champion their cause.

Dani had simultaneously been the head of the department in Tel Aviv, commander of the secret evacuations on the ground, and CEO of Navco – overseeing the 'business' and representing it in meetings with Sudanese authorities. The combination was almost too demanding for one individual to carry out. On Dani's departure, division chief Efraim Halevy decided it would be more practical to split the role and appointed Tarzan to succeed Dani at HQ, with Yuval as commander in the field.

Before Dani's departure, Colonel Mahgoub threw a farewell party for him at his home in Khartoum, attended by senior Sudanese officials and, undercover, a top Mossad figure from headquarters, who came under the guise of working for Navco. Mahgoub and Dani had formed a genuine friendship and had great respect for one another. In a previous year, it had come out in conversation that Mahgoub and his wife, Bedour, were having fertility issues, so Dani had asked Halevy if there was something they could do to help. Halevy agreed and contacted a particular Jewish obstetrician in Harley Street in London, renowned as a place of medical expertise. Dani bought the Mahgoubs business class tickets from Khartoum (Colonel Mahgoub offered to pay his own way in economy but Dani insisted he accept the trip at his expense) and met them in London. Before they arrived, he visited the doctor to brief him on the importance of the relationship and not to talk about Israel. The doctor didn't know exactly what it was about, but he understood it was something for the state and waived his charge. Despite his efforts the treatment was unsuccessful, but the Mahgoubs were deeply grateful to Dani for going to such lengths to try to help.

On the night of his leaving party, Mohammed Mahgoub presented Dani with a gift: a copy of the book *The Blue Nile* by Alan Moorehead. In it, he wrote the following heartfelt words:

My dearest brother, Daniel

On this moment of your departure, I cannot express my real feelings towards you, because I do not trust that you are leaving the Sudan. Anyhow, this is life, but I assure you that all our family, especially Bedour and myself, we will never, ever, forget your kindness, friendship, honesty. You have made a very strong family relationship and we consider you as a member of this family, so do please come back home [to] Sudan again and again.

It is said that anybody who drinks from the Nile, he comes back to it, so we are expecting you very soon.

Good luck. Regards, Bedour and Mohd [*sic*].

14

NICK OF TIME

Whereas a maritime evacuation would take a week, theoretically the more planes that could be used, the more Jews could be lifted out in a single operation. The Air Force wanted to step things up. It should be possible, they said, to evacuate 1,000 people at a time using five aircraft. However, from a practical point of view, they were limited by both the capacity of the agents on the ground to pick up and deliver refugees, and also the imperative to keep their presence in Sudan low-key and avoid suspicious patterns of activity. Each evacuation meant bringing more 'divers' to the village, which at times when there were not that many guests would make no sense to the watchful Sudanese authorities. In the camps themselves, to have hundreds of refugees creeping out every other night would also ring alarm bells among bored non-Jewish refugees with nothing to do but watch any goings on. It was decided to wait several weeks between operations to allow things to settle, so that anyone who had seen anything unusual in the camps would have forgotten, and the sight of white men driving a convoy of trucks would not occur too often.

Although the scheduling of the operations had to be staggered, at least two planes could be used at once.

On 9 October 1983, two Hercules were sent for the first

time, landing in the desert and picking up 308 Jews (the operation was called Opening Gift, as it was the first under Yuval's command, though Dani did participate, in what was his final action of Operation Brothers). When the pilots left Israel, they could only estimate the weight of the aircraft on return because they didn't know how many people they would end up carrying. They were already heavy when they landed because they were carrying extra fuel and equipment. On concrete, the maximum take-off weight was 69,750 kilograms. On sand, it was unknown, and the planes were always at the upper end of the scale or over.

With the passengers on board, the lead aircraft got the signal to raise its rear cargo ramp and readied for take-off. The captain – Squadron 131 commander Lieutenant Colonel Yisrael Ben-Chaim – could not see anything in the pitch black, and asked his co-pilot, Asaf Agmon, who was wearing night-vision goggles, if everything was okay.[1]

'Yes, everything's clear. Go,' Agmon replied.

Ben-Chaim released the brake and the plane started to move. As he accelerated, he felt that something wasn't right – because of the weight, the aircraft was not gathering speed quickly enough to take off.

It passed the last set of lights and overshot the end of the landing strip and was now hurtling along bumpy desert ground.

'It's clear – keep going!' Agmon told Ben-Chaim.

The only other option was to abort the take-off, but the passengers were sitting unsecured on the floor and braking sharply could be fatal.

Suddenly Agmon shouted:

'Ben-Chaim! There's a tree! Right in front of us! Pull! Pull! Pull!'

They both knew that if they hit the tree at their velocity, the plane would crash and go up in flames.

As the aircraft thundered towards it, Ben-Chaim, still with his outside visibility nil, pulled the flight control stick with two fingers, trying to catch the exact moment the aircraft had enough elevation to lift off. 'I played it like an instrument,' he recalls, 'and prayed.'

The nose lifted up with a split-second to go and the plane skirted over the top branches. The C-130 was airborne, but the crew knew how close they had come to disaster.

'We were sure we were going to crash,' recalls Agmon. 'For the next five hours, nothing was said in the cockpit. All of us were in shock, nobody spoke, nobody talked, nobody hardly breathed.'

When the aircraft finally landed at Base 27, the marshaller waved his arms for Ben-Chaim to cut the engines. There was something wrong with the front of the plane. The crew got off and went to look. There, sticking out of the nose landing gear bay, was part of an acacia tree. They had been so close to colliding with it in the desert that when the landing gear retracted it had ripped it in half, carrying its entire thorny canopy all the way back to Israel.

Opening Gift was the last desert airlift that year. It had been delayed due to the sudden arrival at Khartoum airport in August 1983 of two US AWAC aircraft with advanced surveillance capabilities, which Mossad HQ feared could expose the secret incoming C-130s.[2] Another aerial operation took place on 3 February 1984, evacuating 346 Jews, and then some three months later, on 27 April, when a record 380 Jews were airlifted out.

In what turned out to be a stroke of good fortune, one airlift was aborted when Mossad agents arrived at Gedaref with three empty trucks as planned, only to find no Jews at the pick-up point, apart from one Berare. He explained that hundreds had been there but had fled back to the camp when police turned up. The agents had no choice but to leave without any passengers. On their way back to Arous, the front two trucks jumped a checkpoint but Tarzan, in a pickup, and the rear truck were ordered to stop by Sudanese soldiers manning the position who were unusually aggressive that night.

'Lots of them, with automatic rifles, aiming at us, shouting, mad, with torches, with flashlights, yelling at us: "Get off the road! Switch off the engine!"' Tarzan recalls.

Both he and the agent driving the truck pulled over. They were ordered out and held at gunpoint, while a commander grilled them with questions about who they were and what they were doing. Tarzan stayed calm and politely responded with false answers, until, after 90 minutes, the commander decided to let them go. However, at that moment they could not get the truck's engine started because of a flat battery and had to jump-start it with cables from the car.

'You get this bloody engine going or we'll be trapped in this country till we're pensioners!' Tarzan told his colleague tensely. 'After a few attempts it turned on,' he recalls. 'You cannot imagine! We are out of Hell! So I said to the soldiers, very nicely, in a British way: "Thank you so much, gentlemen. Goodnight!"'

Had the truck been carrying its Jewish passengers, they and the two agents would have been caught, with serious consequences. It was a sharp reminder that past success did not mean that things got easier or safer. Just one week after the record-setting airlift, another was launched, on 3 May, but it was struck by disaster and ended up being the final one.

As with all these operations, the Air Force didn't know how many people they would have to pick up until the Mossad informed them (they would send three C-130s – one of which would stay airborne as back-up in case of a problem with one of the other two), and the Mossad themselves didn't know until they collected the Jews. Whatever number they asked the Committee Men to organise, more would turn up. Jews would hear that others were leaving and they would join them. On the night of the final operation, Yuval's team got to the quarry outside Gedaref and waited for the evacuees. The atmosphere was tense. Unlike other times, tonight there were police cars patrolling the area, driving past with their blue flashing lights as the agents hid. At a certain moment when the coast was clear, the Berare showed up with the Jews, only there were many – very many. There were too many to count, but clearly a lot more than they had evacuated the week before. The Jews had had enough of the suffering in the camps. No more waiting. They just wanted out. The agents could not delay – they just had to load and go. There were two trucks – the International and a Dutch DAF – and a Toyota pickup. They did not take Jews in the lead vehicle, which carried the incriminating communication equipment and stick lights, so they packed them all into the other two. Suddenly there was a loud crash followed by screaming and crying. The sheer amount of people cramming into the International had caused one of its sides to collapse, sending them toppling onto one another on the ground.

'The whole truck just burst and everyone fell down,' recalls Itai, who was assigned to the vehicle with Louis. 'It was complete chaos, a catastrophic event.'

There were injuries and pandemonium – and they were reduced to just one truck. The Jews from the collapsed truck then piled into the DAF, on top of those who were already in there. They squeezed into the cabin, hung off the back and clung to the sides. Yuval, who was in charge, told Rubi and another agent to go before the second truck collapsed. Anyone who could not fit inside was pulled off, and as the agents held back the crowd, the DAF rumbled away. Yuval in the pickup followed. The damaged International was driveable, but could take no passengers, and they had to get it out of there to stop people trying to climb back on.

Itai turned to Louis.

'You go,' he said. 'I'll run after you.'

Louis took the International and set off. With the vehicles gone, the Berare started to marshal around 100 people back to the camp.

'It was then an old man came out of the crowd and came up to me,' recalls Itai. 'He said something in his own language which I could tell meant: "Listen, I know I'm not going to Jerusalem, but take this." He handed me a small package, and just said the word "Orit". That's the only word I knew: "Bible".'

Itai took the bundle and ran as fast as he could, catching up with Louis and the International and jumping inside.

Rubi, who was driving the refugees, radioed the command-and-control plane.

'We have a little problem,' he said. 'We are one truck, fully loaded.'

He could not speed up because of the weight and the risk to the passengers. He also had to slalom because of debris on the road – it was a common thing for drivers who broke down to pile rocks as a warning to other motorists but then not bother to clear them away – and dodge oncoming vehicles which also drove without lights. He was behind schedule already, and still had many kilometres to go. There was a chance he would not make it and the aircraft would have to go back. He also had no way of knowing what had happened to the three other agents and the stranded passengers – only that if they had been caught by the secret police it would be a calamity, far worse than the ambush on the beach.

The lead pilot came on the radio.

'Fifteen minutes till landing. Repeat. Fifteen minutes till landing.'

There was a limit to how long the planes could stay in the air because of the fuel they were using up. They needed to conserve enough to be able to make it back to Israel.

Rubi managed to get to the turn-off and lumbered into the desert. A few thousand metres on, he found the landing strip and switched on the lights.

Suddenly he spotted a vehicle which had also turned off the main road behind him and was heading in his direction. There could be no innocent reason as to why he was standing in the middle of the desert with hundreds of black people waiting for a plane to land. Anyone who found them could not be allowed to live to tell the tale. Rubi braced. The two Hercules would appear any second, and the vehicle in pursuit would get there just at the same moment. It came into view, sped towards him and sharply pulled up. It was the Toyota pickup, and behind it, the International truck. All the agents had made it.

The planes arrived, landed and turned around, engines running. The soldiers dashed out, holding up the green stick lights.

'How many?' they asked Rubi.

'No idea!' he replied.

They rushed the Ethiopians onto the aircraft – there was no system, they just had to get everyone in one plane or the other.

After the last soldiers ran back in, the rear doors closed and the first aircraft took off, closely followed by the second. They disappeared into the night sky and silence returned to the desert.

When the team got back to the village they received a message from headquarters.

'Congratulations. Only 312 this time. You didn't break the record.'

That wasn't quite right. They did break a record. Three-hundred and twelve people in one DAF truck.

After this event, it was decided to halt the operations. Hundreds of distressed people would have been seen traipsing back into the camp that night, and the agents were very lucky they themselves had not been caught. The Mossad dared not risk any more runs, at least not for now.

In the course of two years, the joint operations between the Air Force and the Mossad had delivered 1,868 Ethiopian Jews to Israel. Technically, it had tested the pilots and crews to their limits. As one put it: 'We had the problem of flying with not very accurate maps, very primitive navigation systems, to a very inaccurate target. Not only did we have to find the Mossad and the people but then land with no aircraft lights, without any aids, safely, and then take off again.' It is a testament to their extraordinary skills that in all eleven landings, they never missed a runway or failed to arrive dead on time.

That last year of the joint operations, 1984, was the worst of the refugee crisis in the whole of the 1980s, with up to half a million fleeing to Sudan. If Jewish migration from Ethiopia was only a trickle in 1980, by 1984 it had become a deluge. That summer alone, about a quarter of the entire Ethiopian Jewish community was reported to have made the trek to Sudan.[3]

Although the Mossad was still covertly getting Jews out through Khartoum airport via the ICM, the surge meant there were more coming than it was humanly possible to evacuate through that means alone, although the urgency was now greater than ever. Something needed to be done on a much bigger scale, and that meant gambling on getting the tacit co-operation of the Sudanese themselves. A previous attempt at this had not ended well. Three years earlier, Halevy had sent an agent to put feelers out to the Sudanese leadership on the issue, but the reaction was so negative that the Mossad had to launch an operation to exfiltrate the operative before he was arrested. By the latter part of 1984 however, Nimeiri was in a more insecure position – the Sudanese economy was in a state of collapse and government forces were under pressure from the rebel Sudanese People's Liberation Movement in the south. Halevy proposed co-opting the United States, Sudan's ally and its biggest foreign aid donor, to use its leverage over Nimeiri and get him to acquiesce to a massive, clandestine operation which would clear the camps of all the Jews. With the approval of Hofi's successor as Mossad chief, Nahum Admoni, Halevy flew to Washington and held high-level meetings with US diplomats.[4] As a result, the Reagan administration agreed to put pressure on Nimeiri to help. Fearful of domestic and regional consequences, Nimeiri initially resisted, but ultimately relented, enticed by the promise of substantially increased US aid.

Behind the scenes, the CIA and the Mossad (under Halevy's direction) orchestrated a mass airlift of Jews from the camps, with Vice President and head of the State Security Organisation

Omar el-Tayeb in charge on the Sudanese side. It came at a cost – el-Tayeb received payment in cash of up to $2 million, although in the scheme of things, it was a modest sum. US aid to Sudan was also significantly increased. Nimeiri insisted on two conditions: one, that the evacuations be carried out in total secrecy. Sudan belonged to the Arab League and if it got out that he was turning a blind eye to the mass migration of Jews from Sudanese soil to Israel, he would be branded a traitor (he had seen the example of what happened to Egyptian President Anwar Sadat, who in 1981 had been assassinated by an army officer for making peace with Israel). Secondly, as Sudan was technically at war with Israel, he would not permit flights to go there directly. They would have to be routed to Europe first, but where they went from there he did not need to know.

Halevy secured the assistance of the Belgian Jewish owner of Trans European Airlines (TEA), Georges Gutelman, who put at their disposal one of his Boeing aircraft (the airline flew pilgrims from Khartoum to Mecca for the Hajj, the annual Muslim pilgrimage, so its presence there would not appear out of the ordinary), and from 21 November 1984, the plane began spiriting out Ethiopian Jews, hundreds at a time, first touching down in Brussels for as long as it took to refuel and change the flight number, then on to Tel Aviv. Almost every night (there was a pause for the Sabbath, because of the Ethiopian Jews' refusal to transgress religious law by travelling on the holy day) large groups of Beta Israel were secretly bussed from transit points on the outskirts of Gedaref by Sudanese security forces to a remote part of Khartoum airport (under the deal, the security forces got to keep the fleet of vehicles bought with Israeli money). While these Khartoum airlifts were conducted with the assistance of the Sudanese authorities, only two people actually

knew these refugees were Jewish – Nimeiri and el-Tayeb. There
is no evidence that even they knew that the Mossad had been
staging clandestine evacuations for years and was embedded
on their own coast.[5] An important point to underline about it
is that this operation, known as Operation Moses, was carried
out in parallel to the Mossad's Operation Brothers and one was
not part of the other.

However, in a series of disastrous blunders, despite a media
blackout, news of the 'top secret' airlift got leaked – ironically from official Jewish quarters. On the very day Operation
Moses began, the World Zionist Organization issued a press
release quoting allusive remarks by the head of the Jewish
Agency that 'one of the ancient Jewish tribes is due to return
to its homeland'. The information was used by two US Jewish
publications, which ran stories about the dramatic 'rescue' of
Ethiopian Jews, and then by the *New York Times*, though without saying they were being brought out from Sudan. That fact
was revealed one day after the *Times* report, when the *Boston
Globe* identified Sudan, saying 'unmarked planes [were] landing
at night at Khartoum'. It said Sudanese officials were working
with 'Israeli agents' to stage the airlift, and with remarkable
irresponsibility went on to point out that 'American officials …
urged news organizations that found out about the operation,
including *The Globe*, not to print the story prematurely, and
thereby jeopardize its continuation.'[6] Although the information
was now in the public domain, Israel remained tight-lipped
and Sudan did not react. Ultimately it was explosive confirmation nearly a month later from the Israeli Prime Minister,
Shimon Peres, himself that derailed the operation. On
4 January 1985, Peres hastily convened a press conference where
he answered journalists' questions about the secret airlifts.

Ostensibly it was done in an attempt to contain damage after news of the airlifts from Sudan went worldwide following the publication in a little-known Israeli periodical of off-the-record remarks by the Jewish Agency's deputy chairman that most of the Ethiopian Jews were now in the country.[7] Peres' critics, though, saw it as a tactical move by the prime minister, who was also the leader of the Labour party, to take the credit for a mission begun under Labour's political rival, Likud. Either way, the move triggered a political backlash and accusations of blame were flung in every direction.

The debacle was summed up by a frustrated president, Chaim Herzog, who appealed for restraint from all sides, lamenting how 'we have a dubious talent for converting any admirable achievement into a matter of controversy.'[8]

Sudan immediately called off the airlifts. Nimeiri denied any involvement. He said that, while all refugees were free to leave the country, 'If they come and tell me they're going to Israel, I will not help them, because Israel knows that I am its enemy.' The comments were likely made to assuage anger in the Arab world towards Sudan, and in Sudan itself, over the revelations (Ethiopia condemned the airlift, calling it a 'sinister operation').[9]

Despite the recriminations in Israel, the blaze of publicity surrounding Operation Moses created unprecedented global awareness of the previously little-heard-of Ethiopian Jews.

In Western media, the operation was hailed as an epic moment. The *New York Times*' distinguished political commentator William Safire observed that: 'For the first time in history, thousands of black people are being brought into a country not in chains but in dignity, not as slaves but as citizens ... Israel's quiet acceptance of responsibility should say a great deal to

Africa, to American blacks and Jews, and to all who believe that the "Falashas" of the world should be strangers no more.'

The operation had been cut short with reportedly just four more flights to go.[10] The last 494 Jews who had been due to be taken out were left behind. The news was met with anger and grief among the Ethiopian Jews now in Israel, and their supporters, and renewed appeals were made to the US to step in. After a request from Vice President George H.W. Bush on a scheduled visit to Sudan on 4 March, Nimeiri agreed to let the US evacuate the remaining Jews, so long as they were not flown directly to Israel. From that point on, events moved quickly. Milton Beardon, the CIA station chief in Khartoum, flew Omar el-Tayeb to Washington for meetings with Bush, state department officials and CIA chiefs to work out the mechanics of how it could be done. Halevy, representing the Mossad, also went to Washington and held face-to-face talks with el-Tayeb, an old adversary, to iron out details. Once everything was agreed, Bearden and el-Tayeb returned to Khartoum, taking with them a special operations team from Delta Force, an elite commando unit.[11] On 22 March 1985, in a secret operation codenamed Joshua (also known as Operation Sheba) the stranded Jews were brought out on six US Hercules planes, taking off from an airfield secured by the American commandos a few kilometres outside Gedaref. The whole process was completed in just four hours, with planes flying straight to Israel, in defiance of Nimeiri.

Five days later, as Nimeiri arrived in Washington on a private visit, riots broke out in Khartoum over food and fuel prices. Thousands of students took to the streets, chanting anti-government and anti-US slogans. The Army moved in and restored order, at a cost of several lives, but associations of politically influential professionals joined the protest movement, and after days of more clashes and a general strike, Sudan's armed forces, led by Nimeiri's defence minister, announced they had taken power 'in order to save the country'.

15

'SOMETHING IS GOING TO HAPPEN'

The Israeli government and the Mossad monitored the situation closely – it was feared in particular that the toppling of the old order could lead to a resetting of Sudan's relations with Nimeiri's foes, the staunchly anti-Israel Libya and Iran (Libya immediately recognised the new regime, becoming the first country in the world to do so). The agents in Khartoum sat tight, while in Arous things felt strangely closeted from events on the outside. Nimeiri's overthrow coincided with Easter weekend and the village was full of guests. It also meant there were five Mossad operatives there instead of the usual two at quieter times (one actually flew in as support at the beginning of Easter week, an indication that the Mossad still felt that conditions were safe enough to do so). Sudan's new military government declared a state of emergency and took action against the forces and figures who had propped up Nimeiri or were closely associated with him. Old loyalties no longer mattered, and secrets were spilled in their informers' hopes of being spared. Towards the end of Easter week, the Mossad discovered that the authorities had uncovered their long-time charade.

'By pure chance, we got indication that the cover had been blown, that the Sudanese were on to it, that this village was not what it purported to be,' a top official from headquarters recalls. 'It was clear to us: we had to get the people out as soon as possible. I immediately went to Nachum [Admoni, the Mossad chief] and said that we had to get the Air Force in. Admoni said "Do it."'

The order was communicated to the agents at Arous. It would mean they would have to disappear – but the resort was at its busiest, with guests and staff all around. If the management and diving instructors took off together, there was a chance they would be noticed and questions would be asked. From the point of view of the group, if they could stall until Tuesday, a few days away, when the last guests were due to leave, they could then make a clean escape.

Back in Moshav Adanim, central Israel, Squadron 131 commander Ben-Chaim was at home when he got the call. The squadron was on a week's recess, a period during which it was not the norm to be contacted about official business. Yuval, who was in the country after having broken his ankle on a diving trip in Arous, was on the line, and it was serious.

'Listen, Yisrael, something is wrong there,' Yuval said, cryptically. 'I'm going down. I strongly recommend that you be ready.'

Ben-Chaim understood immediately what Yuval meant, and knew it was a big deal if he had called him when it was another squadron that was on duty.

Ben-Chaim had already flown on several missions airlifting the Jews from Sudan. He had landed on the desert airstrips in the dark and made it out again more times than any other pilot.

He left his house and drove straight to Base 27, 25 minutes away. As soon as he got there, he put on his flight suit and reported to the base commander, Avinoam Maimon.

'Something is going to happen, and I want to do it,' Ben-Chaim told him, knowing it was the turn of the other squadron, 103.

'What are you talking about?' replied Maimon. 'There's nothing going on.'

'Something is going to happen, I'm telling you. I have my own information, and I want to be the one to do it,' Ben-Chaim insisted.

'I don't know what you're …'

'Avi, listen,' Ben-Chaim interrupted. 'If you want to continue our good relationship, then I'm going to take that mission, no matter what, and I'm going to wait here in your office. You let me do this, and I will make sure you will be flying number two.'

Ben-Chaim then made a phone call to Ika Brant in operations at Air Force HQ.

'Listen, Ika, I'm here,' Ben-Chaim told him. 'I know something is in the works. Do not let me miss it, because I'm telling you, it will be your end!'

Ben-Chaim waited at the base for 24 hours, without anything happening. It was not uncommon for operations to be put in motion only to be called off. This though, he felt, was something different.

Then Brant turned up. He called Ben-Chaim and Maimon for a meeting. There was going to be an aerial operation in Sudan. The specifics were not known, but it was, they assumed, for refuelling, or a rescue.

Ben-Chaim's persistence paid off. Maimon gave him the job. Ben-Chaim hand-picked his team for the mission – twenty crew altogether – and recalled them from recess.

They started to prepare: gathering data, poring over maps and studying weather reports. Ben-Chaim took out the contingency plans – never rehearsed – for evacuating the team from Sudan and looked through them for the first time. They were known as 'drawer plans' by dint of the fact that they were locked away in a desk and not removed unless and until they were needed for real.

In the meantime, Yuval returned to Sudan to command the evacuation.

On the morning of Monday 15 April 1985, Brant called Ben-Chaim and told him to take his crew to the base of Sikorsky helicopter Squadron 118 at Tel Nof. There he went into a briefing room. It was packed with top brass, including IDF Chief of Staff Lieutenant General Moshe Levi, Air Force chief Amos Lapidot, and head of the Mossad, Admoni. The initial idea was to send CH-53 helicopters (Ben-Chaim would not have flown one of the helicopters but would have refuelled them in mid-air) to pick up the operatives, along with the two vehicles they would be using in the escape, from somewhere near the village. The plan was to lift the cars up and fly with them suspended underneath the helicopters, then ditch them and the communication and other secret equipment which could not be off-loaded out at sea.

Agmon, who was now chief of operations, objected, warning that it was too risky.

'Nobody would survive this kind of operation,' Agmon later reflected. 'It would have been a glamorous disaster.'

Without knowing the weight of the vehicles, he warned, the helicopters might crash struggling to lift them up, or the cars would 'swing like pendulums' and bring the helicopters down into the sea. He advised sending a C-130 instead.

The Air Force chiefs listened, but unlike with helicopters, there was nowhere to land a plane in an untested part of the desert. Agmon was overruled and the helicopters were prepared.

However, minutes before they were due to take off, a communication came through from Yuval in the village. There was, he said, a possible area to land a plane which he had seen a few months earlier while travelling with a newly arrived operative, about 100 kilometres north of Arous.

'Send Ben-Chaim,' he said.

All eyes in the room turned to Ben-Chaim, and Lapidot asked: 'You think you can do it?'

'If Yuval thinks I can do it, I can do it!' Ben-Chaim replied.

It was agreed. They would use two Hercules instead, the first piloted by Ben-Chaim, and the second – at his insistence – by Maimon. Ben-Chaim had kept his word. A rendezvous time was set and the meeting was adjourned. Ben-Chaim and his team went back to Base 27, to get ready to fly after dark. The C-130s were prepared and Ben-Chaim briefed his crew. To find the agents at night-time in the desert was going to be extremely difficult. He did not have pin-point coordinates, only that they would be somewhere in an area about 24 kilometres wide and 80 kilometres deep – more than twice the size of New York. Ben-Chaim planned to fly in a criss-cross pattern, methodically scouring the huge expanse from north to south. On top of that, he would be landing on unknown ground, with the risk of ditches, obstacles or weak sand.

By 16 April, there were six Mossad operatives at Arous – five men and a woman. At the same time, there were three agents in Khartoum. One was Uri, who was in charge of smuggling Jews through the airport. The other two were not connected to the operation.

When the last guests had checked out of Arous, the six agents gathered their belongings and operational equipment and loaded them onto two Land Cruisers, along with as much diving gear as could fit. One took down Chana's hand-drawn map of the diving sites from the dining room wall to keep as a souvenir. Nothing in the village was destroyed, and it was even decided at Mossad HQ, as a gesture of respect to the Sudanese, to leave a calling card on the desalination system, saying: 'This is the contribution of Israel to the wellbeing of Sudan.'

The agents told the staff that now the guests had gone, they were taking a break and going to look for new diving sites. They were expecting a new arrival of tourists from Switzerland and told the staff to tell them that they were gone for the night but would be back in the morning.

'However,' recalls one of the six agents, 'Sudanese time is not very accurate, so they came early and we left late.' As the team was driving out, Ali drove in with the Swiss guests.

'We passed them in the car,' the agent says. 'They waved to us and we waved to them!'

The names of the guests – a man and a woman – do not appear in the log book because they were never registered. The log book, along with other management documents, had been taken. The agents drove north to the rendezvous point and prepared the area, marking the landing site with the same green stick lights used for guiding the refugees. After they had set it up in a rudimentary fashion, they stayed there out of sight for the rest of the day.

With Sudan and Israel in the same time zone, evening fell on both places simultaneously. As the agents waited in the dark in the desert, some 1,200 kilometres away the Hercules engines started up, and, one after the other, the planes (shadowed by a command-and-control aircraft) accelerated down the runway and took off, heading south. The operation, codenamed 'A Sad Sunset' was under way.

What followed were 'hours of deep anguish and anxiety', recalls a top Mossad figure who oversaw the evacuation of the agents, and was waiting with the military and Mossad echelon at the air base for their return.

The team out in the desert somewhere in the north-east corner of Sudan did not have any way to communicate with headquarters, the system they had used at the village having been dismantled. All they had were Motorola radios, which they hoped would be able to make contact with the planes once they came within range. After about four hours' flying time, the aircraft neared the Sudanese coast. Maimon stayed outside the border, on standby in case they needed the second plane to land, and Ben-Chaim continued, crossing over into Sudanese territory.

'Johnson … Johnson … Johnson …' – he called on the radio, trying to make contact with Yuval, using his codename.

'Johnson … Johnson … Johnson …'

'This is Johnson, over,' came the reply.

They continued to converse in English, using coded language in case they were being listened in on.

'Turn your headlights on and off and I'll come and park my car there,' Ben-Chaim told Yuval.

He continued to fly west, then turned and flew back east, then back west again, snaking his way over the area in a southerly direction. After only a few minutes, Ben-Chaim spotted a twinkling speck of light and headed for it.

'Look for the green lights,' Yuval said. 'Can you see them?'

Ben-Chaim did a visual sweep of the area through an infrared illuminator in his night-vision goggles, but could not see the green lights.

'No,' he answered. 'Nothing.'

He continued to search intently but although he could vaguely see the flashing light of Yuval's car, he could not see the green stick lights. The stick lights, it would later turn out, could not be detected on the infra-red system.

Either way, he was going to have to land, and he was going to have to do it blind.

'Listen, put the first car at the beginning of the parking lot and put the other one at the end, so they are facing each other. Keep their lights on.'

It was highly dangerous but with fuel running low it was a risk Ben-Chaim was prepared to take.

Once he could make out both sets of car lights he made his descent. The landing was so hazardous that, as he got closer, he decided to switch on the plane's regular lights – something never done when flying over enemy territory.

The C-130 thundered over the roof of Yuval's car and made touchdown with a deafening noise, whipping up a sand-storm as it ploughed its way towards the second car, coming to a halt just in front of it. The ramp came down and a dozen Air Force commandos dashed out to secure the area. The agents drove the two cars into the cargo bay and the crew strapped the vehicles down. The commandos ran back into the plane and the ramp was raised. Ben-Chaim turned the aircraft around and, with only its own light for guidance, accelerated back down the landing strip and took off, soaring away into the night sky.

Six years after the telegram from Ferede Aklum led to one of the most elaborate ruses ever staged by the Mossad – and carried out not only inside an enemy state but with its unwit-ting collaboration – the spies who ran the holiday village on the Red Sea had got away.

'I felt from Day One that I was taking part in history – some very serious Jewish history,' Ben-Chaim later reflected. 'I'm not the only one. We all felt the same.'

And he wanted a piece of it for posterity.

On the flight back to Israel, he gave an instruction to one of his crew: 'Take the number plates off the cars, front and back, all of them, and bring them to me.'

The crewman removed the plates and gave them to Ben-Chaim, who put them by his side.

After four hours, the planes crossed back into Israeli air space and touched down at Base 27. The crews, commandos and agents disembarked. Two of the agents reversed the Sudanese vehicles back down the ramp and onto Israeli soil.

Ben-Chaim himself had not got off the plane when the officer in charge of field security came to him.

'Yisrael, where are the number plates for the cars?' he asked him.

'I have no idea,' replied Ben-Chaim. 'What's it got to do with me?'

The pilots and the agents were taken to a debriefing at the base, with the heads of the Air Force and the Mossad.

'So, how was it?' was the first question put to Ben-Chaim.

'A piece of cake!' he replied.

Later on, the licence plates were turned into four framed souvenirs, which were given to certain individuals from Operation Brothers. The inscription read: 'April '85 – A Sad Sunset', and next to that the words 'Piece of Cake'.

Although the agents from the village were out of harm's way, the three still in Khartoum were not.

'As a result of the fact that the cover of the village was blown, we reached the conclusion that these people would also be in jeopardy,' recalls a high-ranking Mossad figure involved in Sudan operations at the time.

'They were not part of the village, but they did have contacts with the people who had been there, and we were not sure what might happen. They were in Khartoum, though, and we had a problem with what could be done about it. We just knew we had to remove them.'

The three men were ordered to evacuate and get to Milton Bearden's house. Even by the time they got there, security forces were on their tail.

The elaborate plan to smuggle them out from the embassy in crates was worked out and, with the boxes built, the men (along with the fourth agent who had turned up at Bearden's door) were sealed inside. Because of the heat that would be generated in such a confined space, three of the men wore only their underwear, while Uri insisted on wearing his shorts to preserve his dignity in case they were caught and hauled out.

The boxes were taken down in the freight lift and loaded into a van. Two CIA officers went with them – one in the cab with the driver, the other in the back with the crates. Not wanting to risk drawing attention by his presence in the van, Bearden stayed at the embassy, keeping in radio contact. They drove to the airport, about fifteen minutes away, and stopped at the side gate, as was the procedure for diplomatic vehicles. However, this time, the guards manning the entrance would not let the van through.

The CIA officer up front radioed Bearden to tell him there was a problem.

'Show them your special card,' Bearden told him, referring to an old pass from the palace which said that the holder was on special assignment for the president, 'and bluff your way in.'

It worked. The guards opened the gate and the van went through. As they approached the runway, an American C-141 plane that had been called in from Germany (the flight plan was filed as a diplomatic cargo flight) touched down and came to a stop. It lowered its rear loading ramp and the three personnel transferred the crates from the van to the aircraft, one at a time. Once they were all loaded, and with the plane's engines still running, the pilot requested clearance for take-off.

The response from the control tower came. 'Air Force heavy [call-sign], you're not cleared for take-off, please hold.'

Bearden, who was in communication with the pilot, got word from his people on the ground that there were some Sudanese military helicopters approaching. They were worried that the helicopters had been despatched because somehow the authorities had found out about the spies aboard the plane.

'Move it!' Bearden ordered the pilot. 'Just get out of there before anything happens. Just go!'

The pilot held his nerve. 'Roger, Khartoum tower, thank you very much, Air Force heavy [call-sign] cleared for take-off,' and with that he started to move off.

'Air Force heavy [call-sign], you're *not* cleared for take-off, I repeat, you are *not* cleared for take-off!' the control tower persisted.

'Roger, Khartoum tower, thank you very much,' the pilot replied. He set off down the runway at a rate of knots and took off, climbing into the sky.[1] Inside the cargo bay, the diplomatic sacks were quickly opened and the lids prised off the crates. The four agents emerged and were examined by a doctor.

He declared they had suffered no ill-effects. The plane headed south, out of Sudanese airspace and on to Kenya.

The chapter was over, though even after its exposure and withdrawal, the Mossad returned to smuggle Jews still in the camps out of Sudan in ways which are still secret. In time, they will be told.

President Nimeiri was on his way back home from his truncated trip when he was deposed. He had got as far as Cairo when he took advice to stay put, a fortuitous decision.

In Sudan, there was a clamour to hold the former regime accountable for its wrongdoings and thousands took to the streets demanding Nimeiri's extradition (something which never happened. In the end, Nimeiri was welcomed back to Sudan in 1999 after being granted an amnesty).

For the new rulers, the episode of the airlifts was considered treachery, and before the end of the month an investigation was launched into who had colluded with Israel and the US, and for how much.

The Washington Post reported in May 1985 that the public was 'fascinated by unconfirmed rumours that Nimeiri and key officials were paid $1,700 for each Falasha emigrant. Bankers reported the sudden appearance of fresh $100 bills in plastic packets containing $100,000 in December and again in March, periods coinciding with the Falasha airlifts.'[2]

'We feel we've been fooled. Nobody likes that,' Attorney General Omer Abdelati, head of the investigating committee said at the time. 'We feel we have been fooled by a foreign nation, and we have been betrayed by our president.'[3]

The committee found that airlifts had been going on

since 1981, and its enquiries led to an astonishing discovery. Information reached it about a small holiday resort on the coast run by foreigners which had started up around that time but had been abandoned when the evacuations ended.

Local police reported that staff had been flown out in a C-130 Hercules.

Abdelati sent a team to investigate.

'No one had suspected anything about this resort,' recalls Abdelati.[4] 'Local people would just see people swimming and *khawajat* [white foreigners] going in and out, and nobody thought anything of it. It was completely dismantled in about eighteen hours. There was nothing there. Nobody was there. We just found empty cans of beer and some tissue paper and rubbish. They'd cleaned everything.'

Investigators discovered it had been leased by a company called Navco, which had signed a contract with the director general of the Ministry of Tourism, Mohammed Mahgoub. Navco, they established, had been a front for the secret evacuations of the Ethiopian Jews, and in July, 1985, Mahgoub was arrested.

He was held under house arrest for several weeks, then released. His line of defence was that he signed the contract for Arous in good faith with what he believed to be a European company, that he was encouraged to do so by his authorities and that he knew nothing about their clandestine activity.

El-Tayeb, the vice president, who had been arrested within a day of Nimeiri's overthrow, was charged in connection with the airlifts – the only official incriminated over the issue. Nimeiri himself was investigated but no charges were brought.

After a four-month televised trial, el-Tayeb was convicted of undermining the constitution, instigating war against the state, treason and spying (though the allegation that he took bribes was not proved in court). He was sentenced to two consecutive terms of life in prison (later reduced to ten years on appeal), and was released following the coup which brought Colonel Omar Hassan al-Bashir to power in June 1989.

Considered by the Israeli state as classified material, Operation Brothers was officially kept under wraps for 30 years. The team which had operated the holiday village by day and smuggled out the Jews by night continued working for the Mossad or, in the case of the special recruits, returned to civilian life. In a remarkable moment in the late 1980s, as recounted by a trusted source, one of the agents was walking down a street in Geneva when he heard someone calling him by the cover name he used at Arous. The source said the agent described to him what happened:

'[The agent] said he did not respond and carried on walking, then he said: "I can hear the guy, he starts running behind me, then he stops me and looks me in the eye – 'Mr J. [agent's full name withheld], don't you recognise me? I'm Mohammed Mahgoub, from the tourism ministry,'" and he said: "Ah yes, sorry, now I remember. How are you?", so Mahgoub told him the story, how he was under house arrest, and then [Mahgoub] said: "Where is Dani?" [The agent] said: "Dani, the anthropologist? I think he's in the Amazon, working on some tribe." "The Amazon, huh?" said Mahgoub. "There's an Amazon in Tel Aviv?" So [the agent] said: "I don't understand", and Mahgoub replied: "I know that you're Israelis, but I understand. It's okay." He said: "I love Daniel, he's my brother, but I have only one complaint – and if you see him and talk to him, please tell him: he should have trusted me and told me the real reason why he leased the village and what he was doing, because I think it was a great thing that he did, all of you did, saving those people from the camps and so on, and I would have helped, as much as I could.'"

After the village was abandoned, according to a well-placed Sudanese official in the Red Sea state, the government requisitioned the site and used it as a garrison and training base for Sudanese soldiers. Then, in 1991, in a bizarre twist, the source says, a Saudi dissident and radical Islamist invited to take refuge in Sudan was accommodated there for up to two weeks upon his arrival in the country. His name was Osama Bin Laden, founder of the al-Qaeda terror group, mastermind of the 9/11 attacks on the United States and a mortal enemy of Israel. Later on, Arous was leased to a Sudanese-Spanish company, which revived it as a diving resort, but pulled out after two years because of the old infrastructure problems. In 2000, the village was taken over by an influential family from Khartoum who refurbished it, but owing to problems with a team of foreign contractors, the project never got off the ground, and in 2008 they handed it back to the government. 'It's jinxed,' one of the family told this author, 'I think it just doesn't want to work.'

But the Mossad had come from more than 1,300 kilometres away and made it work, smuggling out 7,054 Jewish refugees in the process.[5]

On 8 January 1985, Prime Minister Shimon Peres spoke in the Knesset about what it meant to secretly bring the Ethiopian Jews to Israel. His concluding words made clear that what had taken place would stand as a seminal event in Jewish and Israeli history for all time:

> This is a moment of pride for the Jewish people. This is a moment of spiritual uplift for the State of Israel ...

With all modesty and humility, it may be said that this is one of the most daring and wonderful acts of self-redemption that our country, and not only our country, has ever known …

For we are one people. There are no black Jews and white Jews: There are Jews. History and faith bind us together forever …

The immigration is continuing, and it will continue.[6]

It did.

Even after the US airlift operation, some 17,000 Jews remained in Ethiopia, consisting of those who could not or chose not to go to Sudan, or those in the most remote communities, such as Quara, who did not even know that Jews had left.[7] In an epic operation six years later, which was completed in just 36 hours, most were finally brought out on a non-stop cycle of flights from Addis Ababa. To make it happen, Israel had paid off Ethiopian President Mengistu (who had condemned the earlier airlift of Ethiopian Jews from Sudan as 'kidnapping') to the tune of $35 million.[8] Operation Solomon, as it was called, was done, as before, in complete secrecy, but this time it was a political deal, not a smuggling operation, and if the Mossad had any involvement, it was only on the fringes. Three days before the first Israeli Hercules plane landed (piloted once again by Colonel Dvir, while Colonel Agmon flew the first 707), Mengistu, the Butcher of Addis, fled to Zimbabwe as TPLF rebels closed in on the capital.[9] From then on, to Israel, he was an irrelevance.

From the time of the first secret airlift in 1977 to when the last aircraft touched down in Tel Aviv on 25 May 1991, at least 28,695 Ethiopian Jews – about 80 per cent of their entire community – had been transported to Israel.[10] They had been spirited out by every means possible, over 14,300 of them through Sudan. At least 16,000 had left their villages in pursuit of the dream of generations; almost a tenth did not make it.[11] Just over 35 years ago, *Cultural Survival* magazine described Ethiopian Jews as 'the most threatened Jewish community in the world'.[12] Today, there are some 140,000 in Israel, four times their number when that observation was made.[13] Their survival is secured. Decades ago, twelve young Ethiopian Jews were hailed as the 'first bridge' to Israel – but it was the second bridge, laid by the handful of daring Mossad agents in Sudan, over which thousands were able to finally cross to get there.

A MEANINGFUL MISSION

by Daniel L., Operation Brothers founder
and first commander, 1978–83

When the Lord brought back those that returned to Zion
we were as in a dream
(Psalms Chapter 126, Verse 1)

Sitting at the table in Israel with my family this past Passover,
I recounted a story from an evening in 1982. My team and I
found ourselves in Khartoum, in between two naval operations.
Despite our being part of an undercover operation in enemy
territory, I couldn't help but think of the parallel between the
Exodus of the Israelites from Egypt and our present activity
bringing out the Ethiopian Jews. I proposed to my colleagues
to hold a Passover Seder (festival meal) adapted to the circumstances. Approval was unanimous.

We booked a table at the Ivory Club (a traditional kosher
Passover meal in Khartoum city centre was out of the question!)
and ordered items off the menu most closely associated with
symbolic food found at a Seder table – fish flavoured with bitter
herbs, boiled eggs and crackers (the closest thing to unleavened
bread, or *matzah*, a Passover staple). We recited, and partly sang

from memory, an ancient text (Haggadah) that dates back more than 1,000 years and tells the story of our ancestors' deliverance from hundreds of years of slavery in Egypt and their exodus to the Promised Land.

The Haggadah, used on Passover by Jews the world over for generations, was unknown to our brothers in Ethiopia, who lived in total isolation. Yet remarkably they have marked the same holiday for the past 2,500 years or more, allowing them to preserve their Jewish identity. How? They did it – literally – from the Bible, whose verses state: 'Everyone shall eat roast lambs that night with unleavened bread and bitter herbs' (Exodus 12:8). 'Eat it with your travelling clothes, prepared for a long journey, wearing your walking shoes and carrying your walking sticks in your hands, eat it hurriedly. This observance shall be called the Lord's Passover' (Exodus 12:11).

This image symbolises the Ethiopian Jews' eagerness and readiness to perform their own exodus, and fulfil their ancient dream of returning to Zion.

On that memorable night in the Ivory Club, with our Ethiopian brothers in mind, we sang the words of the Haggadah out loud in Hebrew, but in such a way that our language would not be recognised by the other clientele. To add to the bizarreness, two tables away sat Fathi Arafat, brother of Yasser, head of the PLO.

It was a conspiracy within clandestinity, and we felt elated. We could only wonder how the other diners – mainly rich Arab businessmen – would react if they discovered that this joyful group of 'European' nationals were in fact Mossad operatives conducting a festival ritual. Then there was the question of what would they do to us back home at headquarters if they knew what we were doing!

I spent five years going to and from Sudan, from January 1979 to October 1983. I had the incredible privilege of being chosen by Yitzhak Hofi and Dr David (Dave) Kimche (bless their souls) to carry out the feasibility study in Ethiopia, then enter Sudan, locate and meet Ferede Aklum, and analyse and recommend ways to operate there. Later on I was appointed by Efraim Halevy to command combined operations with the Navy and Air Force. From day one I sensed that I was part of something more profound and meaningful than just a mission. It can be better understood in relation to the eternal philosophical and existential question: 'What is the purpose of our existence under the sun?'

Conversations with Ferede in the flickering light of the small bonfires we made when spending nights in the bush at the end of days spent combing the camps looking for Jews made me realise that while we were *a priori* very different in terms of origin, background, language, skin colour etc., we had two strong and much more relevant bonds: being Jewish and wanting to achieve the same goal. Above all, we understood the awesome responsibility that was vested in us. We had to combine our capabilities and efforts in order to materialise two complementary dreams. The first, the return of the Beta Israel to Zion, and the second – the very essence of modern Zionism – that the State of Israel should do its utmost to provide a home to any Jew, of whatever origin, who so desires. This is what happened in the course of the coming years.

The friendship between Ferede and myself became brotherhood. After his exposure and evacuation from Sudan, I had a similar relationship with Zimna Berhane, and then with Danny Yasmani and Ezra Tezazou. All of them, as well as many Committee members and young Berare, are heroes of this saga.

This brotherhood deepened as the time passed and the operations developed, involving ever more operatives from the Mossad (including Israeli citizens of Ethiopian origin), as well as the IDF and the Beta Israel in the camps in Sudan. Therefore, it should not come as a surprise that, when still at an early and quite intimate stage, I gave the series of ops under way a common name: 'Operation Brothers'. Its development justified the name. After Operation Moses, operations continued, led by brilliant and courageous men from the same branches mentioned above.

In Israel today, life is not easy for anybody, but the Israelis of Ethiopian origin face more difficulties than most, because, as a society, we are still far from reaching the degree of solidarity, mutual respect and comprehension that we should if we uphold the values of Judaism. Many of the Ethiopian Israelis thrive, though, and some of them are like family to me. They came as children and adolescents. Some were born here. Men and women who are doctors, social workers, high-ranking officers in the IDF, police and firefighters, educators, academics, rabbis, Kessim, former and present Knesset members. They brought with them the scent of ancient history and ethics that shine in the darkness. We should embrace them. After a long life of service, I sleep better knowing that they are an integral part of the future of this country.

Since my first landing in Khartoum, this operation was built upon a series of adapting tactics and decision-making on the ground, which led to an ever-changing modus operandi. But the discovery and subsequent lease and operation of the Arous resort was undoubtedly what kept those who were looking for us, trying to uncover and stop us, from relating us to the disappearance of the Jews from the camps. I give credit to the senior Mossad decision-makers for trusting me to turn this off-beat idea into an asset that gave us the legitimacy to operate for almost five years under an ideal cover story that still today challenges the imagination.

None of this would have happened without the members of my team whom I personally hand-picked, and I would like to acknowledge them, with love and respect: Marcel, Rubi, Dr Micki Nobel, Shmulik Machiach, Yola Reitman, Louis, Yonatan, Bill, Gad Shimron, Apke and Jack, as well as Y.G. and Tarzan, both of whom replaced me and kept going on. And finally, Efraim Halevy, who had the difficult task of being my commander. I wish them all a happy and healthy life.

Equally I would like to pay tribute to the many heroic servicemen of the IDF, only some of whom have been named in this book but who all played a crucial part in enabling this mission to be the success that it was.

The best go first, and some key members of my team, whose contribution was invaluable, are no longer with us: Ferede Aklum, Yaakov Barsimantov, Yossi Ben-Arieh, Zimna Berhane, Jacques Haggai (Holocaust survivor), Uri Sela (Holocaust survivor), Gil Paz, Dr Shlomo Pomeranz and Danny Yasmani. The 'father' of the operation, Dave Kimche – a pioneer and a visionary, whose legacy lives on in many ways, not least through the generations of fully-fledged Israeli Jews of Ethiopian origin – has also sadly passed. I salute their families. They are role models to us all and will remain in our memory for ever. May they rest in peace.

Daniel

AFTERWORD

by Efraim Halevy, Director of the Mossad 1998–2002,
and head of the division overseeing Operation Brothers

The true and most accurate story of the Mossad's operation to evacuate Ethiopian Jews from Sudan ultimately over a period of around a decade has found a gifted and worthy author who deserves high praise for his monumental effort in unearthing so many key aspects that have never been publicly revealed till now.

The operational contours of this unique effort require a quick roundup; it was executed close to 2,000 kilometres away from Jerusalem. Feelers sent out at an early stage clearly revealed that the dictatorial regime in Khartoum would have no sympathy during its first critical years – quite the contrary. Access to Sudan was difficult and foreigners had to undergo serious scrutiny before receiving entry permits – not the normal visas granted in other countries. Security was visibly present especially on main arteries along which both the Mossad agents and the Ethiopian Jews had to be transported to their departure points. We were devoid of any intelligence on this faraway target and had no real means either in place or by other ways to collect it. I recall the briefings at HQ level before every round of activities where the only item mentioned was the weather on the scene.

The mission was launched about four years after the traumatic Yom Kippur War and when Israel's attention was turned to the North, to Lebanon, where PLO chief Yasser Arafat was based in Beirut, from where terrorist activities were gradually increasing both in quantity and quality. Central and Western Europe had become areas where terrorism was a growing threat. Eventually a full-blown war broke out in 1982 in the midst of the Sudan effort and activities had to be temporarily suspended, *inter alia* because Dani, the commander in the field, rushed back to fulfil his role as an officer in his reserve Paratroopers Brigade and saw action in bitter fighting along the Beirut-Damascus highway.

The evacuation operation began in the late Seventies with a small trickle of 30 to 40 Ethiopian Jews making their way out of Sudan among the other refugees receiving entry visas from European countries. At the turn of the Eighties, word of this initial success reached the Jews in Ethiopia and the tens of scores suddenly swelled to three- then four-digit numbers. The Mossad at the time did not have a relevant number of trained officers to handle this operation – neither did it have a quick reservoir of personnel who could 'fit the bill' cover-wise. A decision had to be taken to hastily recruit women and men and to provide them with minimal training. Those who would normally train people for this specialised area of service refused to do so. They did not wish to 'sign off' on such limited training, and rightly so. Rapid recruitment and inadequate training were decisions taken with full realisation of the possible consequences.

The sum total of all these unique circumstances had a direct impact on the choice of officers who were appointed to command the operations in the field. To lead they had to be 'maverick' – a term 'Hebraicised' in the Mossad to specify a

person who is simultaneously brilliant and outstandingly courageous, but who is prone from time to time to treat orders rather
as suggestions.

This was particularly significant, since real-time command
was drastically limited in those days and over those distances.

Who were these 'mavericks'? The two who served under me
were veteran Mossad officers who had 'broken the rules' more
than once. They had performed with valour and distinction in
key military operations and had both been censured probably
more than once.

Ariel 'Arik' Sharon, a famous general and later minister of
defence and prime minister, told me on more than one occasion
that he would never promote an officer to the rank of general if
he did not have at least two censures in his personal file.

There were many retirees who volunteered to serve in Sudan
– Uri, a celebrated case officer who had escaped the Holocaust,
and a former division chief who insisted on serving against the
rules. Both served as drivers, maintaining contact with the Jews
in the refugee camps close to the Ethiopian border, hundreds
of kilometres away from Khartoum. Driving along single-lane
dark highways at night risked a sudden confrontation with a
stray camel with potentially disastrous consequences. And there
was Ruth, who I recruited through a friend in a far-off land
to perform a unique task in Khartoum in broad daylight with
unique distinction.

A special mention should be made of the sons of the small
Ethiopian community in Israel who volunteered to serve and
provide the vital link with the refugees who had crossed the
border, having valiantly made the trek from their homes in
Ethiopia. The volunteers from Israel displayed enormous cour-
age as they went about their task.

This is not of course an official and comprehensive report – it is a very personal attempt to turn attention both to the wider context in which this operation was carried out and to focus on some of the personalised aspects in the eyes of a participant.

In this vein I want to conclude with a final observation. I often thought that were the operation to collapse because of a major failure, it would be unnecessary to appoint an enquiry commission to investigate the reasons and shortcomings that produced the disaster. I was specially conscious of this conviction of mine on the occasions I went down to Sudan.

I understood what were the dangers and what might happen and realised the severe limitations of our control.

For all of the participants in this operation, it has become a lifetime experience that has had an indelible influence on each and every one of them, coupled with a unique sense of pride.

ACKNOWLEDGEMENTS

When I set out to write this book, I was faced with a series of daunting challenges. It was clear to me that in order to tell the story properly and in an original fashion, I was going to need the help of a lot of people – from those who were personally involved in the events on which the book is based, to those with a special expertise in matters I knew little about. Furthermore, it would inevitably mean reaching out to members of the Mossad and Israeli security forces who do not court publicity. So began a process of detective work, which took me from one lead to another, trips to Israel and Europe, and countless electronic communications, telephone conversations and meetings. By the time I finished, I had got to know many remarkable individuals, some of whom I now consider good friends, and without whose willingness to assist, this project simply would not have been possible.

I am indebted to these people and it is with profound gratitude that I would like to give them special mention.

First, my partner in this endeavour, Dani, a most principled individual, with whom I worked hand-in-hand, and who provided the foundations for this story. Humble and heroic in equal measure, Dani is an extraordinary person on many levels and it has been a privilege to collaborate with him. The fact that his name is held in such high esteem among people I met in the course of researching this book speaks volumes, and I offer him my deepest thanks for all his help, expertise and advice.

Secondly, I would like to single out Yola Reitman, an indomitable spirit and one of the first people to recognise the value in what I was trying to achieve. Her help and generosity from the outset has known no bounds, for which I am sincerely grateful.

Thirdly, I must give thanks to Rubi, a talented man of many fine qualities, whose wit, charm and gift as a natural raconteur made our meetings a great pleasure.

Of the many contributors who deserve recognition, it is impossible to apportion thanks proportionately. I extend my gratitude to those members of the Israeli intelligence service and military who took me into their trust and spoke to me on- and off-the-record. Some are referred to obliquely in this book, others wished to remain anonymous, but they should know how much I appreciate their cooperation.

I would also like to pay special thanks to the many Ethiopian Jews who shared personal stories and gave me crucial help. It has been an education, through which I have developed the greatest admiration for this special community. In particular, I would like to thank Rabbi Sharon Shalom of the International Center for the Study of Ethiopian Jewry at Ono Academic College, educator and social activist Rabbi Yefet Alemu and author and activist Shmuel Yilma – as well as tireless advocates Rabbi Menachem Waldman, and the Friends of Ethiopian Jews (FEJ) for their time, wisdom and guidance.

Throughout this book, I have striven to be as reliable as possible with the information which I have presented. Some of this relates to areas such as ancient history and politics where I have sought the insight of academics. Many went out of their way to share their expertise. In particular, I would like to thank professors Steven Kaplan, Michael Corinaldi and Colin Shindler for their invaluable help.

I must also extend my thanks to members of the deep-sea diving and oceaneering fraternity, who provided not only a bank of specialist knowledge but also helped me trace certain people who have been key to uncovering elements of this story never known about before – notably Henri Hemmerechts, Alex Double, Jim Watson, Howard Rosenstein, Aurora Branciamore and Adriano Bicciato.

I also wish to express my sincere appreciation to the Castiglioni family of the Museo Castiglioni for their kindness and for sharing with me many remarkable pieces of information.

Others as well have displayed tremendous goodwill in giving me advice and help with many aspects of this book, for which I am truly thankful. These include Udi Avivi from the Israeli embassy in London, Nicole Greenspan of Ariel University, Gillian Lusk, Angela Berry Koch, Mohanad Hashim, Driss Mekkaoui, Zecharia Yona, Tesfalem Araia, Henri Astier, Vanessa Buschschlüter, Stuart Burns and Kathryn Westcott.

I would like to thank too Belmont United Synagogue in Stanmore for granting me the use of its facilities and whose environment I found most conducive for writing a large part of this story.

My deepest gratitude also goes to my editors at Icon Books, Duncan and Ellen, for taking what began as a concept and nurturing it into a reality. From our first meeting, their unwavering enthusiasm for the story and faith in me has been a great source of encouragement. I owe a great deal to their diligence, ideas and oversight, which have been indispensable.

Finally, I wish to thank those who mean the most to me and have supported me unfalteringly throughout – my wife Suzi, for all her patience, and my beautiful children Anya and Coby. May they be inspired by the people in this book.

NOTES

Introduction

1. Jewish Telegraphic Agency, 15 April 1975.
2. Author interview with Dani, 24 August 2018.
3. Operation Moses was a clandestine airlift by Israel of 6,822 Ethiopian Jews from Sudan between 21 November 1984 and 5 January 1985.
4. Where contributors have requested anonymity, pseudonyms are used in place of real names and appear within inverted commas on first mention outside of direct speech to signify so.

Chapter 1

1. 'Sudan's Probe of CIA Role in Airlift of Ethiopian Jews', *Washington Post*, 20 July 1985.
2. Author interview with Milton Bearden, 29 September 2018.
3. Author interview with Amram Aklum, half-brother of Ferede Aklum, 19 August 2018.
4. Steven Kaplan, *The Beta Israel (Falasha) in Ethiopia*, New York: New York University Press (1992), pp.164–65.
5. Micha Feldman, *On Wings of Eagles: The Secret Operation of the Ethiopian Exodus*, Jerusalem: Gefen Publishing House Ltd. (2012), pp.38–9.
6. Isaiah 11:11.
7. The precise boundaries of Cush are disputed and some sources contend that it included part of present-day northern Ethiopia.
8. Embroideries by Yazezow Aklum are currently housed in the Israel Museum's collection of Ethiopian art in Jerusalem.
9. Law of Return (*Hok Hashvut*), passed by the Knesset on 5 July 1950; amended 23 August 1954 and 10 March 1970.

10. Up to 1977, there were officially 269 Ethiopian Israelis, according to Israel's Central Bureau of Statistics (CBS), although the actual number of Ethiopian Jews in Israel could be around 100 more than that (see Mitchell G. Bard, *From Tragedy to Triumph: The Politics Behind the Rescue of Ethiopian Jewry*, Westport: Praeger Publishing (2002), p.48.).

      Daniel Gordis, *Menachem Begin: The Battle for Israel's Soul*, New York: Schocken Books (2014), p.145.

11. The war is also known as the October War and the Ramadan War.

12. On 5 June 1967 Israel launched a pre-emptive strike against Egypt and Syria, amid signs they were about to attack. A full-scale war broke out, drawing in Jordan on Egypt and Syria's side. The war lasted for six days. By the end, Israel had driven Egypt out of Gaza and the Sinai, Jordan out of East Jerusalem and the West Bank, and Syria out of most of the Golan Heights. For Israel, it was an historic victory, and for the Arabs an ignominious defeat.

13. 'Rabin Quits Over Illegal Bank Account', *Washington Post*, 8 April 1977.

Chapter 2

1. From 1922 to 1948 Britain administered the territory then officially known as Mandate Palestine. 'Palestine' has been used here as a shortened form.

2. Etzel blamed the British authorities for not heeding a 30-minute warning; British Prime Minister Clement Attlee, in a House of Commons debate on 22 July 1946, denounced the bombing as an 'insane act of terrorism'.

3. Lawrence Wright, *Thirteen Days in September*, New York: Alfred A. Knopf (2014), p.75.

4. Avi Shilon, *Menachem Begin: A Life*, New Haven & London: Yale University Press (2012), p.254.

5. There are variations of these remarks attributed to Begin, depending on the source.

6. AAEJ founder and past president Graenum Berger said: 'If it hadn't been for our persistent criticism, they [Israel] wouldn't have done it', reported by David B Ottaway, 'Secret Airlift of Ethiopian Jews Followed a Decade of Divisive Debate', *Washington Post*, 13 March 1985, p.A18.

7. Author interview with source who requested anonymity.

8. Louis Rapoport, *The Lost Jews: Last of the Ethiopian Falashas*, New York: Stein and Day (1980), pp.194–95.

9. Rochelle Saidel Wolk, 'The Falashas Must Be Saved', *The Jewish Veteran*, Vol. 34, No. 4, March–April 1980.

10. 'Museo di populi', or museum of peoples, attributed to Italian anthropologist Carlo Conti Rossini, by Robert Gale Woolbert, 'The Peoples of Ethiopia', *Foreign Affairs Magazine*, January 1936.

11. Aaron Matteo Terrazas, 'Beyond Regional Circularity: The Emergence of an Ethiopian Diaspora', *Migration Policy Institute*, 1 June 2007.

12. Author interview with Reuven Merhav, 26 February 2019.

13. Begin remarks to the Knesset, 20 June 1977.

14. Yossi Melman and Dav Raviv, *Imperfect Spies, The History of Israeli Intelligence*, London: Sidgwick & Jackson (1989), p.173.

15. Ibid., p.275.

16. Author interview with source who requested anonymity.

17. Jennifer Joyce, *Ethiopia's Foreign Relations With Israel: 1955–1998*, Washington D.C.: Howard University (2000), pp.42–5.

18. Mitchell G. Bard, *From Tragedy to Triumph: The Politics Behind the Rescue of Ethiopian Jewry*, Westport: Praeger Publishing (2002), p.32.

19. Eritrea joined Ethiopia as part of a federation in 1952, but Selassie annexed the territory ten years later and declared Eritrea a province, fuelling a secessionist rebellion.

20. Benjamin Beit-Hallahmi, *The Israeli Connection: Who Israel Arms and Why*, New York: Pantheon (1987), p.52.
    Dr. Monty G. Marshall, 'Conflict Trends in Africa, 1946–2004: A Macro-Comparative Perspective'. Report prepared for the Africa Conflict Prevention Pool (September 2006).

21. That Selasie was unhappy about breaking relations with Israel is clear from a letter from his foreign minister Menase Haile to Israel's ambassador to Ethiopia, Hanan Aynor, on 23 October 1973, in which Menase says: 'Every Ethiopian knows your situation and every Ethiopian hopes for your victory, for we know you are right in your war with the Arabs … It is with great sorrow that we do it, and we hope that the breaking of relations will not last long.' Haggai Erlich, *Ethiopia & the Middle East*, London: Lynne Rienner Publishers Inc. (1994), p.173.
    Although diplomatic ties were broken in 1973, Selassie did not

boycott Israel and trade between the two countries actually increased. Joel Peters, *Israel and Africa: The Problematic Friendship*, London: British Academic Press (1992), pp.69–70.

22. Haggai Erlich, *Ethiopia & the Middle East*, London: Lynne Rienner Publishers Inc. (1994), pp.175–76.

23. Author interview with source who requested anonymity.

24. Mengistu became leader of the Derg and head of state after a gun-battle on 3 February 1977 in which his predecessor Brig Gen Tafari Banti and other opponents were killed by officers loyal to Mengistu, reportedly on Mengistu's orders.

25. Author interview with source who requested anonymity.

26. Mutual Defense Assistance Agreement (MDAA), 1953.

27. Author correspondence with Dr Haggai Erlich, professor emeritus, Department of Middle Eastern and African History, Tel Aviv University, 8 December 2018.

   Joel Peters, *Israel and Africa: The Problematic Friendship*, London: British Academic Press (1992), p.71.

28. Author interview with source who requested anonymity.

29. Guevara was a comrade of Fidel Castro, and a revolutionary figure in South America in the 1960s.

30. See note 10, Chapter 1.

31. Chaim Halachmy was the director of HIAS in Israel and split his time between HIAS and the Jewish Agency.

32. Some Hebraicised words appear in the Ethiopian Jewish Orit (Bible) but, as Jacques Faitlovich observed in his book *The Falashas* (1920), Ethiopian Jews 'do not know the Hebrew language, and they are not aware that it still exists in modern times'.

33. Dr Azriel Kamon, *The First Bridge 1955–1995: The Testimonies of Jewish Ethiopian Students from Kfar Batya*, Tel Aviv: Contento, Yad Tabenkin Research and Documentation Center of the Kibbutz Movement (2015), p.69.

34. There are recorded, though few, cases of Ethiopian Jews coming into contact with other Jews outside their country down the centuries, including just twelve years before Halévy's mission when an Ethiopian Jewish father and his son travelled to Jerusalem, but Halévy was the first to make contact with Jews inside Ethiopia.

35. J. Halévy, 'Travels in Abyssinia', in A. Lowy (ed), *Miscellany of Hebrew Literature*, London: Trubner & Co (1877), pp.215–16.

36. It is unclear which waters Mahari reached. Some versions say he arrived at the Tekeze River and mistakenly believed he had reached the Red Sea.

37. Michael Corinaldi, *Jewish Identity: The Case of Ethiopian Jewry*, Jerusalem: The Magnes Press (1998), p.109.

38. Examples of 'mainstream' Jewish festivals they did not know are Chanukah and Purim, although intriguingly Ethiopian Jews observed a fast day, *soma aster* (fast of Esther, the heroine of the Purim story), on or around the same date as Jews in the rest of the world celebrated the latter.

39. Daniel P. Summerfield, *From Falashas to Ethiopian Jews: The External Influences for Change c.1860–1960*, thesis, (1997), p.265.

40. Kasaey Damoza, 'Fragments from a Forgotten Past', *Jerusalem Post*, 24 April 2012.

41. Orthodox rabbis who recognised Ethiopian Jews include Abraham Isaac Kook and Isaac HaLevi Herzog, the Ashkenazi chief rabbis in Mandate Palestine, then Israel, during the period 1921–59.

42. Mitchell G. Bard, *From Tragedy to Triumph: The Politics Behind the Rescue of Ethiopian Jewry*, Westport: Praeger (2002), pp.8–9.

43. The ORT was allowed to operate in Gondar on the proviso that its projects did not favour Jewish over non-Jewish communities. However, Jewish communities were an unspoken priority to the ORT in the course of its work in Ethiopia. It was shut down by Gondar's governor Melaku Tefera at the end of 1981.

44. Four ORT teachers were arrested and jailed in 1979 for teaching Hebrew and Jewish education, according to a confidential ORT source. On another occasion, Ethiopian Jewish spiritual leaders, or Kessim, distributing matzot (a product akin to water crackers, eaten on Passover) brought by the ORT to villages for the first time were arrested by security forces who thought it was a special energy food that would allow the Jews to flee the country without suffering hunger on their way, the source says.

45. *Breakthrough Leadership* (in Hebrew), Israel: Forum Yerusalem (2016), p.33.

46. Author interview with co-pilot Asaf Agmon, 18 April 2019.

Chapter 3

1. Sephardi Jews are those of Spanish or Portuguese descent.

2. Ovadiah Yosef's letter of 3 February 1973 is produced in full in Michael Corinaldi, *Jewish Identity: The Case of Ethiopian Jewry*, Jerusalem: The Magnes Press (1998), pp.199–201.

3. Such as the Italian Ovadia of Bartenura and the chief rabbi of Egypt, David ben Zimra, commonly known as the Radbaz.

4. Scottish explorer James Bruce, who stumbled across an Ethiopian Jewish community in the late 1800s, describes how those he encountered related to him the story of the Queen of Sheba in *Travels to Discover the Source of the Nile*, Volume I, Chapter VI (1790), p.484.

5. Rabbi Yosef's position was mirrored in 1975 by Israel's other chief rabbi, Shlomo Goren, spiritual leader of the country's other main branch of Jews, known as Ashkenazi (Jews of European origin other than the Iberian Peninsula).
   'Falashas Eligible for Israeli Citizenship Under Law of Return', Jewish Telegraphic Agency, 15 April 1975.

6. 'Jewish Exodus from Ethiopia', Ariel University Center of Samaria/ Israel Intelligence Heritage & Commemoration Center (2005), pp.17–18.

7. 'Dayan Discloses Israel is Selling Arms to Ethiopia', *Washington Post*, 7 February 1978.

8. *Keesing's Record of World Events*, Volume XXIV (May, 1978), p.28989.
   Tudor Parfitt, *Operation Moses*, London: Weidenfeld and Nicolson (1985), p.38.

9. For reports of attacks and displacement of Jews, Ibid., pp.28–29.
   Remarks by Yona Bogale to the Plenary Session of the General Assembly, 15 November 1979.

10. This was emphasised by Ethiopian envoy to Washington Tesfaye Demeke and government spokesman Taddesse Tamrat in the 1983 documentary *Falasha: Exile of the Black Jews of Ethiopia*, by Simcha Jacobovici.

11. 'The Falashas – A Background Paper', American Jewish Committee Archives, January 1980.

12. Aksum was the capital of the ancient Ethiopian kingdom and empire. It was, according to the Kebra Nagast, the presence here of the Ark of the Covenant which proved that God had forsaken the 'cursed' Jews and replaced them with the Ethiopian nation as his new Chosen People. This allowed Ethiopian rulers to claim to govern by divine right. Haile Selassie himself adopted the title 'Conquering Lion of the Tribe of Judah, King of Kings and Elect of God'.

13. Howard M. Lenhoff, *Black Jews, Jews, and Other Heroes*, Jerusalem: Gefen Publishing House Ltd. (2007), p.134.
14. *Breakthrough Leadership* (in Hebrew), Israel: Forum Yerusalem (2016), pp.34–35.
15. There were some twenty UNHCR camps in Eastern Sudan as well as unofficial squatter camps around Port Sudan, Kassala, Gedaref and Khartoum.
16. UNHCR, *The State of the World's Refugees 2000: Fifty years of Humanitarian Action*, Chapter 5, pp.110–11.
17. There had been a small Jewish community in Sudan but most had fled by the 1960s because of rising hostility fuelled by Sudan's enmity towards Israel. Few, if any, Jews remained in Sudan by the late-1970s.
18. Howard M. Lenhoff, *Black Jews, Jews, and Other Heroes*, Jerusalem: Gefen Publishing House Ltd. (2007), p.101.
19. Shmuel Yilma, *From Falasha to Freedom: An Ethiopian Jew's Journey to Jerusalem*, Jerusalem: Gefen Publishing House Ltd. (1996), p.11.
20. Some sources report slight variations as to where Ferede sent the three telegrams. The version given here is based on an interview by the author with Ferede's half-brother, Amram, 19 August 2018.
21. Ferede used his father's name, Yazezow, because in Ethiopia it is not the convention to use hereditary family names.

Chapter 4

1. Full-length robe.
2. Also known as Beni-Amer, a nomadic sub-group of the Beja tribe inhabiting Eastern Sudan.
3. Sudan was under Anglo-Egyptian rule until 1956, when it gained its independence. Separately, in Mandate Palestine, barracks built by the British for their garrisons were taken over by the Israel Defense Forces after the establishment of the state in 1948.
4. The story of Shuffa and the journey of Addis, Leul and Negusseh has been pieced together from several sources, including the author's interview with Amram Aklum, 19 August 2018; correspondence with Ferede Aklum's nephew Shmuel Yilma; Yilma's book, *From Falasha to Freedom: An Ethiopian Jew's Journey to Jerusalem*, Jerusalem: Gefen Publishing House Ltd. (1996), pp.10, 68–70; verification by indirect correspondence with Leul Aklum; and *Breakthrough Leadership* (in Hebrew), Israel: Forum Yerusalem (2016).

Chapter 5

1. *Breakthrough Leadership* (in Hebrew), Israel: Forum Yerusalem (2016), p.46.
2. Shmuel Yilma, *From Falasha to Freedom: An Ethiopian Jew's Journey to Jerusalem*, Jerusalem: Gefen Publishing House Ltd. (1996), p.17.
3. 'Jewish Exodus from Ethiopia', Ariel University Center of Samaria/ Israel Intelligence Heritage & Commemoration Center (2005), p.45.
4. Author interview with source involved in evacuation operations who requested anonymity.
5. Author interview with Benny Ghoshen, 11 October 2018.
6. Figure from The Committee for the Commemoration Of The Ethiopian Jews That Perished On Their Way From Ethiopia To Israel Through Sudan From 1979–90, under the joint auspices of the Israeli prime minister's office and the World Zionist Organization. A general figure of 4,000 is frequently cited but this has not been verified.
7. Ibid.
8. Micha Feldman, *On Wings of Eagles: The Secret Operation of the Ethiopian Exodus*, Jerusalem: Gefen Publishing House Ltd. (2012), p.24.

Chapter 6

1. Other than in cases where the eighth day falls on a Sabbath, when Ethiopian Jews postpone circumcision until the day after.
2. The preparation of a festive meal is described in the testimony of an unnamed Kes, at the national memorial for Ethiopian Jews who perished on the way to Israel, at Mount Herzl, Jerusalem.
3. Dani learnt this only days later when he tracked the man down to a prison in Gedaref and bribed a prison guard to let him go. The man subsequently made it to Israel on a refugee flight organised by Dani.
4. The two armed Sudanese men were interested only in catching Ferede and left the Jews in the safehouse alone. All the Jews in both houses at the time of the incident were subsequently smuggled out to Israel as planned.
5. The clandestine operation to evacuate Jews from Morocco was carried out by the Mossad as part of a secret agreement with the king, Hassan II, for payments reportedly of up to $20 million.

Chapter 7

1. The name given to a system of railway rescue transportations in which Jewish children were sent to Britain without their parents to escape Nazi Germany and countries occupied by it, from 1938–39.
2. Bosley Crowther, 'Movie of Undersea Study at Cinema II', *New York Times*, 23 December 1964, p.22.
3. Luigi Balbo, who went on to become a technical advisor and photographer on the Castiglionis' expeditions for the next 40 years.
4. Author interview with Angelo, Stefano and Marco Castiglioni, 22 September 2018.
5. The Navco shelf company bears no affiliation with NAVCO Business Security Services, formerly North American Video Corporation, founded in 1971 in North America.
6. Rama Jan is a mispronunciation of Ramat Gan, a city east of Tel Aviv.

Chapter 9

1. After returning to Israel, Zimna continued working in the service of Ethiopian Jewish *aliya* and as an advocate of the community there.
2. A military campaign waged against Israel by Egypt from 1969–70.
3. The decree, which also conferred upon Tarzan the position of Goodwill Ambassador for South Sudan, was issued in January 2019.
4. The ICM channel functioned for about ten years, although it only provided an exit for a limited number of people per month, typically under 100.
5. Klaus Mommsen, *60 Years: Israel Navy*, Norderstedt, Germany: Books on Demand GmbH (2011), p.215.
6. This was learnt by members of the team who met William for the first time in 30 years at a reunion in Israel in 2015.
7. Mekuria Bulcha, 'Flight and Integration: Causes of Mass Exodus from Ethiopia and Problems of Integration in the Sudan', Scandinavian Institute of African Studies, Uppsala (1988), p.214.
8. Author interview with Rabbi Sharon Shalom, 2 August 2018.

Chapter 11

1. This figure includes the $50,000 spent on equipment at Au Vieux Campeur in Paris.

Chapter 12

1. Ivry's term as head of the Air Force finished in December 1982, where-upon he was replaced by Major General Amos Lapidot. From then on, Lapidot was a driving force behind the airlifts of the Ethiopian Jews.
2. Forward-looking infrared.
3. The reconnaissance unit was commanded by then-Captain Yisrael Ziv, who went on to become the head of the Paratroopers Brigade and was promoted to Major General.
4. Commandos from the Air Force's elite Shaldag unit, deployed in special operations inside enemy territory.
5. The aerial assault was known as Operation Mole Cricket 19.
6. In April, 1983, the naval evacuation by the *Bat Galim* was carried out under the command of Major Uzi Tishel, who had succeeded Major Ilan Buchris as captain.

Chapter 14

1. Agmon had just finished his term as squadron commander and flew the mission as co-pilot as part of a handing over procedure.
2. Two AWACS (Airborne Warning and Control System, capable of monitoring aircraft within a wide radius) were sent to Sudan in the first week of August, 1983, amid US concerns over Libyan bombing raids in support of rebels in Chad, Sudan's western neighbour.
3. Ten-thousand Jews arrived in Sudan June–September 1984, according to Micha Feldman, *On Wings of Eagles: The Secret Operation of the Ethiopian Exodus*, Jerusalem: Gefen Publishing House Ltd. (2012), p.60.
4. Nahum Admoni was appointed director of the Mossad in September 1982.
5. It has been reported that, at a secret meeting with a delegation of Israelis, including Defence Minister Ariel Sharon, in Kenya in May 1982, Nimeiri agreed to a deal allowing Israel to evacuate Ethiopian Jews through Sudan. This is denied by a source with intimate know-ledge of this meeting, who says no such deal was made. According to the source, although Nimeiri did not veto the idea, nothing came of it.
6. William Beecher, 'Israelis rescue thousands of Ethiopian Jews', *The Boston Globe*, 12 December 1984, pp.1, 8.

7. 'Statement in the Knesset by Prime Minister Peres on "Operation Moses"', 8 January 1985, Israel Ministry of Foreign Affairs, 31 January 1985.

   On 3 January 1985, two Israeli mass-circulation newspapers ran the story, quoting the Jewish Agency deputy chairman and reporting the airlift from Sudan. With the lid now off, the *Associated Press* followed.

8. Dan Fisher, 'Israel pledges to rescue Jews still in Ethiopia', *Los Angeles Times*, 8 January 1985, p.5.

9. David B Ottaway, 'Ethiopia Protests Airlift', *Washington Post*, 5 January 1985, p.A1.

10. Steven Carol, *From Jerusalem to the Lion of Judah and Beyond: Israel's Foreign Policy in East Africa*, Bloomington: iUniverse Inc. (2012), p.287.

11. Author interview with sources involved in planning Operation Joshua who requested anonymity.

Chapter 15

1. Author interview with Milton Bearden, 29 September 2018.

2. Jonathan C. Randal, 'A Shaking Off', *Washington Post*, 7 May 1985, p.A21.

3. Christopher Dickey, 'Sudan's Probe of CIA's Role in Airlift of Ethiopian Jews', *Washington Post*, 20 July 1985, p.1-A.

4. Author interview with Omer Abdelati, 6 November 2018.

5. One-thousand-three-hundred kilometres is the distance from Tel Aviv to Arous as the crow flies.

   Four-thousand-one-hundred-and-four Jews were brought out by the Mossad through Khartoum Airport; 1,082 by Mossad-Navy operations; 1,868 by Mossad-Air Force operations.

6. 'Statement in the Knesset by Prime Minister Peres on "Operation Moses"', 8 January 1985, Israel Ministry of Foreign Affairs, 31 January 1985.

7. Stephen Spector, *Operation Solomon: The Daring Rescue of the Ethiopian Jews*, New York: Oxford University Press (2005), p.119.

8. Ibid., p.154.

9. Agmon had been promoted to the rank of colonel in 1987.

10. Seven-thousand-and-fifty-four Jews were smuggled out in Mossad-led Operation Brothers between 1979 and 1984; Operation Moses

(1984–85) brought out 6,822; Operation Joshua (1985) 494; Operation Solomon (1991) 14,325.

11. Sixteen-thousand comprises 14,370 known to have been brought out through Sudan, as well as 1,560 known to have died, plus numbers not in the public domain.

12. Judith Antonelli, 'The Plight of Ethiopian Jews', *Cultural Survival*, September 1983.

13. Israeli Central Bureau of Statistics.

INDEX